THE GOSPEL TRUTH

THE GOSPEL TRUTH

You Can't Make This Stuff Up

PATRICK T. RHOADS

RESOURCE *Publications* • Eugene, Oregon

THE GOSPEL TRUTH
You Can't Make This Stuff Up

Copyright © 2020 Patrick T. Rhoads. All rights reserved. Except for brief quotations in critical publications or reviews, no part of this book may be reproduced in any manner without prior written permission from the publisher. Write: Permissions, Wipf and Stock Publishers, 199 W. 8th Ave., Suite 3, Eugene, OR 97401.

This work extracts quotations from various translations of the Bible. There is no preferred translation, and no argument in this book depends on a particular translation. The principal translations used herein are the King James Version (KJV), the Revised Standard Version (RSV), and the New International Version (NIV), and the New American Bible (NAB).

Scripture texts in this work are taken from the New American Bible, revised edition 2010, 1991, 1986, 1970 Confraternity of Christian Doctrine, Washington, DC and used by permission of the copyright owner. All rights reserved. No part of the New American Bible may be reproduced in any form without permission in writing from the copyright owner.

Resource Publications
An Imprint of Wipf and Stock Publishers
199 W. 8th Ave., Suite 3
Eugene, OR 97401

www.wipfandstock.com

PAPERBACK ISBN: 978-1-7252-7342-9
HARDCOVER ISBN: 978-1-7252-7343-6
EBOOK ISBN: 978-1-7252-7344-3

Manufactured in the U.S.A. 06/22/20

Dedicated to my cousin
Patrick J. Cullen (1948–2011), my mentor.

Contents

List of Tables	ix
List of Abbreviations	xi
Preface	xiii
1 Introduction	1
2 Methodology for Assessing the Historicity of the Gospels	10
3 Getting Started	24
4 The Design of the Gospels	35
5 The Resurrection	45
6 The Initial Idea of Christianity	68
7 The Models of Jesus	93
8 The Teaching Ministry of Jesus	108
9 The Miracles of Jesus	115
10 How It All Comes Together	134
11 The Gospel Truth about the Gospel Truth	164
Epilogue: The Fruition of the Gospel Truth	167
Endnotes	175
Appendix A: A Case Study of a Systems Approach: A Review of Josephus's Words about Jesus	181
Appendix B: Design Parameters for the Four Gospels	187
Appendices Endnotes	193
Bibliography	195
Author Index	199
Subject Index	201

List of Tables

Table 2-1	Elements of an Engineering Assessment Model	12
Table 2-2	The Primitive Historical Claims about Jesus	13
Table 2-3	Nonhistorical and Non-salient Claims about Jesus	14
Table 2-4	Table of Criteria for Historicity	18
Table 5-1	Purported Witnesses to Events in World Religions	56
Table 5-2	Comparison of the Creation and Resurrection Stories	64
Table 7-1	Attributes Ascribed to Jesus in the Gospels versus Attributes Ascribed to Others in the Jewish Tradition	95
Table 7-2	Comparison of Jesus to Others in Jewish History	96
Table 9-1	Miracles Attributed to Jesus in the Gospels	120
Table 10-1	Chronology of Events Paralleling the Formation of the Gospels	136
Table A-1	Comparison of *Testimonium* Versions against the Church's Claims	185
Table B-1	Design Parameters for the Gospels	188

List of Abbreviations

1 Cor	1 Corinthians
1 Kgs	1 Kings
1 Pet	1 Peter
2 Tim	2 Timothy
Col	Colossians
ESV	English Standard Version
Ezek	Ezekiel
Hos	Hosea
Isa	Isaiah
Jer	Jeremiah
KJV	King James Version
Matt	Matthew
Mic	Micah
NAB	New American Bible
NIV	New International Version
NNSA	National Nuclear Security Administration
Zech	Zechariah
Zeph	Zephaniah

Preface

I informed an acquaintance in the religious media business that I was going to write this book. His pleasant response, "Another book about the Bible?" belied his facial expression, which tacitly sported a different question, "Do we need another one of those?"

So, why this book? What distinguishes it from the others?

This book takes a different vantage point. The commonly accepted premise among prevailing elites, scholars, and secularists, often conveniently unstated, is that the Gospels are works of creative fiction—the tools of mistaken zealots bent on proselytizing the Mediterranean world of the first and second centuries CE. The Gospels are not reputable sources of the histories of the life and death of Jesus, so they tell us. In this book I set their premise as a hypothesis to test.

The Gospel Truth: You Can't Make This Stuff Up is not so much about what the New Testament says or how to interpret or apply it. This book is about unpacking the design and the evolution of the stories in the New Testament by extracting from them what can be authenticated as historical. I assess the historicity of the Gospels just as an engineer would assess the performance of a system. As a systems engineer, I apply a systems engineering approach to assessing the Gospels' historical claims. Instead of arguing that the New Testament is basically true, I assume that it is basically false and then seek to disprove this assumption. This approach is the basic scientific method.

I address the text of the Gospels using rigorous, objective evidentiary tests. The tests reveal that the evangelists present their stories not from their imaginations but from their experiences or the experiences transmitted to them. The tests validate the basic historical claims in the Gospels, based on reason alone.

1

Introduction

Here is a man who was born in an obscure village, the child of a peasant woman. He grew up in another village. He worked in a carpenter shop until He was thirty. Then for three years He was an itinerant preacher.

He never owned a home. He never wrote a book. He never held an office. He never had a family. He never went to college. He never put His foot inside a big city. He never traveled two hundred miles from the place He was born. He never did one of the things that usually accompany greatness. He had no credentials but Himself.

While still a young man, the tide of popular opinion turned against Him. His friends ran away. One of them denied Him. He was turned over to His enemies. He went through the mockery of a trial. He was nailed upon a cross between two thieves. While He was dying His executioners gambled for the only piece of property He had on earth—His coat. When He was dead, He was laid in a borrowed grave through the pity of a friend.

Nineteen long centuries have come and gone, and today He is a centerpiece of the human race and leader of the column of progress.

I am far within the mark when I say that all the armies that ever marched, all the navies that were ever built, all the parliaments that ever sat, and all the kings that ever reigned, put together, have not affected the life of man upon this earth as powerfully as has that one solitary life.

—Dr. James Allan Francis, "One Solitary Life" (1926)

James Allan Francis's short essay is remarkable for three reasons: (1) It is as vital now as it was nearly one hundred years ago. The world has evolved radically since 1926, but the insights in 1926 are as fresh as ever. (2) The short essay invites us to question who has impacted history as dramatically as Jesus has. The impact of Jesus's life is so uniquely vast and far beyond any other, at least in the West, that it is difficult to identify which historical figure would rank second to Jesus in importance. The space between Jesus and whoever would be the second most important person in Western history (Caesar? Charlemagne? Socrates? Plato?) remains wide. (3) Making Jesus the cornerstone of Western history would have been anything but expected, given that "[Christianity] has been on the 'wrong side of history' since AD 33. The 'right side of history' was the Eternal City of Rome. And then the right side of history was the French Revolution. And then the right side of history was scientific naturalism and state socialism."[1] One does not need to be a Christian to assert the ubiquitous reach of Christianity's influence on the West. Theologian Don Cupitt, an atheist, makes the point this way:

> Nobody in the West can be wholly non-Christian. You may call yourself non-Christian but the dreams you dream are still Christian.[2]

After reading Francis's short essay, one cannot help but ask the simplest question: Why? How did an obscure person living in an obscure corner in an obscure sector of an obscure people become the singular person in Western history, if not of all history? Any thoughtful person who examines history has to ask this obvious question. The answer a committed Christian would give is simple: "This simple man was the Incarnate Son of God, who came into the world to save mankind and restore his relationship to Jesus's Father, the Creator." To the committed Christian, the paraphrased adage attributable to Aquinas applies: "To one who has faith, no explanation is necessary. To one without faith, no explanation is possible." To people who aren't committed Christians, some answer to this obvious question still seems necessary just to gain a basic understanding of Western history and culture, which cannot be isolated from Christianity nor isolated from our understanding of who we are and what we are about.

Just about anybody born and educated in the West must know the basic outline of the life and times of the itinerant first-century Jewish teacher and presumed miracle worker in the Holy Land in the first century named Jesus. His "solitary life" makes him the most important person in Western history, though he was neither a Westerner nor, by some accounts, even historical. The Reverend Paul Scalia offered this thought in the eulogy for his departed father, the late Supreme Court Justice Antonin Scalia, on February 20, 2016, "We are gathered here because of one man, a man known personally to many of us, known only by reputation to even more. A man loved by many, scorned by others. A man known for great controversy and for great compassion." Father Scalia was honoring his father, yes, but he caused a stir in the audience assembled at the Basilica of the Immaculate Conception in Washington, DC, when the priest finished the thought by redirecting the audience's attention from his father's casket by adding, "That man, of course, is Jesus of Nazareth."

THE QUEST FOR THE HISTORICAL JESUS

Unlike the origins of some religions, the origins of Christianity played out on the stage of a real time in a real place with real people. The author of 1 John explains it as follows: "What we have heard, what we have seen with our eyes, what we looked upon and touched with our hands" (1:1). Despite being rooted in history, the origins of Christianity remain clouded. Believers reports the events some years after they occurred. Their records were embedded within the theological constructs the authors employed for their evangelical purposes. No documentation of Jesus's life is contemporaneous with the events that took place. Likely there were no such documents produced during Jesus's life either. In attempting to recover the events of the origins of Christianity, many people, believers and nonbelievers, have been on a quest to find the historical Jesus. They are known as "the questers." The quest for the historical Jesus must have begun even before the Jewish movement, The Way, splintered away from Judaism to become the distinct Christian religion. One can imagine the quest for the historical Jesus that Paul likely would have undertaken in Jerusalem when he met the apostles there after his conversion a mere two to four years after Jesus's execution. Paul had only known Jesus as his resurrected messiah. Paul would have wanted to know Jesus, the man, from the men who knew him best. Like Paul, the first Christian converts were target audiences for the oral stories of Jesus the man of history. In time, evangelists captured the oral stories in a written form, creating a newly emergent genre of literature, the Gospels.

The quest for the historical Jesus has a long history, beginning with the first converts. The substantive quests for the historical Jesus, though, date only to the modern era. Herman Samuel Reimarus (1694–1768) may have been the first scholarly quester. He was a product of the Enlightenment and likely the first to critically examine the historical content of the Gospels. Many others for the next hundred years would follow in his footsteps. A fellow Enlightenment quester was Thomas Jefferson. One of the private renderings from this most inquisitive and expansive intellect was the rewriting of the Gospels by retaining Jesus's teachings but expunging the miracle stories and the death-Resurrection saga. The result of Jefferson's efforts was a document posthumously known as the *Jefferson Bible*. Jefferson preserved the teachings of Jesus for having such an unparalleled sublime quality to them. He sought to have his collection of Jesus's lessons taught to Native Americans.

The systematic quest for the historical Jesus as a matter of more contemporary scholarship dates back to the early twentieth century, led by Albert Schweitzer in 1906. Schweitzer focused his attention on the growing body of critical reviews of the Gospels that began with Reimarus. Schweitzer concluded that Reimarus and the others who had followed him were mostly guilty of projecting their agenda back onto the Jesus whom they wanted to see. Thus, Schweitzer concluded, the works from Reimarus and others were of limited value. Schweitzer asserted that Jesus was a great visionary and teacher, but in the end a failed messiah, as were many Jews before and after him.

The next wave of questing fell to liberal Protestants. Lutheran theologian Rudolf Bultmann (1884–1976), as an example, concluded that we really cannot know much about the historical Jesus—and it doesn't really matter since Christians are going to believe what they believe, the facts notwithstanding. This wave then moved to Anglicans and to Catholics.

The most recent wave, the third, of the quest for the historical Jesus is the deconstructionalism that began in approximately the 1990s. The Jesus Seminar is the most notable of the scholarly pursuits in this wave. The Jesus Seminar is a collection of mostly secular scholars, some of them apostates, who developed methodologies for assessing which of the Gospels' sayings imputed to Jesus actually go back to him. The scholars determined that few did. The deconstructionalist approach adopted by the Jesus Seminar and peers assessed the New Testament and contemporaneous nonbiblical sources by expunging myth and theology from the existing literature to extract the "real" Jesus. In principle, this method should offer great opportunity to learn who this "real" Jesus was or is.

For a specific subset of recent questers, however, their scholarly pursuits are not agenda-free. Some academics sought to undermine the foundations of the historic Christian faith. Their publications characterized Christianity as a mere myth, developed by obsessed true believers. In this book, I address this subset, even though they are a minority of scholars.

The members of this group of questers often operate far afield from predominant scholarly opinion, which more closely aligns with the one provided by Pope Benedict XVI in his *Jesus of Nazareth* than to the minority approaches of deconstructionalist questers. The reason the minority gets such a billing, as Philip Jenkins reported in his *Hidden Gospels: How the Search for Jesus Lost Its Way*, is that its views have generated quite a stirring among the academic elite, the media, seminaries, universities, and the general public. The seminal exegetical counterpoise to the questers I have mentioned is *A Marginal Jew: Rethinking the Historical Jesus*. This monumental work comes from John P. Meier, a Catholic priest at the time of this writing at Notre Dame University. His work sets the standard of scholarship in debunking much of the hype of his fellow questers. Meier argues from his exhaustive research that a lot more was embedded in the historical record of the New Testament than his peer questers had accepted.

The trend of the minority questers making headlines is in keeping with the thrust of modernity, which targets vestiges of traditionalism. The Jesus whom the minority crowd gives us via its many best sellers spans from a philosophical sage to the Jewish equivalent of a Socrates or a Confucius, to a liberation theologian, to a misguided insurrectionist, to an influential rabbi, and to a failed messiah. None of the deconstructions can ever be made to render the names the evangelists themselves had given to Jesus—like Lamb of God, Lord, Savior, Christ, Son of God, or even the only name Jesus used for himself in the canonical Gospels with any regularity, Son of Man. Meier summarizes very nicely the treatment of the rancorous minority:

> [There is the] perennial desire to make Jesus seem "reasonable" or "rational" to post-Enlightenment "modern man," who looks suspiciously like a professor in a Religious Studies Department at some American university. Perhaps the attempt to see Jesus simply as a Cynic-Stoic philosopher or as an early type of Jewish rabbi active among the common people is a present-day, sophisticated version of the Enlightenment's quest for a reasonable, rational Jesus, the teacher of morality created by Thomas Jefferson's scissors. . . . [However,] the historical Jesus does not square with the view of many a post-Enlightenment academic as to what is reasonable, rational or desirable in religion.[3]

Former Anglican bishop N. T. Wright, a scholar in his own right, summarizes the gestalt of the literary community seeking out the historical Jesus as distinct from the Christ of religion with a sentiment resonating with Meier's words:

> The "liberal" picture of Jesus, early Christianity, and the gospels lives on in the persistent reductionalism of a thousand books both scholarly and popular. For many, in fact, it is the new

"orthodoxy." Unless you say something along these lines, you are likely to be sneered at. You can't be a serious thinker.[4]

Like the elites Wright sets aside, the Jesus Seminar delivered to us a broken-down, itinerant preacher with outsized ambition, whose message had been subsumed by the oppressive, misogynistic orthodox Christian Church. Another of the deconstructors, crafted by no less than a bishop of the Episcopal Church, John Shelby Spong, denies the bodily Resurrection of Jesus, among just about everything else Christian orthodoxy would append to him. A more recent incarnation of the deconstructional motif resides in the best seller *Zealot, Jesus of Nazareth* by Reza Aslan. By Aslan's reckoning, Jesus was dedicated to the overthrow of Roman hegemony over Israel by applying force, as necessary, to do so. Like the other zealots of his day, Jesus failed and received their same fate, death by crucifixion, the ultimate penalty for sedition under Roman law.

The end point of the questers has been to undermine orthodox Christianity, sometimes implicitly and sometimes not. Their radical claims warrant address. Addressing them is the mission of this book.

THE PREVAILING SENTIMENTS ABOUT THE HISTORICITY OF THE GOSPELS

Beyond the deconstructionalists, other forces are at work whose goal is to derail the traditional understandings of Jesus's life and times. They include nihilists, the antireligious, atheists, and secularists. Collectively, they hold significant sway on the academy, the media, and the common culture writ large. The secularists attempt to modulate the role of religion in America by emphasizing rationalism as its tool of inheritance from the Enlightenment. The humbly entitled *Columbia History of the World* captures the secularist motif accurately by disavowing any credibility of the only source documents we have about Jesus and the early Church:

> [T]he sources [of the account of the work of Jesus] are the four Gospels, written in the last quarter of the first century; the Acts of the Apostles, originally a sequel to the Gospel according to Luke; and the letters of Paul, dating mainly from the fifties. These sources disagree with one another, and sometimes with themselves, in many points—for instance, their stories of the resurrection. Further they all represent Christian tradition as it was one or two generations of reflections, controversy, exaggeration, and invention. Finally, they are full of incredible stories ... [which] may be of historical value as reflections of subjective

experiences. . . . Hence the early history of Christianity cannot be followed in detail. We can see that there were in the beginning many conflicting interpretations of Jesus's teaching and career, and that gradually a consensus-a rudimentary church-began to be built up.[5]

The last component of the current trend in the popular understanding of Jesus and his times comes from the antireligion crowd—or, at least, the anti-Christian crowd. Dan Brown's *Demons and Angels* and *The Da-Vinci Code* are two hugely successful works in this regard. Both are excellent novels; they are quick and fun reads, are exceptionally creative, and have been made into successful major motion pictures. They are surely fictions, as Brown acknowledges, and anybody doing even a modicum of research would conclude likewise, but in the mind of the readers, the validity of traditional beliefs are undermined by Brown's novels.

THE CHASM BETWEEN MANY SCHOLARS AND CHRISTIANS' UNDERSTANDINGS OF JESUS'S LIFE

What do we actually know about the real Jesus, this most influential person? Many people are surprised that the list of substantiated and accepted facts about Jesus is short. Was he poor? What was his family life like? Was he literate? Was he connected to religious authorities in Jerusalem? Or the Pharisees? Did he have a formal religious education? Was he a pious Jew? What was his message? Was he a miracle worker? Who were his disciples, and why did Jesus's message resonate with them? What was his own understanding of his mission?

The deconstructionalists reject the historicity of the four canonical Gospel accounts. These are the only substantive sources available about the life of Jesus. In effect, then, they reject the Jesus of the Gospels as well. Their widely subscribed but perhaps tacit thesis goes something like this:

> The Gospel authors, gullible and uncritical as they were, wrote their new-fangled kind of biographies, the Gospels, several decades after the events they reported. During the intervening time, the evangelists reinterpreted and mythologized their source material in an exhaustive way. As a result, we modern readers cannot extract any significant material that can be attested to the actual life of Jesus. The evangelists created the miracle stories to fortify their narratives that their re-created Jesus was the long-awaited Jewish Messiah. The references to existing biblical prophecies were back-written into the Gospel narratives

so the prophecies would have the appearance of having been fulfilled by Jesus.

The evangelists just made it up. They let hagiography masquerade as testimony. Bishop N. T. Wright summarizes the prevailing thoughts among elites this way:

> [The elites conclude that most] of these [gospel] stories must be fictitious, because dead people don't rise, lepers don't get healed, people don't walk on water, and, not least, gods do not appear in human form.... Anyone casting doubt on the gospels [appears] as sophisticated, knowing and clever, someone who isn't going to be taken in by a lot of religiously motivated claptrap. People have thus assumed that it is a mark of intellectual maturity to be able to question the historical truth of any and every statement in the gospels.[6]

A group of secularists and a segment of the antireligious have run with the scholarly conclusions to sport their own syllogism:

- The formative basis of Christianity is the New Testament.
- The New Testament is irrational.
- Therefore, Christianity is irrational.

APPROACH OF THIS BOOK

I attempt herein to reverse the conventional practices of apologetics as I address the minority crowd's positions. I assume that no claim in the Gospels should be accepted as factual, unless the claim withstands the scrutiny of severe evidentiary tests. I ask the question of whether the basic story lines (i.e., the kernels) of the Gospels are based on fact or are fabricated, and I answer the question based on reason alone.

Most of the claims within the Gospels cannot be addressed by the criteria of historic analysis. I limit this book to the set of claims in the Gospels that can be. For the subset of events accessible to the methods of logical examination, we test the hypothesis assuming three premises we can accept as self-evident:

1. The evangelists who wrote the Gospels were clever writers with a gift for spinning a tale.
2. The Gospels were designed to evangelize, and they were edited to achieve this goal.

3. The evangelists were people of their times and places and wrote to the audiences and issues of their day.

Here is another test I use that is perhaps the most intuitive of all: If the evangelists were telling tales unconstrained by facts, would the stories they have written be the same ones we have today? The subtitle of this book provides the answer: *You Can't Make This Stuff Up*. The reader will discover that the writers just would not have made up many of the specifics in the Gospels. These examples show us that the source of the recorded stories is not the creative imagination of the evangelists but rather observations by real people in real times and in real places.

CONCLUSION

This book assesses the historicity of the New Testament accounts in the Gospels by relying upon reason alone; the intent is to address the acute skepticism that characterizes our current body politic. Whereas skepticism can offer a great service by preventing irrationality and mobs from overtaking our civics, the acute skepticism we experience today seems to be devolving to disbelief and, if not arrested, to nihilism. Accordingly, I use the methods of skepticism to challenge the insidious skepticism of our time.

This book asks the modern reader to assess what can be extracted from the Gospel accounts as points of history. The question in this book is not a new question at all, as the evangelists themselves put the same question on Jesus's own lips: "Who do you say that I am?" (Matt 16:15; Mark 8:29; Luke 9:20)

2

Methodology for Assessing the Historicity of the Gospels

I had a lively and enriching discussion with a woman in my church group of twenty-somethings at a dinner theatre in the 1980s. She and I debated how to understand the Gospels. She understood the Gospels to be categories of literature that reflected deep truths about Jesus and the early Church. As to matters of history, though, they were a set of pious musings, like family folklore or the romanticized tales of George Washington's youth. That debate set the stage for this book.

That Christianity is a historical religion, no one seriously denies. Nor does anyone take issue with the fact that the Gospels record some of the foundational events of Christianity. The question really is what kinds of history these Gospels are. As I attempt to show, the Gospels are complex mixtures of history, biography, drama, faith, projection, wisdom, and more. The Gospels are literature—and good literature at that. And like all good literature, they are open to more than one interpretation. To this end, I make no claim that my interpretations are the only or even the best ones. I only assert that they are rational, demonstrating that faith and reason need not be in opposition.

I am a systems engineer. At the term, some readers' minds will jump to images of checklists, clipboards, pocket protectors, and #2 pencils. Instead of these images, think in virtual terms. Systems engineering involves both *analysis* of systems—that is, being able to understand the pieces that make them—and its inverse, *synthesis*—that is, being able to put pieces together to build systems. Using my expertise, I set myself to the challenge of applying systems engineering techniques to assessing the histories embedded within the Gospels.

The systems engineering approach I offer is novel, but using one's professional background and applying it to critically assess the Gospels is not. The idea goes back to Lee Strobel. In his best-selling *The Case for Christ*, the author employed his prize-winning investigative journalistic skills to attempt to get his wife to renounce her recent conversion to Christianity. He was convinced that he could use his highly honed skills as an investigator to get her to revert to her atheism, since, of course, Christianity was just a myth. While doing his research, he began to realize that the Gospels actually did report historical events of Jesus and his early followers. Instead of convincing her to rejoin him in his atheism, he convinced himself to join her in her Christianity.

I offer the reader an objective, no-holds-barred approach for assessing the historical facts (the *historicity*) of the Gospels. I seek to challenge the widely held view by secular elites that Jesus the man of history cannot be reconciled to Jesus the Christ of the New Testament.

I informed a colleague of mine, a PhD engineer and a fellow Christian, that I intended to use my own exegetical methodology (techniques for analyzing text) to demonstrate how the two views of Jesus can be reconciled. He and I are senior staff members in the National Nuclear Security Administration (NNSA), and we have long careers in nuclear engineering endeavors. (The NNSA is the governmental agency within the Department of Energy responsible for the nuclear weapons program, defense nuclear nonproliferation, and the nuclear navy.) I told him I was going to employ the techniques of systems engineering to the Gospels. His puzzled look asked the same question as did his voice: "Is that even possible?" Readers who finish this book can answer the question for themselves.

The particular systems engineering approach I employ is an adaptation of a methodology by which engineers assess the safety of nuclear facilities. The reader must wonder what assessing the historicity of the Gospels has to do with assessing the safety of nuclear facilities, which seem to be as closely related as gorillas and matchsticks. Actually, though, one can use similar methodologies for both assessments. From an engineering perspective, to assess something, one follows an approach similar to the one in Table 2–1:

Table 2–1. Elements of an Engineering Assessment Model

#	Element	For the safety of a nuclear system (an example)	For the historicity of the Gospels
1	Identify precisely what one seeks to assess	Define the boundaries of a system and what one seeks to validate. The example here is the main coolant system attached to a nuclear reactor to assess the adequacy of cooling water flow.	Identify the specific historical, most primitive, and salient claims that the Church makes about Jesus in the Gospels.
2	Establish rules to assure that rigor and objectivity are applied throughout	Follow established pressure and flow models to predict coolant flow, such as using head-flow curves provided by the pump manufacturer.	Set the rules for an objective, methodical process for assuring rigor in critically assessing historical texts. In this book, the rule is to apply presumption against any statement in the Gospels.
3	Establish objective criteria to enable the assessment	Demonstrate that adequate flow is available (say, by determining that there is capacity of X liters of coolant per second).	Set objective criteria for the assessment. In this book, a claim needs to meet evidentiary tests to be considered factual.
4	Render a conclusion	Validate that sufficient flow capacity exists to be safe.	Report how the facts of the case compare against the criteria to support a conclusion.

Despite the similarities between the third and fourth columns in Table 2–1, the reader will intuit that the information used to populate the two right-most columns differ in one dramatic way: the engineer has at her disposal the option of performing actual tests of the coolant system. By contrast, we have no way to perform such tests with history. That difference aside, there is some convergence between the two columns, albeit a counterintuitive one. While the best we can do is to attain educated guesses as to historicity of the Gospels (the fourth column), we also have no objective basis to specify exactly what is "safe" (the third column). What is safe is a matter of perception; your perception differs from mine. Conclusions for both scenarios both end up being assessments, which are informed opinions. The methodologies and the criteria may be wholly objective, but the net conclusion is a subjective judgment in both cases. The commonality of assessments and making judgments makes the analogy between the two sets of columns appealing.

DEFINING THE PROBLEM

Our first step is to state what it is that we plan to assess. In the end, what we seek to assess are the most primitive, salient claims that the Church makes about Jesus. We have to set aside any attempt to validate most of the information of the Gospels because (a) we simply do not have enough information to do so; and (b) we need to limit ourselves to only those matters that are subject to historical analytical techniques. By saying that a claim is salient, primitive and historical, I mean it is one that is the simplest expression of an observable historical aspect (or an observable proxy, if the aspect itself is not observable) that says something fundamental about Jesus or the Church. Table 2–2 is a posited set of seven historical but primitive claims, where "primitive claims" are the earliest, unrefined, and salient claims. A different analyst would come up with a different but comparable list. The order of the claims corresponds to the admittedly subjective likelihood that the claims would be accepted by a skeptic from the most likely to the least.

Table 2–2. The Primitive Historical Claims about Jesus

Claim #	Early historical claims that the Church makes about Jesus
1	Jesus's followers banded together after his death to found the Church.
2	Jesus was a wisdom teacher.
3	The Gospel accounts reflect personal witness of first-century CE disciples.
4	Jesus was a miracle worker.
5	Jesus was resurrected from the dead.
6	Jesus is the Messiah.
7	Jesus's death achieved an atonement for the sins of his believers.

The availability of information to assess the seven claims varies from claim to claim. The first claim has such a high likelihood of truthfulness that we can accept it with no further argument beyond this fact: We know from secular history that the Church that exists today is the heir to the Church founded by the original disciples. I take up the other six claims in subsequent chapters. Claims 6 and 7 warrant specific introductions. Unlike the other five claims, these two claims were not directly observable events, even to the first-century witnesses. They are claims about theological beliefs. Theological beliefs reside in the minds of people, not in human history. They are ideas, not events. So, I make no attempt to assess them directly as points of history. Instead, I assess the claims by the following proxies: The witnesses of the first century believed and acted on the ideas contemporaneously with their personal witnesses. In this sense, the beliefs were *native* to the original understandings of the earliest disciples and were not back read onto the narratives.

The reader notices immediately that many claims in the Gospels are not listed in Table 2–2. See Table 2–3 for those types of claims.

Table 2–3. Nonhistorical or Non-salient Claims about Jesus

What is not considered to be a salient historical claim	Examples	Why not included?
Incidental historical information about Jesus	Jesus was from Galilee.	Incidental information does not get to the substance of what the historical Jesus means to Christianity. The incidental information is collected in chapter 3 for context and completeness.
Theological claims about Jesus	Jesus is the Savior of the world, he is Lord, or he will come again.	Theological claims are generally not points of history and thus are beyond the scope of this book.
Details about what comprise the primitive claims	Jesus performed a particular miracle with specific details or Jesus spoke precisely a set of specific words.	System engineers have much more confidence in assessing common themes than individual details. Accordingly, I keep assessment of teachings and miracles on the thematic level.

Before proceeding further, one needs to understand the relationship between the historical Jesus and Christianity. The former is an essential predicate for the latter. The latter is far broader in scope than just history. One could believe the first five historical claims in Table 2–2 and not be a Christian. One can accept that Jesus was a great teacher, a great miracle worker, and a great prophet. One can even accept that Jesus was brought back to life after death. These are events that played out in human history.

They would have been observable occurrences happening to identifiable people in real times and places. These events underlie the stories of the historical Jesus. To make the distinction clear: Christianity is about faith; the life of Jesus is about facts. Understanding Christianity and understanding the life and death of Jesus are not rival or competing understandings, just different ones. Indeed, they can be fully complementary. My goal in scoping out the assessments in this book is to authenticate the historical claims of the Church about Jesus's life and death and the immediate time after his death. I rely solely on rational criteria and logical processes.

To illustrate the relationship between the life of Jesus and Christianity, we can unbundle the de facto definition of orthodox Christianity, the Nicene Creed. The universal Church devised the formative creeds early in her history. The creeds are accepted by more than 90 percent of people who identify as Christians. Using the following example of the creed, notice how few of the lines (those in italics) relate to observable facts of Jesus's life—just five of thirty-three. Note that one of the five can be considered trivial because Jesus, of course, was a man. Three other statements are not contested—that his mother was named Mary, he was crucified under Pilate, and he was buried. The only debated italicized item is the one in bold. The rest of the statements in the creed are either outside of history or are non-verifiable statements of faith:

> We believe in one God,
> the Father, the Almighty,
> maker of heaven and earth,
> of all that is, seen and unseen.
> We believe in one Lord, Jesus Christ,
> the only Son of God,
> eternally begotten of the Father,
> God from God, Light from Light,
> true God from true God,
> begotten, not made,
> of one Being with the Father.
> Through him all things were made.
> For us and for our salvation
> he came down from heaven:
> by the power of the Holy Spirit
> he became incarnate from the Virgin *Mary,*
> *and was made man.*
> For our sake *he was crucified under Pontius Pilate;*
> *he suffered death and was buried.*
> **On the third day he rose again**

in accordance with the Scriptures;
he ascended into heaven
and is seated at the right hand of the Father.
He will come again in glory to judge the living and the dead,
and his kingdom will have no end.
We believe in the Holy Spirit, the Lord, the giver of life,
who proceeds from the Father and the Son.
With the Father and the Son he is worshipped and glorified.
He has spoken through the Prophets.
We believe in one holy catholic and apostolic Church.
We acknowledge one baptism for the forgiveness of sins.
We look for the resurrection of the dead,
and the life of the world to come. Amen.

Note that there are no words about Jesus's preaching, his miracles, or his public ministry. Most Christians understand that the central value of Christianity is love, a value that Christians credit to Jesus himself, yet the word *love* does not appear in the creed. One can conclude that Christianity subsumes the life and times of Jesus, but Christianity is more about faith and theology than facts and history.

ESTABLISHING THE PROCESS

A systems engineering methodology needs to have objective rules for collecting and evaluating information. Here are the fundamental rules for the assessment in this book.

The burden of proof falls to the claims' proponent, that is, the Church. The presumption rests against the claims.

One cannot accept as factual any information reported in the Gospels unless it passes through one or more rigorous tests to demonstrate its acceptability for being objective. The standard is necessary because of the existence of two overriding obstacles to objectivity. First, the Gospels were devised as evangelical tools and are ideologically predisposed to tell an evangelical story, irrespective of the story's historicity. Second, the Gospels were composed in a time quite unlike our own. The idea that recorded history should reflect what actually transpired is a relatively modern standard. The factual approach to history that we take as a given would have been alien to the authors who wrote the Gospels and to their audiences.

The reader should recognize that these rules correspond to the scientific method. As such, instead of trying to substantiate the claims, I look to disprove their negatives. As an example, I attempt to disprove the claim that "Jesus was not resurrected from the dead." The systems engineering methodology results in something akin to the legal processes for bringing charges against an accused. The accusations are rejected until validated. In our case, biblical claims are rejected unless proven reliable.

One area in particular warrants a thorough discussion since the topic comes up frequently: the concept of *retrojection*. The term has its etymology in two words. *Retro-* refers to an earlier time, and *-jection* means to insert. So, to *retroject* means to intentionally introduce material into a story after the fact. One could posit that some material that might have served a theological or evangelical purpose for the Gospel writer was inserted into the text to bolster the author's purpose. Where we suspect retrojection, we need to avoid taking credit for it.

Anyone tackling the New Testament critically must consider the prospect of retrojection. Here is the sequence of events:

1. Jesus led his public ministry for what seems to have been three years.
2. He died.
3. The disciples evangelized the Hellenistic world for several years by oral testimony after his death.
4. The original orally transmitted testimonies came to be written down.
5. We end up with the Gospels.

The lapse in time from (1) to (5) varies over a range, perhaps thirty to sixty years. A lot of things can happen in that span. In particular, theological and other understandings can settle in. The theorized settlings cause people of our time to wonder whether what came out from (5) was really what resulted from (1) and (2). Modern readers ask whether the original authors or perhaps subsequent editors retrojected information onto the original narratives.

To guard against retrojection, I discount any information in the Gospels that may support settled understandings that may have been back-written by the four evangelists. Note that treating candidate words as retrojections does not imply that the material was actually retrojected. I have no way to make such a claim, nor does anyone else. The treatment of potential retrojections as actual retrojections assures objective treatment of textual material. Here is a specific example:

> Some reports have estimated the probability that Jesus could have fulfilled the prophecies that were written of the coming Messiah in the Hebrew Bible. One such set of predictions is presented by Peter Stoner and Robert Newman in *Science Speaks*. They conclude that there are approximately three hundred

prophecies that pertain to the Messiah in the Hebrew Bible that are realized in the New Testament. In assessing just eight of them, they estimate that the probability of them being fulfilled is the vanishingly small number of around one in 10^{28} (i.e., a "1" followed by twenty-eight zeroes, an astronomically large number). The implied degree of precision is unheard of. The best scientific measurements have a precision no better than around one in 10^{12}. The obvious reason for the incredible degree of conformance to the Hebrew Bible prophecies, some might argue, is that the evangelists wrote them into the script to demonstrate their fulfillment, not because they actually happened. Recognizing this objection, we stand wary about claims attending to fulfilling prophecies and do not consider them in our analysis.

SETTING THE CRITERIA

To assess the historicity of the Gospel information, we need to set rational criteria and apply them rigorously to the Gospel texts. Criteria 1, 2a, 3, 4, and 5 in Table 2-4 come from Meier, who produced an encyclopedia on the historical Jesus. Criterion 2b connects logically to criterion 2a and is placed accordingly. It and the last five criteria are my additions. These criteria are objective. Remember that the criteria support assessing the likelihood, not certainty, of historicity:

Table 2-4. Table of Criteria for Historicity

Title of Criterion	What Is the Criterion?	An Example of the Criterion
1. Embarrassment*	The Church would not choose to report something embarrassing about Jesus, the Church, or the Apostles. Therefore, something embarrassing is probably historical.	The crucifixion of Jesus is an example. This form of execution was reserved for the worst kinds of criminals and slaves. A movement at the origin of a religion would never make up a story of its leader being crucified.
2a. Discontinuity (of the first kind)**	If Jesus said or did things that were in keeping with the Judaism of his time, there is reason to believe they may be historical.	Pharisees debated points of Torah among themselves. That Jesus is reported debating them on several occasions is in keeping with this tradition.

2.b. Discontinuity (of the second kind)	If there is information that provides corroboration with a prior claim, the continuity between the two data points provides an indication of authenticity.	If the Resurrection were unanticipated, you would expect some evidence that shows the witnesses to the Resurrection were disbelieving. This kind of continuity exists in the Gospel texts.
3. Multiple attestation	The more a story is captured in different ways by independent sources, the more likely it is true.	This is the gold standard of criteria, akin to having multiple witnesses who are strangers to one another report the same stories to officers about a crime scene. As an example, in all four Gospels and in many episodes, Jesus preaches about the primacy of love.
4. Coherence	The more a story has resemblances to other stories, the more coherence they enjoy together and the more likely they are true.	If Witnesses A, B, and C are all independent witnesses for the defense, all are known to be of high repute, and all offer stories that show the defendant is a person of a moral character, then the more likely it is that the defendant actually is of a moral character. As an example, the Gospels depict Jesus as a preacher who electrifies his audiences. We see in the Gospels, not just the consistency of the teachings, but all the coherence of the reactions to them.
5. Political acceptability	The Gospel writers would have chosen to write their narratives in such a way so as not to undermine the prevailing views of the Roman overlords.	This is one of five criteria from Meier. I do not use this criterion in this book. I include it here only for completeness.

6. Incidental information	*Incidental information* is information about which we have no reason to doubt its veracity. Such information does not attach to any salient point the Church makes nor does it serve any known evangelical or theological purpose.	Here are some incidental facts: Jesus was from Galilee, his mother was named Mary, and the deputy leader of his group was named Simon.
7. Surprise	If Jesus were to have said or done something that was so far afield of what his audience would expect, such a saying or event would have been particularly memorable and thus would have been more likely to have been captured in the collective memory.	The Parable of the Good Samaritan was an assault on the mores of the day and thus would have been particularly meaningful to the audience. As an aside, this parable also meets the criterion for coherence since it comports with other stories about Jesus. This is an example that shows kernels of stories might be deemed valid by more than one evidentiary test.
8. Nonconformance to design	When we find information that runs counter to the overall narrative, we can have some confidence that it is authentic. A writer would not concoct details that undermine his narrative.	By the time the Gospels come together as one corpus in the early second century, the Church is shedding her Jewish origins and picking up a Gentile character. Yet one of the Gospels retains the passage of Jesus referring to Gentiles as "dogs." The Church of the time would see this term as contrary to her purposes, and she would not have used it if she were making up the details. Therefore, the wording is likely authentic.

9. The credibility criterion	Even wildly fictionalized stories need to be placed within the cultural mores of the audience for whom the tales are spun to be accepted as credible. In other words, the degree of license a persuasive writer has with fiction is limited by the constraint of credibility.	The miracle stories in the Gospels are captured in non-hyperbolic and non-sensational ways, lending credibility to them.
10. Omission of information	If there is an absence of information in the stories whose inclusion should have been included if the story were concocted for evangelical purposes, then the omission may be evidence of authenticity of the residual text.	If the writers were free to draft their Resurrection stories unconstrained by sets of facts, the first thing you would expect in the story is direct eyewitnesses to the Resurrection, yet there are no witnesses observing the Resurrection in any Gospel account. This suggests the writers did not overreach in crafting their narratives, even when doing so would have better supported their objectives. The omission makes the residual information that is reported to be perceived as more likely to be true.

* See Meier, *Marginal Jew*. He expressed his set of criteria to test a text against this question: "Do I have positive rationale to reject the text as being ahistorical?" This convention is the opposite of mine, where I ask of the same text, "Do I have positive rationale to accept the text as historical?" The burdens of proofs for acceptance are reversed in the two approaches, my approach being the more severe. In deference to his work, I keep to his convention in naming the criteria.

** As noted above, Meier and I use opposite conventions for naming criteria. For the discontinuity criterion, I have added the corresponding collaboration element. This addition is not in Meier's work, but it fits nicely here and is included accordingly.

The last criterion illuminates the value in a systems engineering approach. The approach uses checklists to assess not just what is present but also to identify absences. An analyst who reviews only what is present and ignores what might be missing is forgoing important information about those absences.

RENDERING CONCLUSIONS

Having clearly stated the problem, applied objective rules throughout, and assessed the claims via objective criteria, I am positioned to render informed judgments about the six essential and earliest claims that the Church makes about Jesus. The seventh, as already noted, requires no additional argument to establish its veracity. In chapters 5 to 10, I take up these claims in detail and provide conclusions.

No contemporary sources about Jesus have survived to our time that originated from other than Christian writers. The only non-Christian, near-contemporary source is from a late-first-century Jewish author who wrote from the emperor's court in Rome. The short passage relating to Jesus in his writing is controversial. I recount the debate in Appendix A as an example of how a systems engineering process can be applied rigorously. In Appendix A, we discover the source supports at least four of the seven original claims of the Church, and moreover, it counters none of them. The passage is powerful, independent evidence of the historicity of many of the claims presented in the Gospels.

One of the common conclusions I draw in subsequent chapters is that the Gospels frequently do not report what one expects. That is, given the evangelical outcomes that the Gospel writers want in their audiences, there are many instances where the writer goes right when he ought to go left. These contra-narratives lend a degree of authenticity because real stories never unfold as cleanly as fictional ones do. "You can't make this stuff up" is another way of saying that truth is stranger than fiction. I come to this conclusion frequently through this book.

The reader will recognize that the you-can't-make-this-stuff-up principle is not just true for the historical claims of the Church. Indeed, the principle is true for Christianity generally. The idea that God should love the world so much that He gave it His Son for its redemption is itself too bizarre a claim to fabricate. C. S. Lewis argues in *Mere Christianity* that Christianity's outlandishness validates its authenticity:

> Reality, in fact, is usually something you could not have guessed. That is one of the reasons I believe Christianity. It is a religion

you could not have guessed. If it offered us just the kind of universe we had always expected, I should feel we were making it up. But, in fact, it is not the sort of thing anyone would have made up. It has just that queer twist about it that real things have about [them].[7]

Lewis might have been traveling the same road that the theologian Tertullian did in the second century. Tertullian reflected on the claims that Christians made. He determined that the claims were simply too bizarre to have been concocted. Thus, he wrote, "Jesus was buried and rose again; it is certain because it is impossible." Tertullian's principle predates my credibility criterion by eighteen hundred years, but they amount to the same thing. For that matter, the idea that the claims of Christianity are too bizarre to have been concocted are native to the biblical texts themselves. Paul declares that the idea of Christian redemption is an "obstacle" and "folly" to the Jew and Greek, respectively (1 Cor 1:23) . Paul never used the saying himself, but he might as well have: "You can't make this stuff up."

3

Getting Started

Here I establish the core set of information that is widely accepted as factual. Widely accepted points that we assume as facts in this discussion are not necessarily universally embraced. For example, a vocal group contends that the person of Jesus never lived. Professor Bart D. Ehrman, himself no friend to orthodox Christianity, writes an entire book to debunk the contention of this group, whom he calls "mythicists." Ehrman demonstrates and demolishes the poor scholarship that underlies their conspiracy-laden theories. He does so by demonstrating that Jesus's existence is beyond dispute. The mythicists are irrational, but their argument evidences all too clearly that no universal agreement exists on any matter that pertains to the life and times of Jesus. Notwithstanding the occasional divergence of opinion, we can accept a set of claims as facts as we establish the baseline.

    Modern readers might feel dismayed to learn that the accepted facts about Jesus constitute a pretty short list. Christians often find it difficult to reconcile the paucity of information with the fact that Jesus is a singularity in history. How could such an important person be so obscure? Perhaps the dismay is wrongly directed. Some scholars have asserted that we actually know more about the person of Jesus than we know about the person of Caesar Tiberius, a contemporary of Jesus, whose importance was understood in no uncertain terms during Tiberius's own lifetime. Considered another way, we have biographical accounts of Jesus that were prepared in the living memories of the people who witnessed the recorded events. By contrast, such a comparable collection of biographical information about Muhammad was not available any earlier than 100 to 120 years after the Prophet's death.

When you consider that this Jesus was a relatively obscure, unconnected, itinerant preacher from a backward part of Galilee—itself an obscure corner of the Roman Empire in which 97 percent of the people were likely illiterate peasants—the real surprise is how much we *can* take to be factual about Jesus. By *factual* here, I mean that the details of his life can be accepted because are attested to in multiple, independent locations; they are presumptively true, meaning details appear in the narratives that we accept as true, for there is no reason to doubt them; they are attested to by non-biblical sources; or they arise from metadata (meaning data about data) or incidental background material.

The sets of factual data we consider here are the historical facts, or probable historical facts, of the life of Jesus, the events immediately after Jesus's death, the processes of designing and writing the literature of the Gospels, and the influences on the Gospel writers.[8]

THE HISTORICAL FACTS OF JESUS'S LIFE

Following are the principal points I take to be as the consensus points of fact pertaining to Jesus's life and times, recognizing that consensus does not equal unanimity.

1. Jesus was born a few years, perhaps four, before the start of the Common Era (CE) in Palestine (a geographical term that comes from a later time), which was then under Roman occupation.
2. Jesus's mother was a young Jewish girl from a small hamlet in Galilee called Nazareth. She was likely a teenager when Jesus was born. She was probably from a peasant family.
3. Jesus was raised in Nazareth with family members.
4. Jesus was born, lived, and died a Jew. Whatever else one knows about Jesus, his self-identified belongingness to God was manifestly Jewish. Everything he is and was reflected his Jewishness. It has become an all-too-frequent tendency of many Christians throughout history to misunderstand or ignore Jesus's Jewishness. Thankfully, Jesus's Jewishness has been recovered in the last hundred years of scholarship.
5. Jesus was thought to have been a carpenter or at least have learned carpentry skills from his mother's husband, Joseph.
6. At some point in his young life, Jesus apparently moved to Capernaum, a Jewish fishing and trading village on the Sea of Galilee (also known as the Sea of Tiberius or Lake of Gennesaret). Remnants of Capernaum and some of the places Jesus walked to are still visible today.

7. Though Jesus's religious training is not accessible to us, he did seem to have some direct or indirect connections with a group of religious folks, the Pharisees. They were a party of laypeople who were known for their piety and obsequious commitment to Jewish rituals and laws. He would reach out to Pharisees and mimic many of their behaviors during his public ministry.
8. Jesus began his public career as a minister when he was thirty or in his early thirties.
9. The transition to his public ministry began with his baptism by a zealous preacher named John on the banks of the River Jordan in Judea. History remembers him as John the Baptist (or Baptizer, which meant *plunger* or *immerser*), a person whose identity is confirmed by extrabiblical sources. He seems to have preached a fiery message of repentance, capped by plunging the supplicant into the Jordan. John follows a script reminiscent of some of the prophets of the Hebrew Bible. John the Baptist would be executed for religio-political reasons, much as Jesus would be one or two years later.
10. Jesus had some relationship with John, but its nature is unsettled. Whether the two really knew other well is unknown, but Jesus clearly looked to him as something of a model or a mentor for Jesus's own ministry.
11. After his baptism by John, Jesus set out on a formative retreat of sorts, evidently to prepare for his pending public ministry.
12. Jesus believed himself to have a unique vocation, assigned a special role by God to bring forth the kingdom of God (also known as the *kingdom of heaven* in Matthew, in deference to Matthew's very Jewish aversion to using the name of God for that Gospel's decidedly Jewish audience). Jesus would use the term *kingdom of heaven* frequently and passionately. Jesus would obsess (in the positive sense) about his election to his unique vocation and his unique relationship with God, whom he called Father. Jesus's zeal for fulfilling his understanding of his vocation would be his calling card for the rest of his life.
13. Jesus became a traveling teacher in an area centered in the semipagan Galilee. He did travel into the more Jewish area of Judea and even into its capital, Jerusalem, on an occasional basis, particularly for festivals. He also visited pagan areas in a few instances. Galilee contained a mixture of pagan and Jewish peoples such that the "real" Jews in Judea looked down upon the people there as something like second-class citizens. Their perceptions might be similar to how modern urbanites look down at rural residents as uneducated country bumpkins. Jesus was

truly a pilgrim, traveling frequently. He never ventured far, probably never more than one or two hundred miles from where he was born.

14. Most of his outreach and contacts were to fellow Jews. He had limited contact with the "nations" of Gentiles in his public ministry, essentially all of whom would have been pagans, as well as limited contact with Samaritans, who were, in Jewish eyes, despised half-breeds living between Jewish and pagan worlds. Undoubtedly, Jesus would have had interactions with Gentiles throughout his life. His hometown was just a stone's throw from the seemingly prosperous Greco-Roman town Sepphoris. This city's name does not appear in the Gospels, even though tiny Jewish hamlets are called out. Among themselves, the Jews would have used the term "Gentile" as mildly scornful in reference to non-Jews. After all, the Jews were the Chosen People; the other nations were not.

15. Jesus's teaching quickly attracted a crowd. The disciples, for sure, but many folks among bigger crowds of Jews also sensed in his teachings a transcendence they had not experienced before. He mesmerized them with his teachings.

16. His teaching's content was characteristically Jewish. Jesus's teachings emanated from many precedents in Jewish tradition. The composite of his teachings generally remained well within the range of Jewish thought at the time. However, he had many novel or near-novel teachings. I present the novelties in a later chapter.

17. Jesus came to be known as a healer. Christians accept these healings as miracles or "signs" (the Gospel of John's term) or "mighty deeds" (the Jewish historian Josephus's word) or "wonders." Aside from Muslims, who accept Jesus's works, non-Christians often believe these events can be explainable by more earthly, material means; believe that they never happened; or claim them to be overstatements of the reported events. Nevertheless, the purported healings caused his ministry to expand by word of mouth, especially across Galilee and into Judea as well.

18. Jesus traveled continuously, almost always on foot, for what was likely a three-year ministry. He had a range of folks who followed him about, tended to his needs, made arrangements for the group, and performed other functions. They were called *disciples*, meaning *followers* in the sense of students who follow their master's teachings. The disciples were a loosely organized or perhaps even unorganized group, whose composition may have fluctuated as Jesus moved from town to town. This band included family members and others whose identities are lost to history. Evidently, there were many dozens of them. An important subset of the disciples were the women, who play a prominent role among the

19. A specific group of special disciples followed Jesus in a particularly close manner. There were twelve of them, all men. This number is not incidental. It is the number of Hebrew tribes. Jesus handpicked these men. This group would be known as the *apostles*, from a Greek word that means those who are sent out—in modern language, we might call them ambassadors. Eleven of them seem to have been Galileans and one (Judas Iscariot, later known as the traitor) was a Judean. By all accounts, they were a motley assortment of ordinary men with nothing holding them together, except their common tie to Jesus.

20. Within this special group were three principal apostles. The first is Simon, whom Jesus would dub as "Cephas" (English: Peter), meaning "rock." Jesus assigned him the nickname to reflect his steadfastness. His nickname may also have been an indirect knock at the name of the then–chief priest in Jerusalem, (Joseph) Caiaphas, where *Cephas* and *Caiaphas* share the same root. The priest's name meant something like "holed-out rock," leaving it for Cephas (i.e., Peter) to be the intact rock. The other two insiders were a pair of brothers, John and James, whom Jesus nicknamed the Sons of Thunder (in Mark's Gospel only). One can suppose the name reflected their zeal. Peter, John, and James were fishermen on the Lake of Tiberius and may have been in some sort of business partnership together. Peter's brother Andrew, also from the same area, was perhaps a fourth person in the inner circle of Jesus's apostles.

21. In their travels, they attracted the attention of the Jewish religious leaders and also, ultimately, the political leaders of Galilee and Judea. The religious teachings and practices of Jesus and his disciples challenged the religious authorities; the growing numbers of followers threatened the Roman overlords. The political climate in Roman-occupied Palestine was very tense, especially in Judea. The Romans and their puppets in Jewish political circles were always concerned about rising instability that could and sometimes did lead to flash points, erupting in violence. The tension was especially acute in Jerusalem, particularly at festivals. Tensions tended to be most pronounced at the gigantic Temple, which was the center of the Jewish sacrificial cult and religious law at the time.

22. After a three-year journey, Jesus and his fellow pilgrim Jews made their way to Jerusalem for a particular Passover feast. The year was approximately 30 CE, with the best guesses being either 30 or 33 CE. Jesus would find himself on the wrong side of Roman tyranny. With

the assistance of an obliging Jerusalem puppet hierarchy, led by the High Priest Caiaphas, Jesus was arrested, tried, and convicted of sedition (or some similar offense) by the Roman governor Pontius Pilate. Outside of the New Testament accounts, Pilate would be remembered to history as a vile and cruel man, who had nothing but contempt and spite for the Jews. He mercilessly kept them under Rome's military thumb. Jesus was crucified and died an utterly painful death as a broken, lonely soul on a Friday afternoon (April 7, 30, is a likely date), a date we now commemorate as Good Friday.

DISCUSSION ON THE LIFE OF JESUS

That's about all we know about the earthly story of Jesus. We do not know his height, weight, eye color, or much about his person. We do not know his likes or dislikes. We know very little about his personal life. We know he spoke Aramaic. We do not know whether he could speak Hebrew, Latin, or Greek, except for a phrase or two. We do not know for sure whether he was literate. One might levy a reasonable wager that Jesus could read and write Aramaic or Hebrew. He may have spoken some Greek, given that Greek was the lingua franca of much of the Hellenized world. We know little about his family, upbringing, or influences in his early life. We know little about the details of how he ran his ministry, how effective it was, or how big it was. We know very little about the apostles, still less about the rest of the disciples.

The collected record of substantive factual understandings makes for a pretty Spartan narrative to be sure. But compared to the information we have about many other elites of the same era, the information about Jesus is actually much richer than one might expect. We have four canonical sources to draw upon (each with its unique points and perspectives), a host of non-canonical literature, correspondence from the early churches (in particular, the corpus from Saul of Tarsus, better known to us as Paul the Apostle), and a few scattered references in non-Christian sources, such as the record from the Jewish historian Flavius Josephus.

We know that Jesus did not write a best seller, command an army, amass a fortune, win an election, invent any major products, or win a Nobel Prize. He did not accomplish anything specifically in his human travels on earth that would have suggested that his was among the most important lives ever lived. Given the dearth of so-called earthly accomplishments, how did his life migrate to the top of the list in terms in Western history, if not world history?

The answer is that his life story did not end with his life.

THE EVENTS IMMEDIATELY AFTER THE DEATH OF JESUS

We also want to establish a baseline for what happened after Jesus's death, the time that would see the migration of Jesus's followers from the religion *of* Jesus to the religion *about* Jesus, a span that went from around 30 CE until Christianity and Judaism split. The latter date is particularly difficult to establish since Judaism, apart from the effects of the Jewish movement The Way (later to become the distinct religion known as Christianity), was undergoing its own transition from a temple-centered cult to a rabbinically based religion at the same time Christianity was being born. Christianity maintained its decidedly Jewish character in essentially all of its practices and adherents until (at least) well into the middle of the second century. Most early Christians would have been Jews, God-fearers (converts to Judaism), or their associates.[9]

The idea that Jews and Christians were distinct groups would be a futuristic one, not an idea native to the earliest Christians. As such, modern rabbinic Judaism and Christianity are really sister religions, both deriving from the same root: Judaism of the first century—specifically, the Second Temple era before the collapse of the Temple cult in 70 CE. (Jerusalem would collapse even more dramatically about a hundred years after Jesus's death when the Romans would once again demolish the city, this time exiling all Jews from the area. The Holy Land would not be ruled again by Jews as a political state until the United Nations established Israel in the aftermath of World War II.)

Most historians, however, treat Christianity as a daughter religion to Judaism. When Pope John Paul II met with Jewish rabbis in a synagogue in Rome, he referred to them as his "elders in faith." Recognizing Christianity as a daughter of Judaism stands to reason. Judaism is the antecedent of Christianity. But if one means by the statement that *modern* Judaism is older than Christianity, the claim is more dubious. Rabbinical Judaism, the source for what we would recognize as Judaism today, is probably newer than Christianity, coming as it did from the second century CE and later, whereas the substance for Christianity was set in the first century. Interestingly, some of the most complete discussions of Jewish life in the late Second Temple era resides in the New Testament.[10]

The events that would transpire after Jesus's death are those upon which, as the Apostle Paul correctly observed, Christianity rises or falls. People dispute what exactly occurred after Jesus's death, so I leave aside for now what those events were. Suffice it to say for the purposes in this chapter that the apostles and a select set of disciples had a *Resurrection experience*.

This experience centered on purported encounters with Jesus after he was raised from the dead. Whatever that experience was (to be explored later), these people would have their whole worldview change in a radical way. They had a profound religious encounter that would affect them personally and compel them to become proponents for their new understandings of the world. These rudderless, Jewish peasant misfits somehow would become the foundation for the world's largest religion.

We start with Jerusalem, circa April 30 CE. We know that the band of followers—mostly Galilean Jews—of a local charismatic religious leader had just witnessed their leader's gruesome execution. The Romans performed the execution. Jesus's blood is on their hands. Not to be dismissed is the culpability of a small set of Jewish leaders in Jerusalem, especially those attached to Roman rule. They were enablers to the execution, as Josephus himself acknowledges later in the first century (see Appendix A). Now, as the clock runs forward about three years, the following points of history emerge:

- A group of Jesus's followers—weak, frightened, and aimless after the crucifixion—now were locked together as an emboldened and energized team ready to engage their world.
- The group, Jews all and acting pursuant to their heritage and traditions, preached about a risen Jesus. This group became evangelists for The Way, when the concept of being an evangelist within Judaism was virtually unknown. The Acts of the Apostles makes the case that the preaching came immediately after the crucifixion. We cannot know precisely the passage of time from the death of Jesus until when the preaching about a risen Jesus began, but it was a notably short time—certainly compared to the time for so-called myth-making. The time it takes to mature revolutionary social or cultural teachings, absorb them, vet them, propagate them, and acculturate them is typically a multiyear phenomenon.
- Some leaders in Jerusalem, rejecting the claims of Jesus's followers, began to persecute them. The leaders organized opposition to Jesus's followers.
- The persecutions became intense and escalated.
- One of the men selected to participate in persecuting the marginal Jews who followed Jesus was a learned Pharisee, a Roman citizen studying Torah (Jewish law) under an esteemed rabbi in Jerusalem. The rabbi was purportedly the grandson of the founder of Phariseeism, and this Pharisee was Saul. He would come to be better known to us by his Roman name, Paul.

- Temple officials selected Saul to go from Jerusalem to Damascus to quash the Jesus-follower heretics/apostates amassed there.
- On the road to fulfill his task to suppress the dissent, Saul experienced a deep conversion and claimed to witness the resurrected Jesus in an apparition. Saul would become an important peg point for us, not only because of the zeal of his evangelism, but because he left a personal written trail for us to follow and because of the indirect trail he left via the stories that Luke, Paul's fellow traveler, recorded in the Acts of the Apostles.

Beyond these historical points, the nascent Jesus movement began to identify itself as a religious sect within Judaism, conforming to Judaism but adding its new dimensions, too. The following events happened in relatively rapid succession:

- The newly emergent Church developed a theology about Jesus. By *theology*, I mean a religiously motivated or religiously informed explanation for Jesus's life, death, and resurrection. Given its short birthing process, this theology would prove to be remarkably resilient and cogent, lasting as it has now for two thousand uninterrupted years. The markings of Christianity were codified early.
- The Church became a community of believers, bonded together.
- The Church became evangelistic.
- A sacramental understanding of Jesus and the community developed.

We cannot precisely date the development of theology, the rise of a community, the understanding of sacraments, and the beginnings of evangelism. However, we can make some estimates, based on the timing of Paul's conversion. Paul appears as a convert just two to four years after Jesus's death. By then, all of these theological points seem to have already been settled. Indeed, it may well be that there *never* was a time after Jesus's death and purported Resurrection that these four things had not been in place on some fundamental level. The four attributes are of a most primitive origin, predating the emergence of Christianity as anything like the distinctive or organized religion we understand it today.

THE WORLDVIEW OF THE EVANGELISTS

The evangelists did not write their stories from nowhere. They were people of their time and place, and they reflected their understandings, values, history, and language in their texts. In particular, the backdrop for all the writers is a clear Jewish worldview of the first century CE. Their religious sources came from Hebrew/Jewish traditions; they would have

- Accepted the Hebrew Bible as normative; the Torah in the Hebrew Bible would have had principal place, but the prophets and the writings would have held sway as well.
- Believed in one sovereign God of the universe.
- Understood themselves to be God's chosen people.
- Centered their religious cult on the temple and its priests and attendants.
- Looked back at their history for their values, aspirations, identity, and heroes.
- Awaited the Messiah to relieve them from the yoke of Roman bondage.

These heroes of Hebrew/Jewish tradition include the major figures: the patriarchs, Moses, the judges, David, Elijah, the named prophets (Isaiah, Jeremiah, the writers of Daniel and Ezekiel as the top tier of the prophets, with another eight or so lesser ones behind them); and more political activists, such as the Maccabees, a fiery brand of militant Jews dedicated to purging pagan influences from the Temple and from the Holy Land.

The political situation in the Holy Land at the time of Jesus was complex. The Romans had occupied the land, the same land given by God to the ancestors more than a thousand years before as a perpetual gift. The local Jewish leaders and Temple priests were de facto puppets of Rome. They exercised authority over religious matters and controlled the Temple.

The political structure could have led to a stable political environment in *Pax Romana*. Most of the people under Rome's rule lived in peace, and there was wide stability in the Empire at the time. Such was not the case, however, in Judea. Interestingly, religious oppression played no significant role in the unrest in Judea, at least in Roman eyes. The Romans were practical rulers. They allowed conquered lands to practice their local religions as they pleased as long as they did not run afoul of Roman order. Indeed, Rome was very accepting of Judaism. There were at least 2 million Jews (perhaps a few times this number by some estimates) in the 50 million to 60 million souls in the Roman Empire. The Jews were concentrated in the Roman area of Palestine, but they were scattered across the Mediterranean world. Festivals in Jerusalem could draw a quarter to a half million pilgrims. Pagan Romans generally could not understand how the Jews could only have one god, but, in their eyes, if the Jews only wanted one, then so be it. The Romans afforded Judaism a prized place among many religions because Judaism was highly ethical and ancient and had a realness to it that many of the pagan religions and mystery cults lacked. One might even say that the Romans had a certain fondness for Judaism, even if the fondness did not necessarily flow to the Jews as a tribal unit—or, using a sociological term, to the Jewish nation. Judaism had a special appeal to pagan Romans because the pagan gods, unlike Israel's God, could be manipulated on a quid pro quo basis, were petty, and were anything but philosophically based.

There were many Jews in high places in Roman society. Paul's father in Tarsus, which is in modern Turkey, would be one such example.

The Romans saw themselves as accommodating to Jews. Many Jews, though, did not quite perceive it the same way. That Romans would rule the land given to them by God was sacrilege. That the high priest and his minions would be vassals of Caesar and not of God was unthinkable. That Jews would put trust in foreigners and pay taxes to them was heresy. That the Jews would use a Roman currency with an image of a Caesar on it with the appellation "Son of God" was pure blasphemy. The Jews were looking for a break from foreign rule and a restoration of the land to the chosen people. Many Jews looked for redemption in a warrior-king, in the mold of a David, who would restore to Israel what was rightly hers. Tensions between religious Jews and Romans simmered and not too infrequently boiled over.

The Gospel writers were keenly aware of the religious background and the political context of their era.

CONCLUSION

Even though we know more about Jesus's life and the events that followed his death on a relative basis than most people of antiquity, on an absolute basis, the information still seems too precious. We only wished we knew more! We know that Jesus was a charismatic, itinerant, Galilean preacher who, his followers believed, worked great deeds. We know that he was crucified and, quite unexpectedly, his followers did not dissipate into oblivion after his death but nucleated into a new organization that would become the largest and most impactful religion of all time.

4

The Design of the Gospels

Moving past the events in Jesus's life, we need to gain an understanding of how the stories of Jesus were collected and recorded. The only substantive resource to draw upon about the life of Jesus is the four canonical Gospels. If you wanted to capture an earlier or more original record than the Gospels' understandings of Jesus, you will be out of luck. When the Gospels were written, they were a new genre of literature, but they compare favorably with contemporaneous biographies (*bios*) of the same time period that the Gospels were written.[11] To make any substantive claims about the historicity of Jesus relies, in large measure, on the authenticity of the underlying Gospels. In addition, one needs to understand the origins and sources for the Gospels to gain the context. The wealth of historical-critical scholarship in the last one hundred years or so aids us tremendously.

There are many theories about who, how, and when the Gospels were written. All of the extant versions come from Greek, though it is not obvious that Greek was the original language of composition for all of the Gospel accounts.[12] Clearly, the stories about the life and times of Jesus circulated orally before some of the stories were written down in the documents we would know as the Gospels. Notwithstanding an occasional outlier, the consensus of scholarly opinion on many aspects of how the Gospels came to be written is reasonably solid. I follow the consensus chain in what follows, recognizing that it has its eminent, credentialed detractors.

The first of the Gospels to be written was the one we know as the Gospel of Mark. This is not to imply that Mark was written all at one time or that it was written by a particular person named Mark. Seams within Mark suggest that it has more than one source for its narrative. The Gospels of Matthew and Luke came later and draw heavily upon Mark's Gospel. Of Mark's 661's verses, the author(s) of Matthew's Gospel pull in 90 percent of them, and Luke's author(s) pull in 60 percent. The first three Gospels follow the same story line, present the events in more or less the same order, use similar wording, and can be thought of variations of the same narrative. Thus, as a collection, they are known as the *Synoptic Gospels*, meaning that they are "seen together"—their optics are the same. The parts of Matthew and Luke following the Marcan account are considered to be literarily dependent. Matthew and Luke also share another set of verses that are not in Mark. Scholars call this second set of common information "Q," coming from *Quelle*, which is German for *source*. Scholars theorized Q circulated independently in the first century, but this remains a theory. A copy of a manuscript has never been found. The portions of Matthew and Luke that are neither from Mark nor Q appear to have been written independently of one another. It is reasonably clear that Matthew and Luke followed Mark, rather than the other way around, for many reasons, including the basic ones that Mark is the simplest, the least theologically developed, and the shortest.[13] There are more sophisticated historical reasons to conclude this sequence as well, particularly the relatively positive treatments of Jews and Judaism in Mark versus the other two later renditions, where portrayals of Jews and Judaism are not as positive.

Since Mark's Gospel is likely the oldest, we'll start there. Mark's Gospel is probably the least cited, at least partially because almost all of the Gospel is subsumed in some fashion into the other two Synoptic Gospels or, to a lesser extent, in the Fourth Gospel. The Gospel of John. Simple though it is, Mark is nothing short of a literary masterpiece, even when we think of its attributes purely in secular terms. It sets the stage for a new genre of literature. Its impact on Christianity and on history is incalculable. The Marcan Gospel reflects theatrical drama, draws upon the richness of Jewish irony, shows the depth of human pathos, provides stories within a story, and evokes raw, deep, visceral emotion. Its characters are authentic, the scenes vivid, and the plot rich. And not to be missed, by the way, it is the most compelling story ever told.

Here is the basic structure of the earliest of the Gospels:

- It opens with this one sentence: "The beginning of the gospel of Jesus Christ (the Son of God)" (NAB; the parenthetical words do not appear in all ancient manuscripts). So, the reader knows from the outset what the purpose of the manuscript is and who Jesus is. The last part is important to understand. The rest of the Gospel is told from the perspective of the people living in the narrative, who are unaware of Jesus's identity. As a result, the audience reading the story knows the secret that the characters in the story do not. The secret is known as the Messianic (or Marcan) Secret. It is reminiscent of classical Greek plays in which the audience knows what fate awaits the characters, but the characters on stage themselves do not. Whether the Marcan Secret is a literary convention developed by the author for its dramatic effect and later adopted by the other two Synoptics or whether the events transpired as written is hard to know. (John's Gospel contains no such secret. In John's Gospel, Jesus is understood from the beginning to be a man set apart uniquely by God with a unique, divine identity.) In any event, the Marcan Secret convention adds mightily to the drama that unfolds.

- Jesus bursts onto the scene from nowhere as a man approximately thirty years old. He is baptized in the Jordan by the apocalyptic preacher named John, he is commissioned by God, and he prepares himself for his mission. All of this happens in eleven verses.

- Jesus takes off. The actions are breathlessly pressed together and linked with phrases like "suddenly," "straight away," and "then." The writing style makes it feel as if the reader is sprinting along with Jesus. Nary is there a dull moment.

- Jesus speaks in pithy statements, aphorisms, and parables. He is fashioned as a quasi-embodiment of Wisdom. He remains enigmatic, going by the puzzling title of *Son of Man*[14] and doing the work as the servant of his Father. The puzzling title reflects a Hebrew Bible apocalyptic concept but other biblical concepts, too. Jesus, known to be the source of the term, may have chosen it precisely because of its ambiguity.

- Mark arranges his story so that all of the events—the calling of the Twelve, the travels from town to town, the teachings, the miracles and miracles and miracles—are compressed in what seems to be a year's time, though this is not explicitly stated. The time is compressed and restricted to Galilee or surrounding areas, particularly in areas around the Sea of Galilee. The drama builds in the whole Gospel to the climax of the story, which is the fateful departure from Galilee for Passover in Jerusalem.

- Jesus is arrested on what are dubious charges, railroaded through obviously corrupt Jewish and Roman judicial systems, and sentenced to suffer a horrible public execution.

- In clear understatement, Mark includes only the following two sentences to describe the horrors of crucifixion: "Pilate . . . had Jesus scourged. . . . Then, [the Romans] crucified him and divided his garments" (Mark 15:15, 24 NAB). The barbarism and cruelty of the

Roman mode of execution is so horrific it would overwhelm Mark's reader to see the suffering in print. The author reflects much discretion in his descriptions of the horrors of crucifixion.

The disciples, who had been following Jesus, become scattered and overwhelmed by Jesus's cruel and unjust death. After the gut-wrenching emotion of the crucifixion, now the reader is set up for a triumphant ending. Just when you expect the story to reach out and grab you, the original story ends with a jolt: "Then [the women] went out and fled from the [empty] tomb, seized with trembling and bewilderment. They said nothing to anyone, for they were afraid" (NAB). The Gospel writer leaves it to the reader what to do with the story, which concludes without a conclusion. The reader knows Jesus is resurrected. Precursor words in the Gospel say as much, as Mark has sprinkled the words for "raising" and "rising" throughout, and as the first sentence of the Gospel cited above already portends. However, a risen Jesus makes no appearance in the original ending of Mark's Gospel. It is a most fitting sign-off for the drama this writer has crafted: sixteen chapters that can be read in a two-hour sitting. The author leaves it for the reader and his or her faith—in his day and ours too—to ascertain the Gospel's significance.

- Two endings were added to Mark's Gospel to clarify and elaborate on the Resurrection of Jesus so that the reader would not miss the subtleties the original author intended.

- Here are the important takeaways about Mark's Gospel as a literary piece:
    - The manuscript is *designed*. It is not simply a set of awkward constructs of uncoordinated stories (a "kluge") that the author(s) and editor(s) threw together. The stories are crafted together to tell a cohesive story.

        By "design," we engineers mean that "Mark" (the person [or set of persons] who wrote Mark, who may or may not have been named Mark) crafted his Jesus for his distinct purposes. The obvious purpose common to all of the Gospels is they were written as a means for sharing the nascent Christian faith, either to fortify those already Christian or to persuade others to convert. Additionally, each Gospel had its own subpurposes. The specific subpurposes include sharing the author's unique perspective and theology with the author's audience. In Mark's Gospel, the themes are Jesus being the incarnation of Wisdom and the servant of God.

- The Gospel recounts real events observed by real people in real places in real times. The events are not just concoctions from Mark's fertile imagination.
- The Gospels are literature. The Mark who crafted the manuscript breathed the air of his time. The Gospel reflects Mark's personality and his understandings.
- The order of the stories within Mark's Gospel (and the others) is not strictly chronological. Instead, the stories are ordered to support the storyline. For example, we know that Jesus's public ministry was likely three years long and that he frequented Judea and Jerusalem during those three years. Mark suppresses the visits to Judea to establish the drama of the Passion narrative as the climax of the story. Thus, Jesus comes to Jerusalem just once—during his triumphant entry there.
- The stories in Mark's Gospel convey many lifelike, firsthand accounts of the events. Some of the stories sound almost as if they were written by a reporter who is recording the events for a newspaper. In particular, scholars have surmised that the vantage of the stories in Mark's Gospel likely is Peter's. Mark may had other sources as well.

Matthew and Luke follow Mark's lead and then add their own information, spinning the material to fit their own narratives. The theory that Matthew and Luke both draw upon Mark and Q is known as the two-source hypothesis. Scholars have re-created Q, based on back-extracting it from Matthew and Luke.[15] It was a so-called Sayings Gospel, meaning it was principally a set of sayings and teachings attributed to Jesus, though Q does include a short record of miracles too. Q has been likened to an important archaeological discovery in Egypt in the middle of the twentieth century known as the *Gospel of Thomas*.[16] The *Gospel of Thomas* is an apocryphal document of Gnostic origin. It is younger and of inferior quality to the canonical documents. It provides essentially no direct historical information for our use. It does, however, inform us that Jesus's teaching had currency separate from the canonical Gospels themselves. In this regard, the Gnostic literature and its cousins, the pseudo-canonical books, are less reliable and more recent than the canonical Gospels. It has been said about this set of literature that the Church did not deselect them from the canon; the set deselected itself.

One should understand that the Gospel accounts we have today show indications of editing, as we see with the Marcan additions to the original Resurrection story. If one allows for the prospect that the Gospels may have been developed over a period of time by more than one author and could have drawn from multiple sources, then the discussion of literary dependence of the three Gospel accounts has a geometrically greater number of options about how the three documents, and the individual stories within them, relate. Nothing a priori restricts us to supposing the final versions were developed by one author at a time. (Not relating to the Synoptic problem, but John's Gospel has even clearer indications of multiple authors at multiple times. The evidence includes the arrival of the blessed disciple late in the story, the woman in adultery in John 8, the prologue, and the various post-Resurrection stories.) We discuss authorship of the documents presently.

Like Mark's Gospel, Matthew's and Luke's Gospels were also designed. In form, Matthew adds to Mark's version additional teachings, a birth narrative, and a more complete set of Resurrection stories. Matthew recrafts Mark's servant model into his view of Jesus as the new Moses, presented in a royal line descending from King David. Matthew's Jesus is a Jewish priest, prophet, and king. We deduce this because Matthew cites Scripture from the Hebrew Bible (via its Greek translation, the monumental Septuagint) more frequently than the others, shows Jesus being a law-giver, has Jesus speaking with authority from mountains, follows the Moses infancy stories, and reflects the David-king paradigm more directly and dramatically. Peter has a particularly privileged position in Matthew's Gospel.

Luke takes Mark's servant and transforms Jesus into a superhuman in the mode of a true humanitarian and prophet. In terms of form, Luke includes transformations of Mark's Gospel, mirroring what Matthew did: adding teachings and a preadult narrative, and expanding the Resurrection accounts. Additionally, Luke couches Jesus with a mystical, prayerful interiority and a deep empathy for others that are unique to this Gospel. We find the loving and compassionate nature of Jesus most distinctly here. Some of the greatest New Testament literature comes from Luke's Gospel, including especially the parables of the Good Samaritan and the Prodigal Son.

The Gospel of John—the Fourth Gospel, as scholars call it—is enigmatic at many levels. The Gospel of John looks nothing at all like the other three:

- With no birth narrative, John takes us back to the Jesus as the Word of God at the dawn of creation, who takes flesh to live among us in the fullness of time.
- Jesus is a divine, supernatural being who understands and controls all situations.
- Jesus self-identifies as "I am" seven times. The name is a direct take-off of the personal name of God given to Moses. The author chose

the number specifically, we can suppose, since it represents the Jewish number of completeness.
- Jesus's public ministry takes place over three years and is punctuated with frequent visits to Jerusalem.
- Much of Jesus's public ministry is set in Jerusalem and Judea, unlike the Synoptics, which locate essentially all but the last week of Jesus's public ministry in Galilee.
- The public ministry of Jesus is established in the so-called book of Signs, in which John strategically lays out the Christology of Jesus over the course of seven signs.
- The book of Glory follows, in which John lays out how Jesus redeems the world by his Passion-death-Resurrection saga and how Jesus relates to his Father.

John is usually deemed to be the last Gospel written, but the claim is difficult to test directly because the Gospel itself is at once both the most sophisticated and the rawest of the four Gospel accounts. The complex mixture gives rise to the theory that the document may have been drafted over a period of time via a set of authors. John is a "spiritual" Gospel, certainly highly theologized, but its writing style is the least developed linguistically and uses the simplest Greek. It also incorporates some of the most primitive stories of Jesus's public ministry. The theology in John is identified as a high Christology, meaning that Jesus as Christ is proclaimed in unequivocal, dramatic terms, as contrasted in the more subtle pronouncements, like in Mark. The high Christology makes extracting the historical words and acts of Jesus from John's Gospel more challenging than doing so from the Synoptics. Some scholars dismiss John as wholly ahistorical,[17] but this presumption misses much that can be extracted from John with some confidence. We come back to John as a basis for unfolding the other Gospels. To set the stage for John's Gospel, one way to view it is as the author(s) might have meant it to be read: Jesus was God's love letter to man, and John's Gospel is man's love letter in reply.

HOW DID THE GOSPELS COME ABOUT?

Scholars all agree the four Gospel accounts are informed by earlier oral traditions. How did the oral tradition make it to a written form? Given that (1) writing was an intensely expensive and laborious process; (2) the vast majority of people at the time were illiterate; and (3) the idea of a literary genre of a Gospel was a novel one, one has to ask the basic question: How is it that we are endowed with a veritable gold mine of literary sources of Jesus's life? There are several contributing reasons:

- The first witnesses to spread Jesus's story relied upon oral transmission. That was fine for them originally because the Lord was going to return promptly. They need not leave a permanent record because there was not going to be a future to need it. Paul, for one, was pretty clear on the point that Jesus's return was imminent. When the Church began to realize the Second Coming might be later than the Church's original understanding, the need for building some permanence of Jesus's memory began to take hold.
- As we get into the 60s CE, the eyewitnesses and the first generation of believers are dying off. The Gospel writers recognized this. They made a conscious effort to capture the first-generation accounts to memorialize them for perpetuity before the accounts would be lost forever.
- With the thirty-plus years since Jesus's death, the Church as a whole and the writers as individuals had opportunities to reflect on not just the events in Jesus's life but their meaning. Capturing these understandings gave more richness and color to the events the writers recorded.
- The first written account, Mark's Gospel, did not displace the oral tradition but complemented it. We conclude this for two reasons. Jesus says in Mark's Gospel (1:38) that it is for preaching that he has come into the world. Notwithstanding, Mark contains comparatively little of Jesus's preaching. (Most of what we know about Jesus's teachings come from the other three Gospels.) Further, Mark ends the original account of his Gospel without an explicit Resurrection narrative. One surmises Mark may be filling in some of the holes in the oral record for those who were already familiar with Jesus's preaching and Resurrection. The last point correlates with the early Pauline record in which Paul speaks sparingly about Jesus's life but focuses on Jesus's death and Resurrection. One supposes the community of Mark's Gospel had been informed by the Resurrection tale but may not have benefited from a narrative of Jesus's life. Indeed, providing this narrative may be what motivated Mark to write his Gospel.
- With Mark's Gospel in hand perhaps a decade later, Luke and Matthew felt the need to add nuance and episodes for their particular audiences. They also added in much of the preaching Mark did not include, probably because the ability to gather first-generation accounts of Jesus's accounts was quickly evaporating. The firsthand witnesses and the

secondhand hearers of the oral tradition alive when Mark wrote were dissipating.
- John wrote his Gospel, one supposes, as a capstone. It is mystical journey that brings with it an otherworldliness that the author wanted to assure was propagated to perpetuity.

SUMMARY OF SOME OF THE GOSPELS' DESIGN PARAMETERS

We have established that the Gospels were designed, yet we have four of them. Why were they not homogenized to tell one coherent story? Because each Gospel writer developed his manuscript for certain audiences at certain places at certain times. The details of the design parameters are relegated to Appendix B for interested readers. The summary points from Appendix B are as follows:

- We have theories and pious traditions about the authorship of the Gospels. In the end, though, the authors of the Gospels are anonymous.
- We do not know when the Gospels were written. The process of writing, editing, and distributing them may have been years in the making. We only have reasonable estimates when they were completed. Mark was likely finished in the 60s, Matthew and Luke in the 70s, and John about 90.
- We know the authors wrote for their own unique audiences and for promulgating their views of Jesus. The audiences and visions are, respectively: *for Mark*, Romans and diaspora Jews, and Jesus as the servant of God; *for Matthew*, Palestinian Jews, and Jesus as the Jewish Messiah; *for Luke*, humanitarians of the Hellenized Roman Empire, and Jesus as their Savior; *for John*, for all mankind, and Jesus as the divine Lord.

CONCLUSION

The Gospels, arising from oral tradition, are monumental literary works, quite apart from their obvious religious significance. These facts beg the question: What kinds of literature are they? No simple answer presents itself. Dr. Pitre argues that the Gospels look a lot like then-contemporary biographies. There is truth in his conclusion, but we would do an injustice to the grandeur of the documents to relegate them as linear retellings of history. The injustice emanates from asking too little from the documents (they are literary masterpieces, not simply history) and from asking too much from them (what we know as linear history does not appear until a thousand years after the Gospels were written).

If we know that the Gospels are not linear history, we also know that they are not just collections of myths either. The Oxford classicist C. S. Lewis informs us:

> I have been reading poems, romances, vision literature, legends and myths all my life. I know what they are like. I know none of them are like [the Gospels].... Either [a Gospel] is a reportage ... or else, some unknown (ancient) writer ... without known predecessors or successors, suddenly anticipated the whole technique of modern novelist realist narrative.[18]

Starting with the Gospel whose attributed authorship goes to Mark, we see that the Gospels are documents carefully designed to satisfy the evangelical needs of particular communities in specific places at specific times and with specific writing styles to communicate to their intended audiences. The fact that the documents have been carefully designed, in the sense that a systems engineer would use the term, accords us the ability to extract information from the Gospels that we would not have been able to if the documents were loose kluges of uncorrelated tales. We exploit this fact in making the case that many kernels in the Gospels are authentically historical.

5

The Resurrection

The Resurrection of Jesus is the event that launches Christianity. Without the Resurrection, it is fair to say, that Christianity would never have evolved. Predictably, then, we begin our assessment of the historicity of the Gospels with the Resurrection. (Note that I capitalize the *Resurrection* of Jesus. Other uses of the word, such as the resurrection of all believers, are lowercase.)

Consistent with the theme of this book, I assume the Resurrection did not occur and then rebut the premise. But one cannot start a discussion assuming that there was no event that triggered the birth of the Jesus movement that became Christianity because the Church obviously exists today, and it came from somewhere. What we know did happen is the *Resurrection experience*. Soon after Jesus's death, the disciples had an experience that radically changed their worldviews. I posit a scenario that envisions a resurrection experience that does not actually involve Jesus's physical resurrection and then proceed to debunk that scenario. The debunking involves employing the historians' rational criteria from chapter 2. The highest standard for validating historical claims is multiply and independently attested information with collaborating circumstantial evidence. The Church's claim about the Resurrection meet this standard. Beyond this standard, though, the Resurrection stories are not the stories that one would ever have passed down through history if they were constructed to support the Church's evangelical mission. The Gospel stories of the Resurrection are stories that conform to the you-can't-make-this-stuff-up principle, by which we affirm their historicity.

THE FICTION OF THE RESURRECTION

Skeptics, elites, and nonbelievers assess the story of the Resurrection and offer their own explanations. The following narrative can serve as a proxy for their explanation.

After the loss of their beloved leader by his execution on the cross, the group of disciples experienced overwhelming grief in their existential crisis. They wondered how they could go on. One or more of them had a feeling of Jesus's presence. Maybe the feeling came a day later, maybe a week, maybe a month, maybe a year. Maybe the presence was a rich dream. Whatever the psychological phenomenon was, it derived from the incarnation of a memory of Jesus. Jesus had counseled them so many times not to be afraid and fed them with the confidence that he would always be there for them. The en masse delusion among the disciples was a catharsis for them, expiating their fear and anxiety. In the presence of this hugely emotional and relieving moment, even if a delusion, a new warmth arose, and a new calm came. The presence became so real to them they envisioned in their minds that Jesus was alive again, standing right next to them as he had done only a short while ago. He soothed them before in the flesh. Now, he soothes them in memories. The new memories are so strong that they create their own reality of a living Jesus.

The disciples resolved they would not let the execution of Jesus be the end of him. His words and actions were too great to meet an unseemly end in a tomb. They crafted the idea that Jesus rose from the dead. This idea was the balm that they needed to make sense out of an otherwise insensible conclusion to the life of the greatest man they had ever known. They established that Jesus was alive! *Of course, he was alive.* Once they gave it some thought in the light of day, they realized that some silly pagan overlords could never quash their Jesus, their Son of Man. With this understanding, the disciples began to believe their own narrative. Their conception fit together so well. It was as if God had given them the idea. His death, far from being meaningless, was the ultimate expression of meaning. Jesus cracked open for humanity a door to everlasting life in heaven with the Father.

The re-creation of Jesus satisfied the disciples' holy hunger, a hunger only Jesus had filled for them. His loving ways were so rich and so real in the flesh that they had to survive death. All the disciples had to do now was mutually assent to the myth and broadcast it widely. Believers in Jesus reasoned that their mission was to share this feeling of completion with the world. Thus, the disciples launched their scheme to export calm and hope to an awaiting populace. For the first time now, the disciples began to see why the Jews were the chosen people. They were chosen to witness the fullness of God's plan and then communicate it to the nations: God loves us as His children because we are created in His image. He calls us back with unwarranted, reckless, and unbounded love. Jesus's Resurrection was the proof of God's irrational love for humanity. That is the good news, the gospel.

Over time, the disciples expounded upon and embellished their first Resurrection accounts as part of an evangelical outreach to share the gospel. We need not ascribe any malice in the evangelists' telling of their fantastic stories as true events; instead, the stories were concocted with the purpose of instilling hope and joy in the hearts of the hearers. Then as now, the world was full of desperate people. A story of hope deriving from a repressed peasant who scored major points against the despised Romans is the stuff of which hope is made. The Resurrection story could have spread like wildfire among the empire's desperate souls.

The evangelists were not guilty so much of fraud as hyperbole. Their Jesus stories grew out of real-life stories and experiences that became more fantastic with time. The Gospel writers lived in a time when important people were recalled in epic and heroic terms. Accordingly, the evangelists just followed the path for recording the lives of heroes. The Gospels were not told as modern history with an eye toward objectivity. Nobody ran around with steno pads and took notes along the way. The Gospels' accounts of the Resurrection do not lend themselves to acceptance as a factual representation of actual events.

Emboldened proselytizers invented their stories in their post–Resurrection experience world, based upon their invented virtual reality of a present Jesus being with them after his death. One scenario offered by John Dominic Crossan, a former Catholic priest, illustrates the point:

> First, the Easter story is not about the events of a single day, but reflects the struggle of Jesus's followers over a period of months and years to make sense of both his death and their continuing experience of empowerment by him. Second, stories of the resurrected Jesus appearing to various people are not really about "visions" at all, but are literary fiction prompted by struggles over leadership in the early Church. Third, resurrection is one—but only one—of the metaphors used to express the sense of Jesus's continuing presence with his followers and friends.[19]

The Resurrection story is not about what actually happened but about how the disciples *felt* about it. Crossan's summary is consistent with the idea there was a Resurrection experience, but the experience existed within the minds of the observers, not with any events transpiring in the physical world on the planet Earth. As we would understand it today, "The central theological claim (or modern theological tradition) remains constant: The Bible mediates a myth-concept-experience that has the power of revelation, not the biblical text itself."[20]

In Crossan's vein about the subjectivity of the Resurrection experience, there is a book from no less than an Anglican bishop, John Shelby Spong, whose title *Resurrection: Myth or Reality?* intends to answer itself.

With a resurrection of hope, the disciples kluged together sets of fiction en route to becoming the first pan-religion in history.

TESTING THE HYPOTHESIS THAT THE RESURRECTION IS A FICTION

We now have a hypothesis that we can test: The evangelists made up the Resurrection stories.

For the rest of this chapter, we assume that the evangelists retrojected (i.e., made up and inserted back into the record) all the evidence in the Gospels to support their fictions, unless we can provide objective evidence to the contrary. In lay terms, we ask the simple question: If one were making up the Resurrection stories, would an author have provided us the Resurrection stories that we have received through the Gospels?

After Jesus's death, the earliest disciples experienced something revolutionary. We can conclude so without relying upon any subjective Christian testimony of claiming to see a resurrected Jesus. A scholarly answer is that the early disciples had a Resurrection experience. The term *Resurrection experience* does not imply they actually experienced a physically risen Jesus. We have independent strands of historical points leading us to the conclusion of the disciples experiencing a profound, life-changing event for them, setting aside for the moment what that event was. We have these marks to inform us of the Resurrection experience without identifying the event itself:

- The dispositions of the disciples changed from before to after Jesus's death.
- The disciples formed themselves in a distinct organization with a mission.
- The new organization displayed an evangelical and proselytizing spirit that was without any contemporary parallel.
- The post-Jesus teaching motif switches from Jesus's wisdom teaching to the disciples' Christological teaching.

With respect to identifying the source of the Resurrection experience, the reality of an empty tomb might be a matter to debate, but the Church that professed it is not. Luke Timothy Johnson makes the point this way: "Although traditions about the empty tomb are ancient, they are not at the heart of the resurrection experience. . . . The absence of a body does not by itself empower a community. It is a new form of presence that needs explanation, not an absence [of Jesus's body]."[21]

Now we have to locate the cause that triggered the birth of the Church.

REBUTTING THE ARGUMENT FOR A RESURRECTION EXPERIENCE WITHOUT A RESURRECTION

The problems with possible explanations for the Resurrection experience without a resurrection, like Crossan's argument, are threefold. On the first problem, *any possible explanation for a Resurrection experience without a resurrection is speculative*. Never has there been a fulfilling articulation of a scenario that is consistent with the Resurrection experience without a resurrection. Notwithstanding, it would be an unfair burden to place upon skeptics to have them provide such a substantive response. Proving negatives is virtually impossible. Instead, we recognize that the burden of proof about the Resurrection falls to the Christian to substantiate, not to the skeptic to negate. Extraordinary claims require extraordinary evidence. In any event, the reader should know that no acceptable scenario to substantiate the Resurrection experience without a resurrection has ever been argued.

The second problem is that *a Resurrection experience without a resurrection demands a massive conspiracy by the disciples*. If there were a conspiracy, why would the perpetrators have pushed it? What was in it for them? The disciples might have wanted to provide hopeful stories to their peers to make the world a better place, but would they continue their magnanimous endeavor if they were going to be persecuted and killed for what they knew to be false? Not very likely. Throughout history, people have sacrificed themselves for noble purposes, but who sacrifices himself for that which he knows to be a lie?

Last, *the consensus of critical scholarly opinion runs counter to the hypothesis of the Resurrection experience without a resurrection*:

> It is extremely difficult to object to the empty tomb on historical grounds. . . . Those who deny it do so on the basis of theological or philosophical assumptions. By far, most exegetes [learned people who analyze texts] hold firmly to the reliability of the biblical statements about the empty tomb. In fact, in a bibliographical

survey of over 2,200 publications on the resurrection in English, French and German since 1975, the researcher Gary Habermas found that 75 percent of scholars accepted the historicity of the discovery of Jesus's empty tomb.[22]

William Lane Craig has taken up the challenge of considering explanations for the Resurrection experience without a resurrection. In one element of his work, he proposes not trying to prove whether the disciples actually discover the tomb of Jesus being empty. He recognizes that the facts surrounding the event are lost to history. So Craig asks a different question: Which hypothesis is *most likely* to be true among rival hypotheses? The set of hypotheses are as follows:

- The Resurrection Hypothesis: God raised Jesus from the dead.
- Conspiracy Hypotheses: A group of followers conspired to make up the story.
- Apparent Death Hypothesis: Jesus did not die but only appeared to have died.
- Wrong Tomb Hypothesis: The disciples went to the wrong tomb; it was empty because Jesus had never been placed in it.
- Displaced Body Hypothesis: The disciples went to the right tomb where Jesus corpse had been lain, but his corpse was removed to another place to put it into a permanent locale.

Craig concludes that the first hypothesis is simply much more likely to be true than any of its rival hypotheses, and, thus, it should be accepted. Craig's argument only goes so far because the tests of the rival hypotheses fall back on relying upon the reports in the Gospels to provide the evidence he uses to test them. One can quickly see how prospective retrojection of narrative details could have crept into the development of the Gospel accounts. Rejecting rival hypotheses requires one to rely upon accounts of information now resident in the New Testament. A modern skeptic could suppose that such information was back-written into the story line in the first century. The Gospel writers inserted the discriminating information to discount the rival hypotheses when they were first proposed in the first century. In other words, testing the veracity of the Resurrection accounts relies upon accepting the veracity of the information in those same accounts. This is to argue a tautology, of course. To take one example of prospective tautological reasoning, consider this: the New Testament accounts of the Passion include the detail that the disciples watched where Jesus's body had been lain on Good Friday so that they could go to the tomb on Sunday morning to prepare the body for proper burial. The skeptic could argue that the Gospel writers added this detail as a contingency. The evangelists wrote this not because it actually happened but because it rebutted an argument a first-century skeptic might have had. The skeptic's argument might claim that the tomb was empty not for the reason that Jesus was risen but that the body had never been placed in the tomb in the first place. The evangelist's clever preemption moots the objection. Thus, we are left questioning whether the preemption is historically true or a retrojection. Unfortunately, we have no definitive way to know for sure.

The example in the previous paragraph is a classic manifestation of an intellectual problem with assessing the historicity of Gospel texts. We must confront this critical intellectual problem with extracting information from the Gospel accounts: How do we know the information recorded about the events actually happened as stated versus whether they were written back into the story line by the Gospel writers? To establish the historicity of claims, we need to apply the rigorous criteria and methods identified in chapter 2.

TRYING TO "PROVE" THE RESURRECTION FROM THE NEW TESTAMENT TESTIMONY

We twenty-first-century readers might suppose the Gospel writers wrote the accounts to "prove" Jesus rose from the dead. However, this supposition is anachronistic. We tend to read the accounts technically as if the accounts were samplings of modern history. But the Gospels were not written for people in our time but for the people of their own time. Those people primarily received their testimony orally, and oral testimony was often considered the more authoritative venue for them, even for the few who were actually literate. The primacy of oral testimony over written is the opposite of the order we impose in our modern, literate, technical world. The content of oral testimony when the Gospels were being composed, we can be sure, was saturated with Christological understanding, a Christology that rested on the Resurrection. We have confidence that this is true because the most primitive records we have of Christianity are from Paul. Paul's words are replete with Christological content but almost devoid of any information about Jesus's life and public ministry. What's more, Paul informs us that the Christological understanding of the Resurrection accounts predated his conversion to Christianity. Therefore, the Gospel writers would have limited need for written testimony to "prove" the Resurrection to the readers. The proclamation of the Resurrection was widely available orally already when Paul wrote and later when the evangelists wrote. In furtherance of the point that the writers did not seek to prove Jesus's Resurrection, we note the following:

- The original version of Mark ends without a specific Resurrection story at all, yet the author thought the Gospel was complete without it. Why? Because the audience already knew about the Resurrection. Mark's account uses words foreshadowing the Resurrection throughout his Gospel, for suspense and subtlety as literary devices. The story of Jesus's public ministry had not been as widely reported, so that's where the evangelist directed his literary effort. Indeed, Mark may have written his Gospel precisely to document Jesus's public ministry.

- The Resurrection is the cornerstone of Christianity, yet the Resurrection and post-Resurrection stories are small segments of the Gospels. In the original version of Mark with the shorter ending, there are zero references to the Resurrection. In the other Gospels, Matthew offers one chapter of twenty-eight that includes Resurrection and post-Resurrection stories. For Luke, it's one chapter of twenty-four. In John, it's one chapter of the original twenty or two chapters of the later version with twenty-one chapters. This makes for a grand total of just four chapters pertaining to the Resurrection and post-Resurrection, compared to a total of eighty-nine chapters in the four Gospels all told—about 5 percent. The Gospels do not focus on the Resurrection, even if the Resurrection was certainly the central tenet of Christianity when the Gospels were being composed. Why? Because the oral testimonies of the disciples had already articulated the Resurrection thoroughly, so the writers of the Gospels had no need to make a written case for it.

- If you were an evangelist and you had just told a potential first-century convert that Jesus had been raised from the dead, he would have asked the obvious question: "Well, where is the living Jesus now?" The point of the obvious question is, If he rose from the dead, then why not present him to us in his post-Resurrection form? Of the four Gospel accounts, only Luke provides an answer (here, I discount the later accretion to Mark's Gospel that draws upon the Lucan narrative because it is not literarily independent from Luke). Luke provides us the Ascension. None of the other authors offer an answer to the question of where the risen Jesus is now, which implies two things: (1) the writers concluded they did not need to answer the obvious question, which suggests the answer was already widely known and need not be repeated, and (2) they made no attempt to insert any contingency to address this particularly obvious question. If the writers withheld supplying contingencies for identifying what happened to Jesus after he said his farewell, what does the omission say about potentially inserting contingencies into other parts of the Resurrection accounts? It means that the authors took some effort to avoid inserting contingency information into their texts, providing some confidence of the historicity of the (noncontingency) information that actually is recorded.

- The Gospel writers never intended their Resurrection stories to be interpreted simply as history. The stories emote, they spark drama, they inspire us, and they put our humanity in the mirror. Yes, the Gospel writers' accounts of the Resurrection echo the truth Jesus had been raised as a historical point, but the writers demand much more from their readers than assent to historical events, like asking us to
    - Sprint along breathlessly with Peter to the empty tomb (John 20:1–8).
    - Share Mary of Magdala's exuberance when Jesus addresses her as "Mary" and her sincere response, "Rabboni," which the writer retains in its Aramaic original (John 20:16).
    - Have our hearts burn along with those of the disciples on the way to Emmaus (Luke 24:13–35).
    - Be thrice reconciled with Peter at the breakfast by the sea (John 20:15–19).
    - Connect to Thomas's overwhelm when he declared, "My Lord and My God!" (John 20:24–29)
- Psychologists attribute the success of Christianity to its ability to overcome the fear of eternal death. However, if overcoming the fear of eternal death were the reason the evangelists concocted Jesus's Resurrection, then surely they would have had the Resurrected Jesus saying so. Yet, not a single line in the four Gospels explicitly links Jesus's words about his Resurrection to the readers' future afterlives; any linkage is indirect. The connection must have been explicit in the oral testimony that circulated pertaining to Jesus, as we know because the linkage is quite explicit and frequent in Paul's writings, which predate the Gospels by a decade or more (see 1 Cor 15:12–19).

The Gospels' Resurrection accounts may touch at the surface of history, but they stab at the heart of humanity. To understand the Gospel accounts only as proof of the Resurrection misses what the writers intended. It seems the writers started with the understanding that the audience already knew Jesus was resurrected. They didn't seek to prove this point; instead, they tried to capture the meaning of the event more than the event itself.

THE ARGUMENTS FOR THE RESURRECTION

The Argument from Multiple Independent Attestation

The first problem with the hypothesis that the evangelists made up their Resurrection stories is that stories of Jesus's Resurrection abound—from many people in many places in many contexts. The composite brings questions about how all of the incidents could have been concocted and yet share such commonalities. That one person could come up with an outlandish claim is certainly understandable, and it is even understandable how several people attending the same event might make the same outlandish claim. It is, however, an entirely different matter when many people who are separated from one another in time and space make the same claim quite independently of one another. Consider this citation from Paul:

> [Jesus] appeared to Cephas [Peter], then to the Twelve. After that, he appeared to more than five hundred brothers at once, most of whom are still living, though some have fallen asleep. After that he appeared to James, then to all the apostles. Last of all, as to one born abnormally, he appeared to me. (1 Cor 15:5–8)

Paul lists six discrete accounts. The tally does not even include the untold number of oral accounts not explicitly identified. Some of the accounts are attested in more than one location in the New Testament. The appearance to Paul shows up five times in the New Testament (once in Galatians, once in 1 Corinthians, and three times in Acts). Paul's list of six appearances above does not include stories at the end of John's Gospel, nor does it count the appearances to the women followers, who are the first witnesses to the Resurrection in all four Gospel accounts.

Paul almost certainly knew of the appearances to women too, although he did not include them. The exclusion should not be taken to mean that Paul did not believe the women's accounts. Paul is rendering here something akin to a rabbinical statement. He conforms to the rules for making arguments by which rabbis would have abided. The rabbis' rules generally discounted women's testimony.

Additionally, the appearance of the risen Jesus to James (James the Just, whom Paul calls the brother of Jesus) is nowhere attested to in canonical Scripture. It is found, however, in the apocryphal *Gospel of the Hebrews*, one of many early Christian documents that did not make it into the New Testament. The information in noncanonical sources like the *Gospel of the Hebrews* suggests the possibility of other Resurrection appearances beyond those explicitly identified in canonical Scriptures; the surmised oral accounts are implicit examples.

So, if a delusion were spread among many people, it was dispersed widely in geographical and temporal senses. There are many literarily independent sources in the canonical books for the Resurrection: Paul, John, Matthew, and Luke. (The Resurrection stories are an unusual case where Matthew and Luke do not appear to have a common antecedent in Mark. The longer ending of Mark with its Resurrection stories appears to depend on Luke and perhaps other sources.) The probability of all four literarily independent sources coming up with substantially similar Resurrection stories is remote. The far more likely answer is they did not make up their stories at all, but instead the stories were passed down to the writers from earlier, more primitive and common sources. This is precisely what traditional Christian teaching has always posited; moreover, the Church has consistently taught that the source of the primitive witness is the apostles and first disciples themselves.

In response, the skeptic might argue for an early common delusion that then was propagated down the chain of history, but the facts discount this possibility. The appearances to James and Paul could not have been the result of some sort of common delusion among Jesus's followers. Neither of them was a follower of Jesus initially; actually, both were at first antagonistic toward the Church. As a side note, Paul and James would both be martyred for their faith, providing a huge mark of confidence that the faith they sported was genuine. People do not offer themselves for martyrdom for stories they know to be false. Since they were martyred and were eyewitnesses to the events they reported, one has another piece of independent collaborating evidence for the claim of the Resurrection.

There are simply too many independent, uncoordinated testimonies to discount. Can people who are joined together be guilty of groupthink and believe the same thing, even if it never happened? Of course, especially if what they report seeing is what they wanted to see. But how would this point be applied to the many recorded appearances? Since many separate accounts of many different incidents come from many different sources, including one event allegedly witnessed by five hundred, discounting the existence of the testimonies is hard, even if we toss aside the content of the individual testimonies themselves. The interesting point of the five hundred people is that, when Paul wrote these words—in a public document meant to be read aloud—many of the witnesses were still alive. Paul as much as challenges the readers to go and interview one of them to validate the claim.[23]

The foundational myth of Christianity is the witness of the risen Jesus. Here are interesting parallels with some other foundational narratives for other faith traditions:

Table 5-1. Purported Witnesses to Events in World Religions

Event	Religion	Witness(es)
The Ten Commandments	Judaism	Only Moses
The Ascension of Elijah	Judaism	Only Elisha
Revelation of the Qur'an	Islam	Only Muhammad
Revelation of Maroni	Mormonism	Only Joseph Smith
The Enlightenment	Buddhism	Only The Buddha
The Resurrection	Christianity	Dozens (plus the five hundred)

The Stories We Have in the Gospels Are Not the Stories Fabricators Would Have Written

Let's start with the fundamental hypothesis that Jesus's disciples made up the stories of the Resurrection and see if it comports with what we know from the Gospels and historical accounts. To make this assumption, the writers would have served up their concoctions with generous amounts of cleverness and a heaping portion of deceit, and topped it off with some collusion. One might suppose the probability of these things coming together ought to be quite small, particularly the collusion point since the writers are known to be literarily independent. We just assume these constraints away by hand-waving. We consider what we have in the Gospels against the fact that we know the Gospels were designed, meaning they were written to meet one or more specific purposes. We look for these items for concluding that you can't make this stuff up:

- Contra-information: information running counter to the narrative being curated
- Omitted information: information that we should have expected if the stories were concocted
- Novelty information: information that describes events that deviate from then-existing norms
- Complexity of information: the information is unnecessarily complicated just to have been made up.

The Argument from Inclusion of Contra-Information

Assuming the Gospel stories were simply made up, one would think the writers and particularly their later editors would have expunged contra-narrative information. The kinds of contra-information that we should expect to be edited out would be information that could derail the Gospels' messaging, yet we find that such expungement has not occurred. That the Gospel writers and subsequent editors retained the contra-narrative testifies to the Gospels' historicity:

- In all four Gospel accounts, women are the first witnesses to the Resurrection. They are remembered as the "apostles to the apostles." Yet women's testimony was heavily discounted in the first century.[24] Why would the evangelists make up details about women's experiences if they only detract from the evangelists' narratives? Since the writers cannot really not take any credit for the women's accounts, their inclusion argues for authenticity.

- For unspecified reasons, Jesus's identity is obscured in some of his appearances. People do not immediately recognize him. The incidents of Mary of Magdala at the tomb, the two travelers to Emmaus, and the meeting at the shores of the Lake of Galilee are three cases. Why would the authors include these details? They detract from the narratives they are supposed to support. If the evangelists were fabricating, wouldn't they have purged these words, or at least modulated them? Since the potentially undermining information is retained, we have reason to accept the stories' authenticity.

- Even after the Resurrection, the now-Resurrected Jesus rebukes the Eleven for having believed neither the women nor the two disciples who came back from Emmaus (Mark 16:12–15) about his Resurrection. At this point in the Gospel story, couldn't the apostles be portrayed more positively? The readers of the Gospel accounts realize, of course, that the deliverers of the message are ultimately these same disciples. Why would the evangelists choose to make the first witnesses seem so skeptical when the audience is set up to expect total triumph? Why would the authors downplay the apostles at this point in the story when they are being launched on their heroic paths? If their stories were untethered to real events, they most likely would not have retained this information, yet we have this set of contra-information: another suggestion of authenticity.

- Even as Jesus is ready to depart from his friends with his farewell address—the Great Commission—some "still doubted" (Matt 28:17).

Wouldn't the writer want to convey to the reader some assurance about all of the apostles being on the same page with Jesus before he leaves them and commissions them for their mission? Wouldn't this have been the place to steel the resolve in the apostles?

The writers are reporting what they understand to be true, even though their points might potentially distract from their intended purpose. No one would choose to include information that undermines his own narrative if he knew the information were false. Therefore, we conclude that the contra-narrative information must be true—strong evidence in favor of the Resurrection.

The raw, unrefined character of the Resurrection narratives also testify to their authenticity. The stories even convey the kind of ambiguity real stories of this sort would carry. Expunging ambiguity is what you get with a concocted story, because concocted stories are blessed with the predictability of certainty. The people who experienced the Resurrection were overwhelmed and confused. Nothing made any sense. Their confusion is preserved in the Gospels, just as you might expect in any real story, but you would *not* expect in a concocted one—especially one edited and refined over decades, as the Gospels were.

The ambiguities in the individual Gospel stories of the Resurrection are exacerbated when looking across the Gospel accounts. The four accounts seemingly do not jibe with one another to provide a consistent story. Counterintuitively, the lack of precise agreement among the accounts actually authenticates the core accounts' veracity. If the accounts were tightly conforming, one would suspect collusion, but we have no reason for suspicion here. Each account is distinct. It may be an unlikely source to argue for the veracity of the New Testament, but here is a Jewish scholar commenting on the New Testament and its ambiguities, likening them to the same kinds of ambiguities in the Hebrew Bible (the Tanakh), thus suggesting a certain authenticity in the former's divergent renderings:

> Both the Tanakh and the New Testament incorporate multiple, contradictory traditions, as we see when the same story is narrated in Kings and Chronicles, or among the four Gospels. This is very different from modern books, which typically, especially when they deal with the past, take a single viewpoint. The variety of opinions on crucial ideas in the Tanakh anticipates the variety of ideas in the New Testament.... Both the Tanakh and the New Testament do not participate in the either/or world of the twenty-first century.[25]

Finally, divergences are not the same as disagreements. Sometimes there are divergences that are real disagreements, but the recorded divergences we see in the Gospels do not derail the basic stories recounted. Amy-Jill Levine, a Jewish professor of New Testament studies at Vanderbilt and the coeditor of the *Jewish Annotated New Testament*, writes,

> A number of my students get very worried when I point out differences [between Gospel accounts]. They fear they cannot trust the Gospels, or that Matthew or John somehow got the details wrong. There are some biblical studies experts who delight in pointing out discrepancies in the texts, as if a different perspective would serve like a thread that, when pulled, would unravel the entire picture. Nonsense![26]

As an example of how divergences do not negate the big picture of history, consider this example: How many people still harbor dissenting views on the assassination of President Kennedy in 1963? There is a cottage industry in conspiracy theories about it. How many shots? From where? From whom? Was the CIA involved? The Cubans? The Russians? Jack Ruby? Whatever divergences exist, in the end, all the theories still conclude that President Kennedy was fatally shot. So it is with the Resurrection stories in the four Gospels: There may well be divergences about *how* it happened, but not *whether* it happened.

The Argument from the Omission of Expected Information

Consider what is *not* in the Gospels. The authors and editors had significant opportunity to include information into their story lines that would have greatly increased the ability to sell their stories, if the Gospel accounts were fabricated. That the authors were reluctant to include such information tips off the reader that the content preserved in the accounts is more likely to be authentic. Here are some examples:

- If you are trying to convince people of the Resurrection and you have the luxury of writing the story as you wanted, the first thing you'll likely do is to include a firsthand, direct eyewitness to the Resurrection. However, none of the Gospels include any firsthand account of Jesus's Resurrection.
- The evangelists would have more than ample opportunity to create characters or events to serve their evangelical needs, whether they existed or not. Yet there is a remarkable lack of such information in the Gospel accounts. Consider this example, in which Luke could have

inserted in Acts a counterfactual (shown in italics) that would have significantly enhanced the story's marketability:

> The priests and the captain of the temple guard and the Sadducees came up to Peter and John while they were speaking to the people. They were greatly disturbed because the apostles were teaching the people, proclaiming in Jesus the resurrection of the dead. *The apostles were so effective in their preaching that members of the family of the captain of the temple guard themselves became evangelists in Egypt.*

Inclusion of the italicized words would have added a dose of leverage without having to defend anything. After all, thirty or forty years after the fact, if Luke were just making up the story, who would be able to challenge the claim about the temple guard's family? Luke holds true to his source material and the facts, taking no liberty in adding information that would have served his purpose. If a writer avoids embellishment, we have evidence of the faithful transmission of information entrusted to him.

- If you were an evangelist writing about the most dramatic action in the history of the world, you would be expected to include a lot of hyperbole. Here is a man who just rose from the dead, directing his disciples to preach, baptize, and forgive sins. Yet there is a paucity of triumphalism, meaning something glorious in human terms. Furthermore, no direct words from the Resurrected Jesus tie his Resurrection to believers' future resurrections—yet this connection is exactly what the reader should expect since it is the central theological claim of Christianity. By comparison to the mild proclamations from the Resurrected Jesus, consider these instances with much higher degrees of triumphalism: Abraham was gifted with descendants as numerous as the sands on the sea, Moses was granted a promised land flowing with milk and honey, and David was promised a dynasty that would endure forever in which all of his enemies would be put under his feet.

  There is an acute lack of parlaying the Resurrection to any direct personal benefit for the witnesses. The commentary from the Resurrected Jesus resides in the spiritual rather than the earthly realm. Here is what the Gospels *don't* have Jesus saying to his disciples, which are examples of claims a reader would expect to come from Jesus if the stories were mere concoctions:
  - How and when will Rome be overthrown?
  - How do my followers take over the world?

- How will we get even with Caiaphas and Pilate, the Jewish high priest and the Roman governor, respectively, who were responsible for Jesus's death?
- How will current and future disciples benefit from their experience?

This set of questions might seem speculative for us to ask so long after the events, but such queries are actually native to the stories preserved in the Acts of the Apostles. In Acts, the apostles explicitly ask Jesus when Israel would be restored. Jesus sets the question aside, noting that the answer rests with the Father. He redirects them to the spiritual domain, saying to them that they have their appointed roles. "Follow me" is his command, even if he never quite specifies where the following leads.

One can come up with dozens of more immediate or urgent statements the evangelists should have wanted to put on the lips of the risen Jesus, but they don't do so. Instead, they keep to the spiritual domain: "Peace be with you," "Do not be afraid," "Do not be troubled," "Follow me," "Feed my sheep," and "Receive the Holy Spirit." These are mild sentiments by worldly standards. Since the Gospel writers self-suppress, the few words that *are* preserved have a heightened probability of being authentic.

The Resurrection claim is audacious, yet the post-Resurrection stories are the opposite in their subtlety.[27] We can explain the divergence by concluding that the writers kept to what they knew or understood to be true, which meant not inserting concocted or audacious claims into the post-Resurrection stories. In other words, and in keeping with our theme, the evangelists felt no compunction to make this stuff up.

The Argument from Novelty

If the evangelists were writing stories to convince their audiences to join their nascent faith, they would have sought to draw from cultural mores and understandings. They would have planted their seed in ground that would support germination, but that is not what happened. Their stories have no precedent. Instead of conforming to cultural mores and taboos, the authors challenge them. The stories run counter to expectations. The evangelists are not grafting onto safe perches; they are hanging out on the peripheral, dangling twigs. They spun their tales the way they did not as a matter of choice but because they were recording what they saw or heard. They are recorders of history, not makers of it.

The expectation of a risen Messiah really comes from the early Church more so than the Hebrew Bible. The understanding of a resurrection by the early Church comes from reading the Hebrew Bible *retrospectively* and then finding prophecies buried (pun intended) deeply within. The other Jews read their Scripture *prospectively*. They had no specific reason to interpret old prophecies as did their Christianized Jewish peers. There are no specific Hebrew Bible passages predicting the particular Resurrection that is recorded in the Gospel accounts. The Resurrection of Jesus has a parallel to the story of Jonah and the whale, but nobody before Jesus would have interpreted this story to presage the resurrection event of a savior.[28] Notwithstanding the lack of any specific prophecy, the disciples could see the Resurrection foretold in their Hebrew Scriptures. The difference from understanding Scripture retrospectively by the disciples versus prospectively by other Jews can be likened to the following analogy:

> A *retrospective* biographer of Abraham Lincoln might look at his childhood in Kentucky and observe how splitting logs contributed to his personal sense of independence, self-reliance, and determination. These qualities, the biographer might argue, would serve him well when he assumed the presidency at the rockiest point in the country's history. By contrast, a *prospective* colleague of Abraham Lincoln from Lincoln's childhood in the 1820s might have observed Lincoln's log-splitting capability and expected him to become a successful pioneer. The same observer would have had no reason to project how these qualities would have parlayed Lincoln into the White House in March 1861. Looking backward, seeing how the pieces fit together was easy. Looking forward, it was nearly impossible to do so.

The 2001 Pontifical Biblical Commission makes clear the difference between prospective and retrospective understandings of Scripture:

> Although the Christian reader is aware that the internal dynamism of the Old Testament finds its goal in Jesus, this is retrospective perception whose point of departure is not in the text as such, but in the events of the New Testament proclaimed by apostolic teaching. . . . It cannot be said, therefore, that Jews do not see what has been proclaimed in the text, but the Christian, in the light of Christ and in the Spirit, discovers in the text an additional meaning that was hidden there.[29]

Given the difference between prospective and retrospective understandings of Scripture, the following verse from John 20 has to be a candidate for one of the greatest understatements in literature in the last two thousand years. In this verse, Peter and the disciple whom Jesus loved

(John?) are dazed as they look into the empty tomb: "For they did not yet understand the scriptures that he had to rise from the dead."

Similar words appear at Luke 24:26–27 and 1 Corinthians 15:4. The text from Luke evidently is a restatement of the latter words from his mentor, Paul. Paul's words predate Luke's by twenty or so years. The latter content is especially important because of the source. Paul writes in 1 Corinthians: "[Jesus] was buried, that he was raised on the third day according to the Scriptures."

These words convey more than they appear to since the person writing them was a contemporary scholar of the Jewish Scripture in Greek, for sure, but likely also in Hebrew or Aramaic, the local dialect of Judea at the time. Paul was studying with some of the best Jewish minds in Jerusalem and under a great Jewish Pharisee. He understood very well how Jews of his day interpreted their Scriptures. He was a self-described zealot of the law of the Jews. While Paul did not identify the explicit source of his "according to the Scriptures" statement, given his background and credentials, we can be sure his words are not just mere filler. They even have a rabbinical ring to them.

We are left wondering how Paul deduced that the Hebrew Scriptures foretell the death and Resurrection saga. There are many allusions and passages to prompt the faithful to make the connections, but one cannot arrive there just by proof-texting. The inclusion of a new creation via Jesus's Resurrection as foretold in the Hebrew Bible is subtle and easily missed. The fact that Paul did not grasp the nexus to prophecies quickly is obvious since he was originally a persecutor of the early Church. Paul came to understand prophecies in the Hebrew Bible retrospectively, that is, given the Resurrection, he answered for himself and presumably shared the answer with his audiences orally. Unfortunately for us in the twenty-first century, his writings only provide hints.

Readers should not presume that the Hebrew Bible fails to provide a substantive, prophetic basis for the Resurrection. Nor should readers presume that the Hebrew Bible is inconsistent with this interpretation. Rather, one needs to be circumspect in finding the linkage. One can see the Resurrection prophecy in the Hebrew Bible in several places—for example, in the Psalms and by parallel to Jonah in the belly of the whale. Another way to approach the prophecies in the Hebrew Bible derives from comparing the Resurrection saga to the creation story (see Table 5–2). The degree of coincidence makes one consider the prospect of providence.

Table 5-2. Comparison of the Creation and Resurrection Stories

Day of the Week	Genesis	New Testament
Friday	The creation of humans is the apogee of creation. God's work is finished. Everything is very good, just as God willed it.	The accomplishment of the new man (Jesus) is the apogee of a new creation. Jesus's work is done. Everything is very good, as the Father wills it.
Saturday	God rested. The day is blessed.	Jesus rested. The day is blessed (doubly so as Passover and a Sabbath).
Sunday	The world is created, light floods the world, and chaos is vanquished. God sees how good it is.	Man's world is re-created. Light refloods the world. Chaos (sin/darkness) is vanquished. God *and* man see how good it is.

Another coincidence is the duration of the time between Jesus's death and when he was next seen alive. The span is from 3 p.m. on Friday until 7 a.m. on Sunday. This is exactly forty hours—forty being a perfect number for a vigil for the Jews, as in forty days and nights of rain or forty years wandering in the desert.

Skeptics argue that the fulfillment of Hebrew Bible prophecies in the New Testament is simply a case of retrojections into the New Testament. How better to show a particular prophecy is satisfied than to back-write it into your script! However, nobody can make such a claim about the bodily Resurrection of Jesus from the dead. There was no belief among the Jews, then or now, that a Messiah would come, die, and then be resurrected. As an aside, there was no such story line among pagans either, despite the specious claims by some scholars and elites that the early Church adopted pagan myths and absorbed them into the Christian Resurrection.

Non-Christian, late Second Temple Judaism was confused about what a resurrection was. The issue of resurrection of the body is mentioned briefly in Daniel 12:1–3, voiced in prophetic, apocalyptic, and obscure language. The idea of the resurrection of the dead only began to firmly take root in Judaism contemporaneously with—or more likely after the birthing of—Christianity. The topic of resurrection was not then and arguably still is not central to Judaism. If you were to do a web search today related to the Jewish conception of resurrection, you would get some equivocal answers and citations. Any Hebrew Bible discussion of resurrection is late in development and not well articulated. Indeed, as reported in the *Catechism of the Catholic Church*,[30] the clearest revelations of resurrection come from 2 Maccabees 7:9 and 7:14 ("The King of the Universe will raise us up to an everlasting renewal of life because we have died for his laws," and "One cannot choose to die at the hands of men and cherish the hope that God gives of being raised again," respectively) and Daniel 12:2 ("Multitudes who sleep in the dust of the earth will awake"). These books are very late books, dating from the first or second century BCE, and Maccabees is not even included in the Jewish or Protestant biblical canon. The verse from Daniel is in a discourse about the end-times, a discourse never intended to be literal. Modern conceptions of resurrection in Judaism may draw more from the Christian traditions of resurrection than the other way around.

Even for those of Jesus's contemporaneous Jews, like the Pharisees, who might have subscribed to a resurrection concept, the event would likely have been expressed as a national resurrection at the end of time and certainly not attached to some agent to usher it in and probably not a bodily resurrection either. Almost everything about Jesus's Resurrection would have been novel to his Jewish peers—a personal (not collective) resurrection, a bodily (not just a spiritual) resurrection, and its occurrence in human (not mythical or millenarian) time. None of Jesus's contemporaries had any expectation of the kind of resurrection we read about in the New Testament accounts. Therefore, the evangelists could not have back-created their stories to reflect some prophecies of old. No such prophecies existed. Nothing in the Hebrew Bible compelled the central claim of the New Testament. Nobody expected it, sought it out, needed it, or copied it.

Given the lack of precedent, where did the idea of Jesus's bodily resurrection come from? Its novelty attests to its authenticity. If the story delivered to us were predictable, we would be asking ourselves whether the tale was back-created to conform to the agenda. The Resurrection stories, however, are entirely unexpected and thus convey a sense of authenticity.

The Argument from Complexity

If starting with the assumption that the Resurrection was just made up, then one is compelled to ask the obvious question: *Why* did the authors (the plural implies a conspiracy) make it up?

Coming up with the tale of a resurrection could have been a useful marketing ploy for evangelists. After all, a resurrection would have been proof positive that God rested His favor on Jesus and that Jesus's mission survived his earthly life. The Resurrection of Jesus could have been written in simpler terms and achieved much the same result. The story the evangelists wrote requires a resurrected body, personal visits by Jesus to the disciples, and Jesus's arrival to them in an unexplained glorified state. None of these attributes would have been necessary for the evangelists to reach their desired conclusions that God favored Jesus and that his mission would continue via the disciples. Yet the evangelists offer us deeply complicated and bizarre resurrection stories. Complexities make selling the story more difficult. Instead of a corporeal Resurrection in a glorified state, the rising-to-life narrative could have been crafted in a simpler way to make the story easier to sell and having much less to defend. Jesus could have been resuscitated, he could have appeared as an apparition, or he could have been reported as being raised by unidentifiable witnesses who relayed the information to the apostles. These are examples of simpler approaches that would have pushed the story to the same end: a risen Jesus. A modern skeptic would protest that my posited scenarios are just hypotheticals or counterfactuals, but, alas, they are not. All three modalities already appear in the New Testament: the raising of a child at Nain (a resuscitation, Luke 7), the appearance of Jesus to Paul in a nonphysical form (an apparition, Acts 9), and the Ascension reported by a third party (Acts 1).

The writers did not take the easy route in establishing their resurrection stories. Why would an evangelist offer up more than he needed to in order to make his case? After all, the more you propose, the more you have to defend and the more you risk your credibility. Then, once you answer the question of why *one* evangelist would be so outlandish, then you have to answer the next question, which is why they all did so. They did so because the writers reported what they observed or what was transmitted to them. This comports with our you-just-can't make-this-stuff-up principle.

CONCLUSION

The hypothesis we started with is that the evangelists made up the Resurrection. Do the data fit this hypothesis? They absolutely do not.

- We have many literarily, temporally, and spatially independent accounts to dismiss the Resurrection accounts.
- We find many instances in the Gospels where authors include details that are contrary to the stories they would have narrated if they were just making up the stories.
- We are missing many items that we would expect to be included if the stories were fabricated.
- We have no reason for the stories to have been made up the way they have been recorded.

We can debate the details of the Resurrection experience of the first disciples, but it misses the first and more basic point. If you were an evangelist crafting the story line, you would not have chosen to present the Resurrection story the way you did. If you wanted to create a story about your leader and the impact on his followers after his death, why go to the trouble of crafting a story about the physical resurrection of Jesus's body? Nothing would have led you to craft your story the way it was told; indeed, all of the precedent you inherited would have argued against writing your story the way you wrote it. So why would you compose it that way? Quite simply, you recorded what you observed or heard. You did not develop the story line; it came from observations (yours or others), not imaginations.

As the saying goes, you can't make this stuff up. The Resurrection is too rich, too complicated, and too bizarre to have just been imagined. This is what Tertullian meant when we he said in circa 200 CE, "The Resurrection is impossible, therefore, it must be true."

When Jesus walked about, the Resurrection concept was poorly defined and not widely understood or accepted among the Jewish people. Nobody who walked, worked, or ate with Jesus expected him to rise from the dead. In other words, the writers of the Gospel accounts certainly had no compulsion to write into their stories the Messiah had to rise from the dead. Including a story like the Resurrection in the Gospels would go well past anything anybody then had been waiting to see. The unlikelihood of the Resurrection stories all coming together the way they did mimics this quip about such stories just being made up:

> I am reminded of Talleyrand's famous answer to an earnest revolutionary, who asked him for advice on how to start a new enlightened religion to replace Christianity. Talleyrand responded, "I recommend that you be crucified and rise again on the third day."[31]

Perhaps the most unequivocal argument for the Resurrection from history is the existence of the Church. That Jesus was crucified is not doubted. That the proto-Church sprang up immediately after his death is also not doubted. By themselves, these two facts would diverge. Something had to bridge them and the Resurrection is that something. We have established the Resurrection, but we have not established why there was a resurrection. This answer resides in the next chapter.

6

The Initial Idea of Christianity

We can confidently state that, after approximately 3 p.m. Jerusalem time on the day we now know as Good Friday, zero people alive on planet Earth understood what a resurrection was. Jesus's followers had no expectation of a resurrection. The Resurrection was a wholly unexpected phenomenon thrust unto them. It came without precedents and without any instruction manuals. The charge to write the instruction manuals fell to the Church over the next two thousand years, which she has done with such verve that one can understand the hyperbolic words near the end of the Fourth Gospel as prophetic: "If every one of the [things about Jesus] were written down [. . .] even the whole world would not have room for the books that would be written" (John 21:25 KJV).

Over the next two millennia, the Church has ended up answering many questions pertaining to the Resurrection, among them: What did the Resurrection mean, and what were Jesus's follows supposed to do with it? The central question the Church answered, though, is the why question: Why did God raise Jesus from the dead? I call the Church's earliest answer to the why question the *initial idea of Christianity*. The answer is contemporaneous or near contemporaneous with the Resurrection, meaning it is primitive and did not evolve. It is an idea (not something observed); and the idea was the divide that would ultimately separate Christianity from Judaism. It is why the religion *of* Jesus became the religion *about* Jesus, and why Jesus's followers cast him as a singularity. The answer to the why question is a theological one; that is, the earliest disciples from the inception of the Church were crafting their understandings in theological terms. They were offering theological answers to the question Jesus asked his apostles a few months earlier while they rested together at Caesarea Philippi: "Who do you say that I am?" Such answers would have been unimaginable those few months before (Matt 16:13–16 / Mark 8:27–29 / Luke 9:18–20). I show in this chapter that the initial idea of Christianity, like much else in this book, conforms to the conclusion that you just can't make this stuff up.

IDENTIFYING THE INITIAL IDEA OF CHRISTIANITY

The Resurrection was a physically observable matter; the answer to what to do with the Resurrection is not. The answer is an idea. Ideas are virtual, not real or tangible, things. For clarity, I assert what I consider to be the initial idea of Christianity up front. Later I offer a rationale to validate the assertion.

The initial idea of Christianity can be expressed in many but equivalent ways. Here is a simple rendition:

> Jesus, as the Resurrected *Messiah, remits the sins of the believers* by their *faith* in Him, offering them *eternal life with God*.

None of the italicized words are directly observable things. When we discuss the foundation of Christianity, we are talking about ideas, not events. Observable events underlie ideas, of course, but events do not substitute for ideas. Ideas can answer why questions; events are empirical matters, not direct conveyors of meaning. The principal questions religions purport to answer are, What are the relationships between humans and nature and/or God, between one another, and between good and evil; and how should we conduct ourselves in response to those relationships to find purpose and meaning? The answers Christians offer to these questions revolve around a singularity, Jesus. *Singularity* is used here to mean that Jesus has no peer, akin to the singularity that cosmologists believed was the universe before the Big Bang, approximately 13.7 billion years ago.

The initial idea of Christianity formed quickly and has been retained in a stable manner ever since. Christianity has evolved significantly over two thousand years, but the initial idea has not. The initial idea has three characteristics:

- The earliest followers of Jesus developed the initial idea of Christianity very quickly after the Resurrection (a few days).
- They promulgated the initial idea very quickly after it was formulated (a few days or at most a few weeks).

- The Church has retained the initial idea in a more or less stable manner down to our time (many centuries).

How common is it for a world revolution movement, of which Christianity is one, to have all three of these characteristics? Christianity is rare, if not unique. The following revolutions, all of which had staying power, had incubation and promulgation periods of many years, not weeks, and, once the movements took hold, they often drifted widely from their foundational idea:

- Judaism
- Islam
- Mormonism
- Hinduism
- The Reformation
- Marxism
- Socialism
- Capitalism
- Mercantilism
- Nationalism
- Science
- The American Revolution
- The French Revolution
- Democracy
- The Enlightenment
- The Renaissance

These revolutions span all manner of human thinking—from science, to culture, to economics, to politics, to religion. Christianity stands apart from all of them by its unparalleled short gestation and infancy periods with a continuous adherence to its unaltered foundational principle.

THE ORIGINS OF THE INITIAL IDEA OF CHRISTIANITY

I begin the argument by establishing two essential points:

The Resurrection was not the initial idea of Christianity. The Resurrection of Jesus may be the singular event in human history by some accounts, but the Resurrection is an event, not an idea. Facts do not a religion make; ideas do that. Ideas, not naked facts, are what speak to people's visceral needs. Ideas answer the question that motivates people's core behaviors. To transfer the Resurrection fact to a religious idea, the adherents needed to establish an answer for why God raised Jesus from the dead.

The why answer came very quickly. The answer is built into Christianity; Christianity was seemingly born with it. Christianity did not evolve to answer the question with the luxury of time, vetting, contemplation, or debate. We know of no time in which the Church existed but the answer to the question did not also exist.

Suppose for the moment that Jesus was resurrected. Good for Jesus, for sure, but we need to understand what it meant to the apostles, to the Jews at that time, and to everyone else since then. The Resurrection of Jesus is God's validation of Jesus's earthly ministry and of Jesus himself. Perhaps, too, Jesus's Resurrection might be a glimpse of a resurrection that would be reserved for those Jews who followed in Jesus's path. But these points still do not directly answer the why question. Without an answer to the why, there is no Christianity.

Suppose there really had been an itinerant, firebrand Jewish preacher who performed miracles and even rose from the dead. The story could have been uniquely inspiring. Jesus could have been remembered in a thriller along with other superheroes of the past. Perhaps this Jesus would have been something like the Jewish version of Confucius. But that is not what happened, not even remotely. Or suppose Jesus's story could have been captured in the collective memories of those around him and who followed after him. Perhaps this Jesus would have been something like Abraham Lincoln, the Buddha, or Socrates. But that is not what happened either. The story could have been a great tribute to Second Temple Judaism and remembered in the tribal memories of the chosen people. But that is not what happened either.

Suppose the Resurrection story were the story of Jesus being killed and then raised by God for his faith. This would not be a *Christian* story; it would be a *Jewish* story. What kind of narrative could be more inspiring to the Second Temple Jews, who lived under occupation by a hated Roman Empire, than that one of their own, who was killed by the oppressive Romans, was brought back to life? This would be an incredible validation of Jews overcoming their pagan masters, as did the judges and prophets of old. It would be Maccabees on steroids, Ezekiel's bones in the desert coming to life, the long-awaited answer to Jeremiah's lamentations, the animation of Job's story, Jonah's story, or Elijah's prevailing over the pagan gods. Jesus would be a new Esther in saving the Israelites. It would comport to the basic story of Israel: try as the pagans may, but despite short-term superficialities that might suggest their advancement over Israel, Israel and her God prevail in the end. Jesus's Resurrection story is an epic Jewish superhero story. David Gelernter, a Jew, makes the point (italics in the original):

Christianity is a dialect of Judaism, is profoundly Jewish, not *just* because Jesus answered the famous question about how to merit salvation ("Master, what shall I do to inherit eternal life?"; Luke 10:25) with two Hebrew verses. Jesus responds, "What is written in the law? how readest thou? And he answering said, Thou shalt love the Lord thy God with all thy heart, and with all thy soul, and with all thy strength, and with all thy mind; and thy neighbor as thyself." (Luke 10:26–27, citing Deut 6:5 and Lev 19:18)

Not *just* because the man Jesus and his mother, Paul and Peter, and so many other Christian founders were Jews. Most important, "Christianity is a dialect of Judaism" because the story of the intermediary sent by God to man whom pagans tortured to death but who would not and could not *remain* dead, who could be killed but never die, is the story of the Jewish people. For Jews, Jesus is *klal Yisrael*, all Israel in the form of one man: Jesus is the Christian name for "the Jewish people." And the Passion is Christianity's recitation and sacralizing of Jewish history. (The Jews, of course, are repeatedly called the Lord's firstborn son in the Hebrew Bible.)[32]

The worst the Romans could do is to kill Jesus by their most barbaric methods. Yet, Jesus, the Jewish uber-superhero, ultimately wins anyway: He was resurrected to a new beatific state. He would be the embodiment of the Jews' ultimate victory over the cursed pagan Romans. Israel would be redeemed, and under God's terms! The Jews could jump on this story and meld it into their ancient covenant.

I recall a conversation with a twenty-first-century Jewish woman who stated, "Jesus. I love Jesus. It is Christianity that I reject." Her statement is the same as a first-century Jewish woman would have made, the only difference is one spoke the words in English; the other would have spoken in Aramaic.

Notwithstanding the Jewishness of Jesus's story, most first-century Jews did not rally around this story line. Indeed, Jesus's witnesses, all Jews, were dismissed as rogues, if not heretics, by the power centers of Judaism. This fact compels us to ask how the best Jewish story that ever could have been told did not become a Jewish story at all. In other words, we ask ourselves how did it become the "greatest story ever told" for non-Jews, to borrow a title from a famous movie? We need to explain how the Resurrection of Jesus became a Christian story.

To get from the Jewish story of the Resurrection to the good news of Christianity, we need something beyond the Resurrection. The Resurrection story by itself is not a story of human redemption. The Resurrection alone does not cause disciples to become evangelists. Premises are missing in the logic train. How do we go so very quickly from premise A (we know the disciples experienced the Resurrection) to premise B (we know they became evangelists)? Here are some of the missing points in the logic path:

- Is the merit of Jesus's Resurrection passed along to others?
- If so, why?
- If so, how?

The initial idea of Christianity, as I have identified it, explains the observation of the Resurrection of Jesus and how it launched the religion: Jesus's death was redemptive and salvific for believers by enabling the forgiveness of their sins. Consider alternative explanations for connecting premises A and B:

- Some might argue that the understanding of the special relationship between Jesus and his Father is the initial idea of Christianity. However, efforts to understand this relationship would require significant theological development. Being able to decipher the relationship between Jesus and his Father did not happen overnight, as did the initial idea expressed earlier. Even today, Christians consider the relationship between Jesus and the Father to be a mystery—something to apprehend, not comprehend.
- Another candidate for the initial idea of Christianity is the inauguration of the kingdom. Jesus spoke plainly and frequently about the kingdom of God (or the kingdom of heaven, in Matthew's account). Now that the Resurrection has been revealed, one might think that the kingdom of God ensues. However, we can dismiss this alternative because preaching the kingdom alone does not get the preacher afoul of the authorities, does not isolate religious sentiments of the vast majority of contemporary Jews, and does not cause its acceptors to be liberated in a way the evangelists had supposed. Whereas the claim of the coming of the kingdom surely has a primitive origin in its adoption by the Church, it is not enough to explain how Christianity emerged from Judaism.
- Another option for the initial idea of Christianity is a variant on the kingdom of God notion above. Going back to Albert Schweitzer and following the line of thought to current times through scholars such as Bart D. Ehrman, Jesus, they say, should be understood as a Jewish apocalyptic enabler—a preacher and an usher for the final apocalypse where the reign of God would be installed once and for all. The good

news was that the apocalypse was imminent. To bolster their argument, much evidence from the Gospel accounts substantiates Jesus's apocalyptic message,[33] but like the kingdom of God candidate immediately above, we are left with an inability to understand how such apocalyptic messaging would have accounted for the historically validated Resurrection experience, the purported singularity of Jesus, and the dissonance with Jewish religious authorities.

Nothing in the claim that Jesus rose from the dead would have offended Jews of that time. Rising from the dead would have been unexpected, to be sure, but wouldn't contradict Torah or any fundamental Jewish premise. Indeed, the Resurrection could easily have been understood in Jewish terms as a continuing affirmation of God's interactions with his chosen people. Most of Jesus's contemporary Jews did not embrace this interpretation of the Resurrection story, though. Why? Because the Resurrection story was not presented simply as a miracle performed by a Jewish God for a Jewish people in a Jewish place in a Jewish time; instead, it was presented with the initial idea of Christianity, an idea untenable to many of them. The initial idea was too fantastic to believe. Thus, the Jews rejected the Resurrection because they could not accept the apostles' allied answer as to why God raised Jesus from the dead.

THE EMERGENCE OF THE INITIAL IDEA OF CHRISTIANITY

What we have established so far is that the incipient Church shared her message with the world with these characteristics:

- The message was joyful and merited communicating widely to change the hearers' world.
- The message's origin was primitive, predating any opportunity for substantive myth-making or theological development, and it has endured in a substantive form for two thousand years.
- The message offended a large swath of the Jews at the time, such that the Jews of The Way were rogues among their kin and co-religionists.

The original disciples immediately looked for meaning in Jesus's death and Resurrection. Whatever the time between the experience of the Resurrection and finding its meaning in the initial idea, the duration must have been preciously short.

You may have read that Paul, the self-appointed apostle who never met Jesus in the flesh, founded Christianity. This claim to having founded Christianity is demonstrably false from history. We know that Christianity predates the arrival of Paul. Paul says as much in that he had relatives who were "in Christ" before he was (Rom 16:7). Obviously, the initial idea of Christianity did not originate with Paul. Notwithstanding the falsity of the claim, there is a kernel of truth in the argument for Paul being the founder of the Christian religion in some sense. Paul was the first person to pull together the philosophical basis that would found the basis of Christianity as an enduring world religion. We could make a reasonable claim that Paul was the world's first systematic theologian. To him belong the claims for having developed the basis for justification, the adoption of man by God through Jesus, the mystical body of the Church, the cosmic Christ, the extension of the claim of election from the Jews to Gentiles, and many other novelties and innovations. Even still, Christianity's initial idea predates Paul.[34]

Since Paul's conversion was only a few years after the Resurrection and we know Paul received the initial idea already formed, we know that the initial idea of Christianity has primitive origin. We can assert that some of the essential principles of Christianity were espoused remarkably quickly after the Resurrection. If we believe the story of Pentecost and the story of Peter speaking boldly immediately after it (Acts 2:37 NAB: "Repent and be baptized, every one of you, in the name of Jesus Christ for the forgiveness of your sins"), then we would need no further evidence. However, the Pentecost story could be a retrojection Luke made to sway his peers about atonement theology. Some might wonder whether the atonement theory arose later but was emplaced earlier into the record to make it seem more primitive than it actually was. So we need to look for something more objective and more defensible than Peter's speech that gets us to a similar point of linking Jesus's death and Resurrection to the forgiveness of sins.

We find such a story beginning with the story of the martyrdom of Stephen (Acts 6–7). We cannot really assert the historicity of Stephen either. One could suppose it is also a retrojection. The Stephen character looks like the prototype of a faithful Hellenized Jewish-Christian. His group was one specifically targeted by the evangelists while Luke is writing his Gospel. Accordingly, a skeptic could argue, Luke could have invented this character by back-reading him into the account for evangelical advantage, whether he was real or not.[35] Maybe we can't conclusively validate the Stephen story per se, but we can validate its backstory. The backstory involves Saul, better known by his Roman name, Paul. We can validate it because Paul's story is so well attested and is not a story that anyone would have been concocted. No Christian would make up a story about Paul being a persecutor of the early Church, knowing that he became one of its principal proponents. His awkward story is captured in Acts in multiple places and is captured in Paul's own words in his epistles.

Here is the sequence of events that had to have happened in three or at most four years after the Resurrection. The sequence becomes an anchoring point for us to understand the similarly short window of what happened between the Resurrection and Paul's conversion.

1. The Jerusalem Church recovered from the shock of the Resurrection experience.
2. The Jerusalem Church organized herself as a unit. We know this because the apostles remained as a unit, The Twelve, for many years after the Resurrection. The Twelve were reset with the replacement of Judas Iscariot.
3. The Jerusalem Church formulated her ideas to be substantial, coherent, and exportable.
4. She spread them locally in Jerusalem, for sure, but probably elsewhere in Judea and in Galilee, too. The ideas flowed out regionally.
5. Audiences in some locales distant from Jerusalem accepted these ideas in sufficiently concentrated numbers to make their impacts felt.
6. Those audiences, like the followers in Damascus, organized themselves locally.
7. The newly organized Christians in these remote areas—the term *Christian* is a bit anachronistic here because it would not be applied to them for some while—were sufficiently disruptive within their synagogues that their goings-on had to be assessed, determined to have some sort of adverse impact on the local Jewish community, and then reported back to the Sanhedrin in Jerusalem for direction or disposition. (The Sanhedrin was the ruling council in Jerusalem that acted as the religious authority for Israel.)
8. The Sanhedrin accepted the reports, then made the determination that Jesus's followers were so far afield from acceptable Jewish thinking that they needed to be quashed. The span of then-acceptable Jewish thought involved all of the following far more fundamental doctrinal points than the state of affairs of an itinerant Jewish preacher from Galilee.
    - What makes a person a Jew in the first place?
    - What documents would be counted as authoritative Scripture?
    - Is there a resurrection and life eternal?
    - Is it licit to cooperate with Roman hegemony? If so, under what conditions?

- Who has authority within Judaism to make definitive pronouncements?
- What allegiance do diaspora Jews owe to the Holy Land?

Thus, to say that some Jews had strayed so far from acceptable thinking was really saying something.

9. That the Jerusalem hierarchy would have felt compelled to quash a local, trifling matter in the world of the diaspora would have been highly irregular when so many more fundamental points presented themselves. All of this is to say that the affront in Damascus—and likely elsewhere, too—must have been quite severe for the Sanhedrin to consider the doctrinal matter pertaining to Jesus, particularly given the urgency of Israel-Roman geopolitics and the fulsome sectarian debates then in play.
10. The Sanhedrin organized bands of representatives to quash those remotely situated Jesus followers, such as the ones in Damascus. The Sanhedrin would have carefully selected its confidants to go out from Jerusalem. This was a sensitive, religious mission, after all, with the imprimatur of the Sanhedrin. As such, the Sanhedrin selected only highly qualified, trained, and disciplined candidates for the mission.
11. Saul, a young, zealous Pharisaic student in Jerusalem under a renowned scholar of Torah, was set on his way with a group of like-minded Jews to persecute the Christians in Damascus. He received a thoroughly unexpected appearance of Jesus, an apparition, on the way there. We date this event between three and four years after the Resurrection.

If we work backward in time from step 11 back to step 2, we realize that the ideas in step 2 had to have been established soon after the Resurrection. More importantly, we know that the formulated ideas had to have been disarming to the Jewish authorities. The Resurrection story by itself would not have caused the Sanhedrin to react so deliberately. Therefore, we conclude that the initial idea of Christianity did not evolve over some protracted period of time but was born into the Church; alternatively, if the Idea did evolve, it matured promptly and was preserved in substantive form thereafter.

An early date for the initial idea of Christianity argues there was insufficient time for mythologizing or theologizing to make the huge jump from Judaism to Christianity. The time span to develop substantive, normative myths is much longer than the scale we contemplate here for the advent of Christianity's initial idea.[36]

Imagine yourself with the apostles in those first days after the Resurrection. You would have asked yourself and your colleagues the obvious question: Why did Jesus rise from the dead? It would have taken you no time at all to conclude that the Resurrection was not an accident. Resurrections just don't happen every day. If it were not an accident, then it was intentional. If it were intentional, then what was the intention? If the Resurrection were no accident and the Resurrection naturally required Jesus to have died first, you would quickly deduce that Jesus died for a purpose. Since his death was an injustice, undoing his death works to restore justice. Restoration abolishes sin. Voila, we have the linkage between Jesus's Resurrection and the forgiveness of sins. It is a nexus of pure genius.

The apostles could not lay claim to this genius. The initial idea is too rich and too nuanced to have been crafted among a few untrained and scared fishermen and other commoners in—at most—a few days, even while they were running for their lives one step ahead of Jewish religious and Roman political authorities. These apostles are described in at least two places as uneducated men (once in John and once in Acts). Most were illiterate, as were 97 percent of the peasants of the time; as far as we know, all lacked any substantial religious training. If the initial idea of Christianity did not evolve with the luxury of time, where did it come from?

It is hard to escape the premise that the idea goes back to Jesus himself. None of the eleven surviving apostles had the kinds of theological insight to connect Jesus's Resurrection to the forgiveness of others' sins. Perhaps Paul could have had the insight to devise the initial idea of Christianity after his extensive contemplative time in Arabia. Paul had significant biblical and other religious training and was literate and an intellectual. However, the initial idea of Christianity predated his arrival on the scene. The only credible source is Jesus himself. This conclusion is a separate and independent argument for the Resurrection: if the early Church taught an atonement theology from an early date—a separately provable historical fact—then there must have been a basis for atonement, which leads back to the Resurrection as the atonement's source. Without a Resurrection, where does one come by an atonement theory?

No less a biblical scholar than Pope Benedict XVI makes the point that the genius behind the theology derived from Jesus himself:

> The anonymous community [of the early Church] is credited with an astonishing level of theological genius—who were the great figures responsible for inventing all of this? No, the greatness, the dramatic newness, comes directly from Jesus; within the faith and the life of the community it is further developed, but not created. In fact, the "community" would not even have emerged and survived at all unless some extraordinary reality had preceded it.[37]

ARGUMENTS FOR THE HISTORICITY OF THE INITIAL IDEA OF CHRISTIANITY

Sin is not usually an objectively observable thing, never mind the forgiveness of sins, which is even more rarely observable. The direct effects of a particular sin are sometimes noticeable, but that's more the exception than the rule. How could you ever conclude objectively that somebody's sins have been forgiven? You can't. If our argument is about the historicity or nonhistoricity of the Gospels, how can we discuss sins or, even more abstractly, the forgiveness of sin? We cannot. What we can do is ascertain whether the earliest Church held this belief and communicated this message to the Greco-Roman world in which she evangelized. Whether sins are actually forgiven via the Passion of Jesus is left to the realms of faith and theology, not history, and so is beyond the scope of this book.

So far in this chapter, the arguments about the historicity of the initial idea of Christianity are largely circumstantial, meaning we do not depend upon any personal testimony but instead rely upon the circumstances then at play. We now migrate to considering additional or supplemental evidence that follow the evidentiary tests for historicity in chapter 2.

The Argument from Multiple Attestation

Each of the Gospel accounts identifies Jesus's death as sacrificial and links it to the forgiveness of sins. In Luke, the connection is quite explicit (24:47). In Matthew and Mark, the nexus is more indirect as accomplished via baptism in Jesus; baptism conveys the efficacious capability in overcoming sin. In John's Gospel, the power to forgive sins, via Jesus's merits, is explicit enough, and the power is even extended to the apostles (John 20:22–23). Moreover, one need not wait for the Gospels to come upon belief in the forgiveness of sins appearing in writing. Paul's epistles are replete with such references, and Paul's work predates the Gospels by approximately ten to fifty years. Indeed, one of the criticisms of Pauline literature is its focus on the Resurrected Messiah as Savior in washing away sins while ignoring the human person of Jesus.

Paul's epistles do not introduce the theory of atonement; they just record what was already understood when these letters were written in the 40s and 50s CE. Paul's words may have codified atonement theology, but they didn't invent it. Furthermore, we have the words that Luke put onto Peter's lips in the immediate aftermath of the Resurrection–Pentecost sequence (Acts 3:19 NAB), "Repent, therefore, and be converted, that your sins might be wiped away." It is another primitive attestation of the origins of the initial idea.

So we have multiple independent attestations to the concept that Jesus's death–Resurrection saga was linked to the forgiveness of sins. But the belief goes deeper. The Gospel stories reflect a Jesus whose teachings are characterized by love, forgiveness, reconciliation, and mercy. Even the most earnest negations of Christian interpretations of Jesus's life concur on this point. The Jesus Seminar cofounder Robert W. Funk's *Honest to Jesus* contains a table at the end listing the sayings that the elitist group, not the least bit friendly to orthodox Christianity, conclude go back to the historical Jesus. Dozens of such citations in the table specifically link Jesus's words to the motif of forgiveness. The disciples, it seems, were effectively being trained to continue Jesus's teachings after his departure. The disciples may not have had comprehended Jesus's new values paradigm when he taught it to them, but Jesus had planted the seed deeply during his public ministry about looking to forgiveness as a behavior ideal. These seeds bloomed in the light of the Resurrection.

Even so, one has to be judicious in sorting through the Gospels for forgiveness stories because one needs to guard against the prospect of their being retrojected after atonement theory was set, which came after and in response to the Resurrection. Many passages about forgiveness are well attested and deeply woven into the story lines, and we should conclude they are authentic, not retrojected. The passages include elements supported by the criterion of surprise, both by actions of Jesus being connected to reviled gluttons, drunkards, tax collectors, and sinners (Matt 11:19) and by words by requiring forgiveness for as many as seventy times seven occasions (Matt 18:22). If the primary purpose of the Gospel writers were to devise a Resurrection-cum-forgiveness saga into Jesus's public ministry as understood after the Resurrection, they did a very nice job of disguising it. The passages below are just a few examples where the forgiveness motif is well entrenched in the story, versus being added to it later, such that we are compelled to accept their authenticity.

1. The "Father" or "Our Father" prayer with versions in Luke and Matthew, respectively, and perhaps contemporaneously in the Didache, a first-century Christian catechism. This version is from Matthew 6:9–13 (NIV; italics added for emphasis):

> This, then, is how you should pray:
> "Our Father in heaven,
> hallowed be your name,
> your kingdom come,

> your will be done,
> on earth as it is in heaven.
> Give us today our daily bread.
> *And forgive us our debts,*
> *as we also have forgiven our debtors.*
> And lead us not into temptation,
> but deliver us from the evil one."

The forgiveness motif in italics is deeply embedded into this Jewish prayer as recorded by Matthew. The prayer was offered by a Jewish rabbi for a Jewish audience in a Jewish time and place. Christians often refer to these words as the "Lord's Prayer." From a Jewish perspective, the Christians' title belies the prayer's Jewishness. Christians attribute the prayer, not to Jesus the Jew, but to Jesus the Lord, thus minimizing its inherent Jewish heritage. On the point of how the Our Father is fundamentally a Jewish prayer and how it comports with other Jewish prayers, one of the prayers in the Jewish liturgy on Yom Kippur focusing on repentance and forgiveness is the *Avinu Malkeinu*, which means "Our Father, Our King."

The Lord's Prayer contains many essential themes, forgiveness being but one. It is hard to believe that clever interpolators would have added the forgiveness motif into the prayer simply to retroject it back into Jesus's public ministry. Therefore, we can have confidence that the forgiveness motif goes back to Jesus and was not added by Matthew, Luke, or some later editors.

2. *Healing of a paralytic in all three Synoptics.* This extract is from Luke 5:17–26 (NIV):

> One day Jesus was teaching, and Pharisees and teachers of the law were sitting there. They had come from every village of Galilee and from Judea and Jerusalem. And the power of the Lord was with Jesus to heal the sick. Some men came carrying a paralyzed man on a mat and tried to take him into the house to lay him before Jesus. When they could not find a way to do this because of the crowd, they went up on the roof and lowered him on his mat through the tiles into the middle of the crowd, right in front of Jesus. When Jesus saw their faith, he said, "Friend, your sins are forgiven." The Pharisees and the teachers of the law began thinking to themselves, "Who is this fellow who speaks blasphemy? Who can forgive sins but God alone?" Jesus knew what they were thinking and asked, "Why are you thinking these things in your hearts? Which is easier: to say, 'Your sins are forgiven,' or to say, 'Get up and walk'? But I want you to know that the Son of Man has authority on earth to forgive sins." So he

said to the paralyzed man, "I tell you, get up, take your mat and go home." Immediately he stood up in front of them, took what he had been lying on and went home praising God. Everyone was amazed and gave praise to God.

This story, one of the first miracle stories in the earliest of the Gospels (Mark 2), serves multiple purposes—including Jesus as healer, as prophet, as preacher, as counterpoise to the Pharisees, and as the Son of Man—in addition to the forgiveness theme. In this account, the concept of forgiveness of sins is so deeply embedded it seems unlikely the story was back-written primarily to establish a post-Resurrection forgiveness motif. So, again, the forgiveness theme seems to be native to the historical account, not a retrojection.

3. *The parables.* Many of the parables relate to forgiveness and reconciliation. The one that conveys literary grandeur like no other is the parable of the Prodigal Son (Luke 15:11–32). In this parable, the father waits most anxiously for his errant son to return from a life of dissipation. The story line is moving and authentic. This parable is to the New Testament what Psalm 51 is to the Hebrew Bible. Both identify the necessity of contrition as a means for obtaining repentance. But one cannot miss to whom Jesus directs the parable, as is clear in the introduction in Luke 15:1–2 (NAB): "The tax collectors and sinners were all drawing near to listen to [Jesus], but the Pharisees and scribes began to complain, saying, 'This man welcomes sinners and eats with them.'"

The purpose of the parable is to dislodge the legalisms of the Pharisees and the scribes. Jesus saw the Pharisees and scribes as being obstacles to obtaining forgiveness of sins from those most in need of it. We can conclude that the purpose of the parable is not to retroject some post-Resurrection understanding into the story but to establish the centrality of forgiveness to Jesus's public ministry.

The Argument from Purpose

Suppose the forgiveness of sins manifest by Jesus's death and Resurrection was a creation of later Christians and not native to the initial Christian stories and most tellingly not native to Jesus. Let's run with this scenario and see where it leads.

If the purpose of the evangelists were to convince their audiences to revere their master and to increase their own numbers, the fabrication of the forgiveness of sins would have wide appeal. After all, who does not want healing? Who is not a sinner? A message of healing and hope could be a great seller—then as now. You might say, in modern parlance, they had a good marketing plan to capture market share. But the posited marketing plan collapses upon inspection.

If we assume that the earliest disciples concocted the remission of sins story, they would have defaulted to simple tales. The early Church would have adopted the kind of reasoning the Buddhists used in their religion: Jesus could be the revealer of resurrection (or Enlightenment), but not be its agent. In other words, Jesus could reveal to us how we can be resurrected following his example. In this regard, our personal resurrection need not be dependent upon his.

Similarly, in a concocted story, the Resurrection message could flow from the motif of the Hebrew prophets of old. Jesus could be delivering God's message. In this vein, Jesus would be the messenger, not the message. Selling the revelation of the forgiveness of sins and the resurrection without invoking Jesus as a mediator would have allowed the followers of Jesus to avoid putting themselves at risk with the Jewish or Roman authorities. But the story did not unfold this way—not even close. The apostles took a far more difficult path: Jesus did not just reveal a way to achieve forgiveness of sins (easy) but a path that passed uniquely through Jesus (hard). Moreover, Jesus was captured as a singularity (impossibly hard; this path would require that Jesus be a scandal of particularity within the scandal of particularity that Judaism already was and is). How non-Jewish would this narrative be? And where did the idea or a need for a mediator come from anyway?

You can read the Gospel accounts about Jesus's predictions of his death and his rising from the dead, and maybe you even assign them as retrojections. Even so, where did the idea come from that one person's death could be redemptive for the people of Israel in their relationship with God? It was an utterly unimagined thing before Jesus's death. There had been plenty of Hebrew/Jewish martyrs before and since, and many just and holy people were executed in the fateful history of the Jews, including in the ghastly horrors of the Holocaust in the twentieth century. We needn't look far from Jesus to find one of those unjustly executed. John the Baptist's memory looms large to the apostles, some of whom personally were followers of John earlier. How many of these cruel execution acts were ever paired with an understanding that the deaths were redemptive for the individual, let alone others? None. So we need to ask ourselves where the idea came from that Jesus's death would broker the redemption of his followers, or as Mark has it, that Jesus would be "ransom for the many."

If the early followers were looking for a Jewish precedent from the world view to link to the Passion account as redemptive, not only would they not have found any, but they would find story lines that go in the opposite direction. The antithetical story is in Genesis. Abraham is tested by God to sacrifice his son. In the Genesis telling, Isaac is saved by the intercession of an angel. By contrast, in the Passion account, no angel appears, no intercession occurs, and the victim is slaughtered. (A family member of mine is deeply troubled by the Genesis account. He wonders what kind of God would require His adherent to sacrifice his son and what kind of adherent would entertain such a demand. There are Jewish answers to these questions, but a Christian answer to it is particularly informing. The Christian answer is that God would not allow you to sacrifice your son for Him, but He would sacrifice His son for you.)

Another Hebrew Bible parallel to the Passion narrative is the slaughter of the Passover lamb. Whereas the analogy to the lamb readily translates to a Christian context, the slaughter of the Passover lamb is not purgative in any way, that is, nobody is freed from sin by virtue of the lamb's demise. The Passover lamb is about redemption for the Hebrews as a matter of election, not as a matter of freeing them from their sins. The Hebrew feast pertaining to atonement is Yom Kippur in the fall, not Passover in the spring. In the Yom Kippur celebration, an animal makes an appearance as a scapegoat to carry away the sins of the people as it scurries after the high priest lays his hands on it. But the goat is not sacrificed in this sequence in any event. There is no mechanism to render justice for sins via the scapegoat. Thus, Judaism leaves us without a precedent to draw upon for the Christian concept of redemption.

If the early Christians made up the idea of redemption via Jesus's death, the idea seems to have come from nowhere. We are led to conclude it was revealed to them, not something of their own making. To the point Pope Benedict made before, the theological genius to make the linkage goes back to Jesus personally. On point, note that nowhere in the Gospels is doctrine of atonement attributable to anyone other than Jesus.

The Argument from Novelty

If the Gospel passages followed prophecies written earlier, one might be suspicious the story was back-written to match them. However, the idea that there should be an agent to act as a mediator between man and God for the purpose of redeeming man has no antecedent in Judaism. The story line is wholly new. Still, the Hebrew Scriptures can be read retrospectively to see how the plan of salvation has played out. After all, Christians have done precisely that for two thousand years.

Before Jesus's time, though, no Jew expected a mediator for his sins, except perhaps, incidentally, in the role of the high priest. But the high priest's position was a weak analogy to the Christian understanding of Jesus's mediating role. The high priest presided over sacrifices of animals and cereals. The faithful Jews probably understood that sacrificing animals did little in the way of setting their heart right with God or being a real sacrifice from the supplicant. The sacrifice is the animal's, not theirs.

Before Jesus's Resurrection, nobody sought an atoning death, nobody knew one was needed, and nobody had an inkling to create one. The Jews already had their operative means of atonement, which they deemed sufficient. They had prayers, almsgivings, and fasting (which, by the way, are still retained by Jews today and borrowed by Muslims and Christians into their traditions as well for similar purposes). The Jews had their Yom Kippur, the holiest day of the year, the Day of Atonement. They had ritualized cleansings. They had the sacrifices in the temple. They did not have any need for a new kind of atonement.

The story of David's reconciliation with God is illustrative for Jewish understandings of atonement. Psalm 51 is attributed to David and is considered to be a model of public forgiveness by the king for his egregious sins of adultery and his complicity in the murder of Bathsheba's husband, Uriah. The psalm conveys true contrition that Jesus's peers would have understood to be an operative example of how contrition led to God's forgiveness of sins. This psalm is required reading for anyone seeking reconciliation with the Almighty:

> Have mercy upon me, O God, according to thy loving kindness: according unto the multitude of thy tender mercies blot out my transgressions.
>
> Wash me thoroughly from mine iniquity, and cleanse me from my sin.
>
> For I acknowledge my transgressions: and my sin is ever before me.
>
> Against thee, thee only, have I sinned, and done this evil in thy sight: that thou mightest be justified when thou speakest, and be clear when thou judgest.
>
> Behold, I was shapen in iniquity; and in sin did my mother conceive me.
>
> Behold, thou desirest truth in the inward parts: and in the hidden part thou shalt make me to know wisdom.
>
> Purge me with hyssop, and I shall be clean: wash me, and I shall be whiter than snow. Make me to hear joy and gladness; that the bones which thou hast broken may rejoice.

> Hide thy face from my sins, and blot out all mine iniquities.
> Create in me a clean heart, O God; and renew a right spirit within me.
> Cast me not away from thy presence; and take not thy holy spirit from me.
> Restore unto me the joy of thy salvation; and uphold me with thy free spirit.
> Then will I teach transgressors thy ways; and sinners shall be converted unto thee.
> Deliver me from blood guiltiness, O God, thou God of my salvation: and my tongue shall sing aloud of thy righteousness.
> O Lord, open thou my lips; and my mouth shall shew forth thy praise.
> For thou desirest not sacrifice; else would I give it: thou delightest not in burnt offering.
> The sacrifices of God are a broken spirit: a broken and a contrite heart, O God, thou wilt not despise.
> Do good in thy good pleasure unto Zion: build thou the walls of Jerusalem.
> Then shalt thou be pleased with the sacrifices of righteousness, with burnt offering and whole burnt offering: then shall they offer bullocks upon thine altar. (Psalm 51 KJV)

Last, that any person would be considered a singularity was a nonstarter. While God has called individuals to unique missions and vocations, like Moses and Elijah, none of the prophets was anything like a mediator between God and his chosen people in the sense the Christians' Jesus is. The Israelites were chosen as a nation. The blessing of election flowed to the nation, not to a set of individuals. The prophets were the voices of God. But Jesus's death and Resurrection were not captured as a means of transmitting a message. If that had been the case, it would have been easy to consider Jesus as another prophet. Instead, though, Jesus was not delivering a message; he *was* the message. This doctrine would have been an impossibly hard pill for Jesus's contemporary Jews to swallow. Here is an analogy to make the point:

> When Moses opened the Red Sea for Israel, none of the Israelites ever thought of Judaism being a religion about Moses. The religion was always about God; Moses was just a messenger. By contrast, after the Resurrection, the Church's religion was about Jesus, not just as a messenger but as the message.

The Argument from Difficulty

The need for a mediator between God and his people would have been a complex and novel one to concoct. It was also an unnecessary one too, as the Jews would have already understood themselves to have recourse to achieve remission of sins. Once the initial idea of Christianity was formulated, it would have been an affront to many Jews. Among other possible reasons, many Jews would have rejected the attachment of the forgiveness of sins because

- Evangelists were taking godly Jews away from God by abandoning the covenant and their inheritance.
- If Jesus were a mediator to God for sin, then Jesus must have had some sort of divine relationship with God since only God can forgive sins. But ceding such a relationship to Jesus would be sacrilege, crediting to a man what is solely God's. To his many Jewish peers, the atonement looks like paganism, wrapped in a pseudo-Jewish blanket.
- The whole economy of the temple, the priesthood, and the Jerusalem sacrificial cult would be rendered moot—but this economy was set in Torah by Moses himself!

The Synoptics all tell us that Jesus himself instituted a new covenant (or the English term, *testament*). The Jews who were Jesus's contemporaries would have wondered why Jesus chose to institute a new covenant when the original from Moses worked perfectly well. Shunting the Mosaic covenant would have unthinkable. If the original followers of Jesus retained their allegiance and identity to their ancestor faith—and clearly they did so—they would have had a lot of explaining to do regarding how Jesus's covenant coexists with Moses's. Here are the verses from Matthew's recounting of the Last Supper (italics added for emphasis):

> While they were eating, Jesus took bread, and when he had given thanks, he broke it and gave it to his disciples, saying, "Take and eat; this is my body."
>
> Then he took a cup, and when he had given thanks, he gave it to them, saying, "Drink from it, all of you. This is my blood of *the covenant*, which is poured out for many for the forgiveness of sins. I tell you, I will not drink from this fruit of the vine from now on until that day when I drink it new with you in my Father's kingdom." (Matt 26:26–29 NIV)

We have it in writing much earlier than the Gospels about how primitive the representation of the Lord's Supper is from Paul. Paul's words predate Matthew's account by several years. The following passage comes from a letter that appears to have been written by Paul in the middle to late 50s (italics added for emphasis):

> For I received from the Lord what I also handed on to you that the Lord Jesus, on the night he was handed over, took bread, and, after he had given thanks, broke it and said, "This is my body that is for you. Do this in remembrance of me." In the same way also the cup, after supper, saying, "This cup is the *new covenant* in my blood. Do this, as often as you drink it, in remembrance of me." For as often as you eat this bread and drink the cup, you proclaim the death of the Lord until he comes. Therefore whoever eats the bread or drinks the cup of the Lord unworthily will have to answer for the body and blood of the Lord. (1 Cor 11:23–27 NAB)

These words are remarkable in a number of ways. Notably, the institution of the Eucharist clearly predates Paul, and he claims it originated directly from Jesus. Paul uses rabbinic language ("received what I also handed on"). Again, to Jewish sensibilities, it looks as if Jesus is usurping the sacred Mosaic covenant. Altering their "perpetual" (the word from Exodus) covenant with God was just not something most Jews would ever consider. Paul would have known this, too, which is probably why he challenged The Way in Jerusalem and why the Sanhedrin commissioned him to go to Damascus and quell the uprising there before his conversion en route.

If one were making up the scheme of the Christian atonement, it would have been a very heavy lift. The story is far too complex if the purpose were simply to get the audience to accept the resurrection of Jesus, seek repentance with God and each other, and live a holy life. All of these goals could have been accomplished while resting solidly within Judaism. The story might have taken off among the Jews and been normative to Jews to this day. But this is not the simple story that was told. Instead, the story was a complex one about how Jesus was the unique and sole mediator for the forgiveness of sins. He inaugurates a new testament, supplanting the old. These complexities make the story harder to tell and harder to sell.

We conclude here that the writers would not have presented their stories the way they did if they were making it up. We revert to our common theme: you just can't make this stuff up. They would not have chosen to make the story harder than necessary. They need not have crafted a new covenant nor created a new paradigm of an intermediary to God for the remission of sin. The evangelists had no specific desire to set aside the Mosaic covenant. They did not choose to write the story of the forgiveness of sins because that is how they wanted to tell the story. They told the stories the way they did because the stories were revealed to them that way. The Gospel writers are recorders of history, not makers of it.

Argument from Surprise

The Gospels have Jesus reciting seven utterances ("words") from the cross, pending his death. Seven was considered to be a perfect number of completion. One might suppose that the number of utterances was contrived to get to seven, but this is not the case. The Gospel authors could never have contrived that there would be seven. The number seven only revealed itself after the four Gospels were assembled, which did not happen during the lifetimes of the Gospel writers. The first of the seven is in Luke 23:34: "Father, forgive them, they know not what they do" (NAB and others). Many things about this line are ambiguous. The first is whom "they" Jesus refers to. They could be the Roman soldiers who were about to torture Jesus to death. They could be pagan Romans more generally. They could be the Jewish leaders. Perhaps it is a nondescript reference to everyone. The second ambiguity is whether the words are even native to the Lucan accounts. Not all ancient versions of Luke's Gospel contain these words. Last, assuming we accept their inclusion in the original versions of the Lucan accounts, ambiguity exists on whether the words are a retrojection by Luke or a later editor.

In this case, whether the words were actually retrojected or not does not matter to the obvious conclusion about what these words convey regarding the consensus of Christian understanding of Jesus's teaching. Jesus was about forgiveness. This conclusion is unmistakably authentic to the earliest Christian understanding of Jesus. This follows directly from Luke 23:34, if Jesus were the source of the words, or indirectly, if the source were Luke himself (or a subsequent editor). The sentiment is native to the meaning Luke conveys, independent of attribution.

A characteristic of the Judaism of Jesus's day—like the Judaism of today, too, but quite unlike the pagan religions of the first century—was its ethical composition. One of the most foundational ethics in Judaism is the ideal of justice or divine justice. As an heir to Judaism, Christianity inherits the ethics of the Jews. It is appropriate, therefore, to refer to Judeo-Christian values collectively. In their common Judeo-Christian heritage, Christians and Jews share the belief that justice trumps mercy. Indeed, Christians and Jews realize that a flourishing society could not survive if justice was not primary over mercy. The acute exception in the shared ethics between the two religions is how Christians and Jews understand the way in which mercy modulates and tempers justice. The difference can be so acute in some instances that it is almost a difference in kind more than a difference in degree. Christians attach a far more heightened value to mercy than do Jews. The difference between the Jewish sense of justice as opposed to the Christian sense of mercy is memorialized in the famous scene (Act IV, Scene 1) in Shakespeare's *Merchant of Venice*. The Jewish sense of justice is rendered ignobly by the Jewish moneylender Shylock as depicted as attempting to extract a pound of flesh, when exercising a modicum of Christian-like mercy would have served him better. The source of difference is Jesus. He taught about the centrality of mercy-forgiveness-reconciliation. The divergence from the Jewish norm to the Christian motif meets the criterion of surprise.

Jesus taught his disciples to think of mercy as the mortar to hold a community together; earthly justice just would not suffice. In this regard, Jesus presents himself as a foil to the Pharisees, who were driven by obsequious commitment to keeping the law. In Jesus's view, keeping to the law (Torah) should not be conflated with keeping to justice. A real, sustainable justice requires the modulating influence of mercy to uphold a moral society. What justice looks like absent of mercy is the character of Inspector Javert in *Les Miserables*. Raw justice, sans mercy, is a sterile dystopia, as Inspector Javert learned too late to save himself in Victor Hugo's classic tale.

In the Jewish magazine *Commentary*, the author of an article titled "May God Avenge Their Blood" provides these words in his reflection on the horrific killing of eleven Jews at a synagogue in Pittsburgh in 2018 (italics in original):

> Jews do *not* believe that we must love the sinner while hating the sin; in the face of egregious evil, we will *not* say the words ascribed to Jesus on the cross: "Father, forgive them, for they know not what they do." We believe that a man who shoots up a synagogue knows well what he does. . . . To forgive in this context is to absolve; and it is, for Jews, morally unthinkable.[38]

Contrast the expressed Jewish sentiment with the Christian one. For the Jew, to offer the prospect of absolution is morally unthinkable; for the Christian, to withhold the prospect of absolution is unthinkable. The juxtaposition between these two facts satisfy the burden of the criterion of historicity for surprise. The difference between the Jewish and Christian views gets to the primal, historical influence of the ability to seek the forgiveness of sins merited by Jesus's death. This is the initial idea of Christianity.

CONCLUSION

Among my aims in this book is verifying the historicity of seven of the Church's elemental claims in the Gospels. This chapter has focused on the Church's claim that Jesus death atones for sin. As noted in chapter 2, the forgiveness of sins is not a matter for the historian; such a claim abides in the domain of the theologian—and this book is about history, not theology. To validate the claim of historicity of the forgiveness of sins, I have adopted a proxy claim that is testable with the tools of the historian. The proxy claim is that the belief in the atoning death of Jesus can be located in the earliest days of the Church. I have validated the proxy claim in two ways. The first is based on circumstances, which one might call an empirical approach. The other is based on reasoning alone and comes from applying the chapter 2 criteria for historicity.

Connecting Jesus's death to the forgiveness of sins involves stringing together a series of abstract and previously unimagined thoughts. The connection would have required substantive genius and time to concoct, neither of which was available to the disciples. We can account for the emergence of a theory for Jesus's atoning death in the narrow time period in which we know it was promulgated only if we assume that a source exogenous to the first disciples provided it to them. We conclude that this exogenous source must have been Jesus himself. This conclusion from circumstantial evidence maps exactly to the testimony in the Gospels, and all four Gospels explicitly identify Jesus as the source of the theory. If we believe that the theory of atonement came from Jesus, we have independent evidence for the Resurrection because, obviously, Jesus needed to be alive to deliver the theory to the apostles.

Our starting hypothesis is that the first disciples made up the atonement theory. I have provided the logical bases to reject the hypothesis, which follows these lines of argument:

- Linking Jesus's death to the forgiveness of sins enjoys independent and multiple literary attestations and separate corroborating evidence. This is the gold standard we seek for demonstrating historicity. The Synoptic accounts, the Lucan narrative in Acts, the stories in John, and multiple locations in the Pauline letters all count as independent literary sources. The corroborating evidence comes from the responses of the believers who experience intense joy, and the responses from the disbelievers who reject the notion intensely.
- The first Christians had no particular reason to propose linking Jesus's death to the forgiveness of sins. Modalities for achieving atonement

already existed, and nobody believed a new one was needed. Actually, the specific linkage proposed by the earliest evangelists ran contrary to their preexistent Jewish mores. Accordingly, the linkage greatly complicated the first evangelists' intended outreach to their fellow Jews. We can be clear that the first evangelists would not have concocted an atonement theory that would have alienated their targeted audience, yet their posited atonement theory did precisely that, which is how we can conclude it must be authentic.

We come to the same conclusion as we have in assessing other primitive claims of the Church: you just can't make this stuff up.

7

The Models of Jesus

We have discovered how Jesus's Passion–death–Resurrection saga became the foundation of the faith of the Church. She came to realize how Jesus had won cosmic justice for the world by his Resurrection. The apostles and the disciples were launched down a path they never could have anticipated. They had a mission and they proceeded to fulfill it. They preached about Jesus in "Jerusalem and in all Judea and Samaria and even to the very ends of the earth" (Acts 1:8).

The Church now had her Resurrection and her initial idea. What she lacked, though, was a simple, concrete description to communicate her Jesus to the world. The Church needed what we engineers would refer to as a *model*. Models are descriptions that help understand and predict phenomena. In engineering applications, models can be equations, drawings, or other representations of a system. This chapter provides the answer to what model the Church centered on and how she did it.

In the first days after the Resurrection, there would had been no theological development or myth-making; both demand the luxury of time. Yet, the Church must have characterized Jesus quickly. She had to come to some understandings promptly because the Church was a proselytizing and evangelizing community from or nearly from her inception. The members of the Church needed a tale to tell their Jewish brethren. No doubt, the Church would later expand, clarify, and refine her models of Jesus. Indeed, the Church enjoined in three to four hundred years of theological debate and introspection via several ecumenical councils to develop more refined models. But the Church had to start somewhere. Here I try to tease out the early models the Church used to tell the world about Jesus.

POSSIBLE SOURCES FOR INITIAL MODELS OF JESUS

The earliest disciples would have drawn predominantly upon three sets of inputs to understand Jesus: what they personally observed or knew of Jesus, what artifacts or instructions Jesus had left them with, and the thoroughly Jewish culture and heritage in which they lived. They would have reached into their past to explain their present. They would have looked to their heroes and figures from their past in order to characterize Jesus for their peers—and for themselves, too. They would have drawn upon their past for understanding, not only because that is what the disciples had as their resource, but also because that is what the disciples' audiences had as their resource as well.

Let's compare figures from Jewish traditions to the Jesus of the Gospels. We can argue the comparison from two perspectives. In one case, one can look at an attribute-by-attribute comparison of Jesus as reported in the Gospels versus people in the Hebrew Bible and some other Jewish sources (see Table 7–1). In the other case, one can make the comparison on a person-by-person attribute of some of the leading people and figures from Jewish traditions (see Table 7–2). These are complementary ways of looking at the same data.

The tables reveal that there never had been any hero among the Jews like Jesus before and nobody like him since that time either. Here are some salient takeaways:

- Many of Jesus's attributes have parallels to other figures, but Jesus is a complex compilation of many figures. Jesus takes on attributes of all of the figures in Table 7–2, but no single person in Table 7–2 is a peer or parallel to Jesus. The closest parallel might be a combination of Moses and Elijah, who, incidentally, make appearances with Jesus at the Transfiguration, as recorded in the Synoptic Gospels. With this point in mind, maybe the Synoptics' identification of the other two with Jesus in the Transfiguration is telling.
- Jesus has unique attributes. Clearly, the Gospel writers were not restricted by precedent to describe Jesus.
- Jesus does not foment violence to people as a means or as an end in his work; a fig tree, some pigs, and some moneychangers' tables might be considered victims of Jesus's violence, but they are not people. Contrast this with the characteristic penchant for Jewish heroes to incite or use violence against people to advance Israel's supposed geopolitical aims. The list is not short. It includes: Moses, Joshua, the Judges, Elijah, David, Mordecai (from the book of Esther), and the Maccabees. The list spans the entire range from the dawn of the Mosaic covenant to the intertestamental period, more than a thousand years.

- Jesus is depicted in a way unimagined before his time.
- The combination of attributes puts in him a wholly unique category.

Table 7-1. Attributes Ascribed to Jesus in the Gospels versus Attributes Ascribed to Others in the Jewish Tradition

General Attribute	Specific Attribute	Jesus	Selected Jewish/Hebrew Persons, Figures, or References
Teaching	Wisdom	X	Writers of the books of Job, Psalms, Proverbs, Wisdom, et al.
	Social justice	X	Prophets, such as Amos and Isaiah
	Prophecy	X	Jeremiah, Ezekiel, et al.
	Holiness of God	X	Moses and later prophets, including John the Baptist
	Confront authorities in advocating for God/Torah	X	Jeremiah, John the Baptist, et al.
	Morality and ethics	X	Moses, judges, and later prophets
	Good versus evil	X	Implied in many places but usually indirect in the Hebrew Bible, whereas quite explicit tension between good and evil in the New Testament
	Apocalypse	X	John the Baptist and events described in the book of Daniel and, to a lesser extent, Maccabees
	Teaching by one's own authority	X	None
Actions	Miracle worker	X	Elijah, Elisha, and Moses
	Building lasting coalitions	X	Moses, Isaiah, David, et al.
	Law-giver and covenant maker	X	Moses
	Resurrection or resuscitation	X	Enoch and Elijah
	Using violence as a means or end	No	Moses, Joshua, the Judges, David, Elijah, Mordecai, and the Maccabees

Roles	Priest	X	Aaron
	Prophet	X	Many
	King	X	Saul (of the Hebrew Bible) originally but primarily David and subsequent figures from his dynasty
	Founder of a new social structure	X	Abraham, Moses, and possibly the returnees from the Babylonian exile
	Sacrifice	X	Passover lamb and possibly the Suffering Servant in Isaiah (but no actual human person as the sacrifice, given the Genesis admonition against human sacrifice)
	Political-military leader	No	Moses, Judges, David, the Maccabees, Mordecai, et al.
	Dismissal of sins	X	Scapegoat
	Singularity (having a nature entirely unique)	X	None

Table 7-2. Comparison of Jesus to Others in Jewish History

Person, Figure, or Reference (presented in approximately chronological order)	Attribute Shared with Jesus
Abraham	Founder of a new social structure
Moses	Miracle worker, law-giver, provider of covenant, founder of a nation (in the political sense and also, possibly, in the social sense), fulfillment of ancient promises
Aaron	Executed priestly functions (intermediary ministerial functions)
Passover lamb	Election and sacrifice
Scapegoat	Removal of sins
David	King; Son of God; source of prayers, psalms, and wisdom
Wisdom	Deep understanding of humanity
Prophets (Isaiah, Amos, Jeremiah, Micah, Elijah, et al.)	Miracle worker, teaching, prophesy, insistence on the holiness of God, continual call to return Israel to its covenantal relation with God, moral and social justice teaching
Characters in the book of Daniel and John the Baptist	Apocalyptic teachings

We have the intellectual problem of trying to discern how each evangelist chose the characteristics he wanted to report to create a given model of Jesus—but we are getting ahead of ourselves. The authors of the Gospels have decades to pull their narratives together, but the first evangelists had only a few hours or at most a few days to make their case. Peter and his colleagues faced their Jewish co-religionists in the days immediately after their Resurrection experiences. Somebody (or a set of people) had to devise the models in the first place to evangelize Jesus to the Palestinian Jews immediately after the Resurrection

So, in trying to deduce the original models for evangelizing about the risen Jesus, we have an acute problem of retrojection. The Gospels were all written when the models were already articulated. This creates a chicken-and-egg problem for us as we try to determine whether the evangelists came up with their models for Jesus and then wrote their accounts to conform to the models or whether the process went the other way around.

Wikipedia reveals that Jesus is referred to by 198 different names or titles. History passes down to us many models of Jesus: Lord, Messiah, miracle worker, Alpha and Omega, Son of God, Lamb of God, among many others. Our task is to discern which ones are from the oldest, rawest traditions. When Peter was first addressing the Sanhedrin a few weeks after the Resurrection, we can be confident he was not referring to Jesus as "Lord of Lords and King of Kings" from Handel's *Messiah*. The theological developments to get to those names would take centuries for the Church to work out. But Peter did not have hundreds of years; he might not even have had a hundred hours. In his first speeches, Peter and his associates must have had a simpler, very raw, non-mythological, and a theologically unrefined model. Some sort of word picture model was required to make sense of it all.

INITIAL MODELS

We cannot confidently identify all of the models on which the first disciples might have built their rendering of Jesus. They are lost to history. However, we have a specific few we can assert with confidence. One model that could have been employed is identifying Jesus as the "Son of Man." We have every reason to believe this because it comes from Jesus, it appears in so many contexts and places in Jesus's public ministry, it is a distinctly Aramaic expression that falls into the Greek of the Gospels only as a clumsy idiom, and the title itself is so mysterious. The term *Son of Man* conveys the nondescript meaning of "somebody" or "a human being." As clear as it is that the name is applied by Jesus to himself, there is no indication the Church ever employed this title into any creedal or doctrinal form.

In our quest for a primal model of Jesus, we look for it to satisfy these criteria:

- It is primitive.
- The Church employed it in her evangelical pursuits.
- We can establish its historicity.

If we found a model that satisfied these criteria, we can have some confidence that it predates any supposed myth-making or theological development. The quest for a suitable model renders a readily identifiable candidate. The model is Jesus as the "Messiah" (Hebrew) or "Christ" (Greek). The word *Messiah* means "anointed one." The term is used in the Hebrew Bible to refer to several folks who had been anointed for the roles they played. King David is the ultimate example, but Cyrus, the emperor who freed the Israelites from the Babylonian exile, is also referred to in messianic terms. Cyrus was a Gentile.

When we refer to *Messiah* with respect to Jesus, though, we do not mean *a* messiah; we mean *the* Messiah. Here are the first words of the first Gospel (Mark), which makes the point plainly: "The beginning of the gospel of Jesus Christ (the Son of God)" (NAB).[39] It may well be that other models exist contemporaneous with the one referring to Jesus as the Christ, but demonstrating their origin is less obvious—and if they existed, their significance is overwhelmed by the use of the model of Jesus as the Messiah.

THE MESSIAH MODEL

Associating Jesus with the Messiah is automatic in our era, but it would not have always been so. The model's creation had to begin somewhere.

In Jesus's time, the Jews had clear understandings what they were expecting in their long-prophesied Messiah. The Messiah would be a descendant of the great King David. Additionally, he would restore Israel to her rightful place among the nations, the worship of God would be universalized, and God's peace would rest upon the world.

The era in which the Church first preached was one of great messianic expectation. The Romans occupied Israel. The deepest longings of the pious Jews of that time were that God would send his Messiah and redeem Israel by ousting the dreaded, arrogant pagan overlords. Thus, the idea that Jesus would have been pitched by the Church as the Christ should not come as a total surprise to a people who were burning in expectation of the Messiah.

Jesus conveyed so many holy attributes, as Tables 7–1 and 7–2 indicate, that the Church must have considered labeling Jesus as the Christ all along.

Notwithstanding the incredible tales about Jesus, let us examine how they compare to the expectations of the Messiah from the Tanakh, the Hebrew Bible. Tracey Rich is a modern-day Jewish author who takes up the case to assure his fellow Jews that Jesus was *not* the Messiah. As Rich states, the Messiah was the long-sought person whom the Jews looked to accomplish the following:

> When the messiah does come, he will inaugurate the messianic age (sometimes called the Olam Ha-Ba, World to Come). The Tanakh employs the following descriptions about this period:
>
> - Peace among all nations (Isa 2:4; Mic 4:3).
> - Perfect harmony and abundance in nature (Isa 11:6–9) (but some interpret this as an allegory for peace and prosperity).
> - All Jews return from exile to Israel (Isa 11:11–12; Jer 23:8; 30:3; Hos 3:4–5).
> - Universal acceptance of the Jewish God and Jewish religion (Isa 2:3; 11:10; 66:23; Mic 4:2–3; Zech 14:9).
> - No sin or evil; all Israel will obey the commandments (Zeph 3:13; Ezek 37:24).[40]

Here are the exact words from Ezekiel (37:24–28), the last entry above. These words sum up many of these messianic requirements (I italicize some words to inform the discussion below):

> And David my servant *shall be king over them*; and they shall all have *one shepherd*. They shall also *follow my judgments and observe my statutes,* and do them. And they shall dwell in the land that I have given to Yaakov [interject for Anglicanization: Jacob] my servant, in which your fathers have dwelt and they shall dwell there, they and their children, and their children's children forever; and *my servant David shall be their prince forever*. Moreover, I will make a *covenant of peace* with them, it shall be *an everlasting covenant* with them, which I will give them; and I will multiply them and I will set my *sanctuary in the midst of them forevermore*. And *my tabernacle shall be with them*: *and I will be their God and they will be my people*. Then the nations shall know that I am the Lord who sanctifies Israel, when My sanctuary will be in the midst of them forevermore.

Rich's point is that Jesus did not fulfill the list of Tanakh prophecies about the Messiah and therefore could not be the Messiah. Rich makes this point in the twenty-first century. The Jews of the first century must have performed a similar calculus. Accordingly, one wonders how and why the Church chose to connect Jesus with the prophesied Christ for the Jews of her time. Remember that the Jews to whom Peter and his fellow Church members preached would have understood a messianic urgency at least as much as the Jews of our day.

In answering Rich's objection to the lack of fulfillment of prophecies, how one reads the italicized words in the passage from Ezekiel is telling. The words above from Rich are from a twenty-first century Jew to explain how Jesus was *not* the Messiah, an explanation he provided in way of protecting his co-religionists of our day from falling prey to Christian evangelists. Rich's argument is meant to be a categorical demonstration how Jesus failed to conform to the criteria the Jews had in place for a person to qualify as the Messiah. Thus, Rich's unequivocal conclusion is that Jesus was not the Messiah. The irony is that a moderately well-catechized Christian could easily read this same list of prophecies and draw a conclusion precisely the opposite of Rich's. Christians can interpret all of the italicized words or phrases from the Ezekiel passage as stories and promises in the New Testament. Indeed, not only *could* these words be interpreted by Christians to be prophesying about Jesus, but they *are* invoked explicitly so. To take a specific example from the set of prophecies cited above, the words from Isaiah 11 are read in Christian liturgies in the Advent season as prophecies that Jesus specifically satisfied. So much for the author's assertion of the words being unequivocal rejection of Jesus's messiahship!

To follow Rich's reasoning, though, at a plain reading, these prophecies are not fulfilled. They become fulfilled only when one begins to interpret and apply them through the lens of theology. Suffice it to say that the apostles would not have devised the theology to bridge the gap from the plain reading of Scripture.

The first Christians must have applied a complicated and esoteric reading of their existing Scripture, the Hebrew Bible, in contrast to the literal reading of it, to understand their Jesus. But, the reader will recall, the first Christians were about as far afield from being professional theologians as one could imagine.[41]

Not to put too fine a point on the matter, but prior to the Resurrection, one might say theology as a discipline did not exist. The advent of theology as a discipline was likely an incidental and unplanned adjunct to the evangelical mission of the Church, akin to the development of calculus by Isaac Newton while he was devising the fundamental laws of mechanics in physics. To claim Jesus is the Messiah is one thing; proving it is quite another. The claim to messiahship for Jesus was anything but a slam dunk for the Church. By making the claim of messiahship, the Church created for herself a heavy lift in having to force reinterpretations of messianic prophecies in a wholly new and revolutionary manner. The new manner would have conflicted with the understandings of the Jews of the day and, as Rich makes clear, the Jews of our day as well.

As a sign of how deeply embedded the Messianic model was within the early Church, you will not find an explicit argument in the Gospels why Jesus meets the criteria for being the Messiah. The Church simply asserts it, having no need to prove it. Rich states further:

> The notion of an innocent, divine or semi-divine being who will sacrifice himself to save us from the consequences of our own sins is a purely Christian concept that has no basis in Jewish thought. Unfortunately, this Christian concept has become so deeply ingrained in the English word "messiah" that this English word can no longer be used to refer to the Jewish concept. The [unperturbed Hebrew] word "mashiach" [is] used [for us].

The author's claim the notion is "a purely Christian concept" is patently false. The idea the author denounces as non-Jewish originated as a Jewish idea, was nurtured that way, spread that way, and was accepted that way. It was developed by Jews and for Jews, perhaps with an occasional Gentile at the periphery. Only later would the Jews who originated this notion become a distinct group separated from other (mainline) Jews. Setting Rich's false statement aside, his underlying argument should not be missed. What he states above—the initial idea of Christianity—has no obvious nexus to the messianic prophecies from the Hebrew Bible. The Church bet her future on the initial idea of Christianity. Given this fact, we are left wanting for a reason why she chose to muddle the idea with the added messianic prophesies. There is no a priori reason that the deliverer of spiritual salvation must also be the biblical Messiah. David Novak is a rabbi and a professor. He makes the point of the Jews' rejection of Jesus's Messiahship quite clearly:

> I cannot accept the Christian claim because Jesus of Nazareth did not fulfill the necessary messianic criteria: He did not restore kingship to Israel, he did not rebuild the Jerusalem Temple, and he did not bring about the universal realm of just peace or peaceful justice, when "the earth will be filled with the acknowledgment of the Lord as the waters cover the sea" (Isa. 11:9).[42]

But Rich and Novak need not make their point that Jesus was not the Messiah by testing Jesus's Messiahship against Hebrew Bible criteria. Their argument could even be simpler than that. If the Gospel writers were going to make up the position that Jesus were the Messiah, the Anointed One, then the writers would have included compelling stories of Jesus being anointed, where anointing is a public display of conveyance of sacred authority. All four Gospels do in fact have stories of Jesus being anointed. In all four of them (which may or may not be retellings of the same event [cf. Matt 26:6–13; Mark 14:3–9; Luke 7:36–50; John 12:1–8]), a *woman* does the anointing. If the first, most basic requirement of being the Messiah is being anointed to the position, Jesus did not meet even this basic requirement. Augustine, the great doctor of the Church, admits as much himself in his magisterial *City of God*.[43] No right-thinking evangelist would create the concept of Jesus being anointing by a woman. Women were second-class citizens. They had no authority to convey. So, one is left wondering whether Jesus, the Anointed One, was anointed authoritatively. In words put upon Jesus's lips in Luke's Gospel (4:16–21), the anointing that Jesus himself takes credit for is a non-anointing (i.e., there is no physical anointing):

> [Jesus read from a scroll of Isaiah to those assembled in the synagogue], "the Spirit of the Lord is upon me because he has anointed me." . . . He said to them, "Today this scripture passage is fulfilled in your hearing."

Debate surrounds the differing interpretations of messianic prophesies between Jews and Christians. I do not intend to attempt to resolve that debate here but rather make a different point. With so much to convey about Jesus, as noted in the tables above, not the least of which was a wholly unanticipated Resurrection, why would the Church latch onto the problematic messianic claim so tenaciously? To deconstruct Christianity to its basic elements, why was it strictly necessary for Jesus as the Redeemer and Savior—not to mention prophet, charismatic leader, and miracle worker—to also be the Messiah? Remember that the Church is assumed here to have made all of this all up. If that were the case, what was the specific advantage to the Church to have Jesus wear so many hats? And why would the Church assign Jesus a messianic hat? Identifying Jesus as the Christ would be a deeply controversial and difficult decision. Simpler and more effective ones were available. After all, none of the criteria for being the Messiah were satisfied by Jesus in any concrete, observable way, as Rich and Novak state. Furthermore, to the Jews looking for *their* kind of Messiah, they had no need for a crucified messiah. A dead messiah would be, as Paul would plainly say it later, "folly to Jew and Greek." The claim that Jesus was the Messiah would have no credibility for those who first heard the pitch.

The expectations were not merely hypotheticals either, as a host of claimants identified themselves to be the king of the Jews (a pagan term) or king of Israel (a Jewish term). (Jesus was executed for being "King of the Jews," the title the Romans hung on the cross with him.) Many of these claimants took up arms against the Romans. The Acts of the Apostles (21:13) even records the events of one such claimant, called "the Egyptian." Josephus, the Jewish warrior, Roman confidant, and historian, identifies no fewer than six nominal messiahs existing during the Roman occupation from the mid-first century BCE to the late first century CE, which is when he wrote. Another claimant came shortly after Josephus named Simon bar Kokhba, who was widely thought to be the messiah at the time. The messianic fever would become so intense that the Jews revolted in 66–70 and then again from 130–135 CE (under Kokhba). The results would be devastating. The first revolt ended in the collapse of the Temple; the second, the expulsion of Jews from Jerusalem. The Jews would not find a political home in their ancestral homeland again until after World War II.

Reconsider Rich's extract from above in which he discounts the "messiah" term entirely because of what he considers to be the term's corruption by Christians. Then look back at how his fellow Jews nineteen or twenty centuries ago might have heard the initial Messianic claims attached to Jesus. Imagine how much more difficult a sales job it would have been for the first evangelists. They would have been burdened with trying to sell the Messiah appellation to an audience that had a radically different understanding of messiahship. Presenting Jesus as the Messiah would likely have been counterproductive to the first evangelists' purposes; at a minimum, they would certainly have had a significant amount of explaining to do.

Being a messiah or even *the* Messiah is a seemingly modest claim, in comparison, to the initial idea of Christianity. Looking back from our point of history, we might say the Church had a poor public relations campaign with mixed messaging. Invoking the Messiah label would have only raised issues the evangelists were not prepared to answer, and, besides, the Messianic claim is arguably tangential and thus potentially a distraction to the bigger claims being made. From the Church's perspective, yes, it would have been nice to run the story with Jesus as the Messiah, but the Jesus as the Messiah in the New Testament is much grander than the Tanakh Messiah. Jesus is, as Handel puts in his choral arrangement, the eponymous *Messiah*, "King of Kings. Lord of Lords. And he shall reign forever and ever."

Yet that the Christians called Jesus the Messiah (Christ in Greek) is an undisputed fact of history. The term *Christian* comes from the very word *Christ*, of course. In the Pauline epistles alone, the authors use the term *Christ* 382 times.[44] The great prevalence identifies its ubiquity and original nature. In Paul's writings, which are the earliest written documents preserved in the New Testament, Paul uses "Messiah" as a virtual synonym for Jesus. Without question, the criterion for multiple attestation of a claim in the New Testament is satisfied not only in Paul but in the Gospels and even Josephus. So thorough has the connection between Jesus and Christ become that many folks today unwittingly understand the title "Christ" to be a name. They will refer to Jesus as "Jesus Christ" as if "Christ" were a surname for Jesus. In a similar vein, for the *Merriam-Webster's Dictionary* entry "Messiah," the first definition is "anointed"; the second, "Jesus."

We do not know precisely when the Church began calling Jesus "the Christ." It seems as if the Church adopted the name very soon after the Resurrection. We know of no time after the Resurrection when Christians didn't refer to their risen Jesus in this manner. Peter explicitly connects Jesus with the Messiah within days of the Resurrection (Acts 2:31–32). Pope John Paul II claimed the risen Jesus was always understood in Christological terms.

We have reason to believe that the Messiah title seems to have been applied to Jesus during his lifetime, not just after the Resurrection. From the Passion stories, we know Jesus was executed for being "King of the Jews," which is tantamount to having identified him as a Messianic claimant. Furthermore, all four Gospel accounts identify Jesus being referred to as the Messiah during his life. However, we cannot ascertain from our modern perch whether these Gospel invocations were retrojections or not (see Mark 8:38, which is a clear candidate for retrojection). What we can surmise without much risk of being wrong is that the idea of Messiahship must have been circling in the disciples' minds frequently when Jesus was with them in his earthly life.

The disciples latched onto the title "Messiah" very early and held to it tenaciously in their post-Resurrection reality. This extract from 1 John 2:22 (KJV) could hardly be clearer in how the Church had labeled Jesus as the Christ: "Who is a liar but he who denieth that Jesus is the Christ?" The Church held this position even when jettisoning the title would have been easier and seemingly more effective in way of meeting her objective of evangelization, but she didn't jettison the title. It was not her title to discard. She did not make up the title of Messiah. It had been given to her. If the Church had made up the title, she would be free to have recycled it for a more apt and useful descriptor. She might have done so, if she believed she had the degree of freedom to pick the vocabulary on her own. We know for certain that the Church did not adopt the Son of Man model, whose origin can confidently be traced to Jesus personally. This is the point. The disciples did not have the degree of freedom to pick the model. It was given to them. The following passage from Matthew applies:

> When Jesus came into the coasts of Caesarea Philippi, he asked his disciples, saying, Whom do men say that I the Son of man am? And they said, Some say that thou art John the Baptist: some, Elias [interject for Anglicanization: Elijah]; and others, Jeremiah, or one of the prophets. He saith unto them, But whom say ye that I am? And Simon Peter answered and said, Thou art the Christ, the Son of the living God. And Jesus answered and said unto him, Blessed art thou, Simon Bar-jona: for flesh and blood hath not revealed it unto thee, but my Father which is in heaven. (16:13–23 KJV)

The author states that Jesus is Christ as a revealed point, not a derived one. None of the evangelists or Paul attempts to make the case of Jesus's Messiahship on a criterion-by-criterion basis ala Rich's or Novak's lists above. Instead, the evangelists take it as an established point that Jesus was the Christ because Jesus (or his Father) provided this fact to them. They did not need to create any test on how to get to this conclusion. The first believers left it for another day to determine *how* Jesus was the Christ. That he was the Messiah was the salient point. How he acquired the Messiahship does not seem particularly relevant.

CONCLUSION

After the Resurrection, the Church felt a deep compulsion to evangelize her Resurrected Jesus. She needed one or more models to focus her messaging. The Church had a variety of choices, many of them deriving directly from their personal experiences. Among the many models the Church would employ to describe Jesus, though, none had the carrying power for the original model of Jesus that Christ did. That Jesus should be captured in such terms is anything but self-evident. The then-expectant attributes for the Messiah differed markedly from the Jesus whom the disciples knew personally. Adopting the model of Jesus as Messiah would have conveyed with it much baggage the Church would not necessarily have chosen to carry. This approach also would have complicated selling Jesus to their Jewish co-religionists, the Church's principal targets. This audience, though, was committed to experiencing a different kind of Messiah than the kind Jesus's disciples were selling. And the concept of a Jewish Messiah would have been gibberish to pagans, so the model of Jesus as Messiah would not have been a useful one to concoct to evangelize Gentiles either.

Tying the Resurrected Jesus to the model of Christ would require a wholly new reckoning of Scripture and a rethinking of Jewishness. As history reveals, the Church grasped the Jesus-as-Christ model and held it firmly. We conclude the Church would not have made up and retained the Messianic claim if evangelization were her aim, which it clearly was. The source to validate Jesus's identification as the Christ is Jesus himself. The Church kept to Jesus's claim, quite apart from whether she actually understood it.

Adopting the Jesus-as-Christ model implies the following significant points:

- The Church understood Jesus as the Messiah from an incipient stage. Modern readers might think this conclusion is totally unremarkable, but this understanding is not correct. Jesus looked very unlike the Messiah of the Hebrew Bible.
- Adopting Jesus as Christ means also adopting the source of the Christ motif, that is, the Hebrew Bible.
- The apostles kept true to Jesus as their source in employing a Messiah model. Adopting the model would have been done at the risk of undermining their evangelical position with the Jews and providing no evangelical benefit among the Gentiles, who had no idea what a Messiah was. To wit, the Church put primacy on what she considered to be revealed to her as true, not what would have been expedient or effective.
- The worldview of the Hebrew Scriptures would need to be reconsidered in light of the truth of the Resurrection and Jesus's revelation of his messiahship. The Church realized that the Hebrew Scriptures were fulfilled in Jesus, not set aside by him. The Church would have to reconcile her presuppositions about Scripture with her understanding of Jesus as the Christ.
- The messiahship of Jesus could only be comprehended via faith; the Church did not connect Jesus to messiahship by performing logic tests or confirming prophecy-by-prophecy predictions of the Messiah's coming. To understand Jesus necessitates linkages to the spiritual (i.e., nonhistorical) world. The Church would have to construct theological understandings of how the Jesus story makes sense in light of Jesus's and the disciples' Jewishness. The demand for a theological understanding of Jesus led to the formation of theology as an intellectual effort, arguably a wholly new discipline. In other words, the Church already knew what the right answer was: Jesus was the Christ. Now she took to determine how it was so.[45] The early doctors of the Church and

the ecumenical councils would work these points out over the next three or four centuries.
- The idea that Jesus the man of history could be segregated from Jesus the Christ of faith is debunked. There is no light between Jesus the man and Jesus the Christ. They are the same person. They always were. The Church did not evolve to a model of Jesus as Christ; it started from there, a point she would not have made up on her own.

The net from the Jesus as Christ model is retaining the Jewish religion but radically reinterpreting it. As such, the evolving Church in the middle decades of the first century had a terrific intellectual challenge. How would she differentiate Christianity (then a sect of Judaism) to her co-religionist Jews (and additionally, to the Gentiles) with the Resurrected Jesus as Christ while retaining the disciples' Jewishness? The objectives do not readily comport. The Church had to walk a very tight line between affirming her Jewishness and affirming the faith in the Resurrected Jesus. It seems to be an impossibly over-constrained set of principles. Consider for a moment how the early followers of Jesus could keep to their own faith traditions with a cogent Judaism and yet answer the fundamental questions of life with this new, totally unexpected, totally radical concept of a Messiah as a singularity in his relationship between man and God. The ability to hold the newly revealed answers and retain the prior faith understandings simultaneously is almost miraculous in and of itself. No reasoning person would have concocted Christianity to walk this kind of tightrope.

We reach the same endpoint we have reached elsewhere: you just can't make this stuff up.

8

The Teaching Ministry of Jesus

The preponderance of historians accept Jesus was a great wisdom teacher, just as the Gospels depict him. This puts him in league with the Buddha, Confucius, Socrates, and perhaps the Hebrew sages of yore. Jesus would merit inclusion into the history books based on his teaching content alone. The corpus of sayings, teachings, and stories attributed back to Jesus has been enormously important in the development of a common morality in Western civilization. The majesty of his words includes the examples below. Their impacts on the development of our culture's ethics are immeasurable. Their ubiquity is evidenced by their familiarity to any classically educated Westerner, Christian or not:

- The Our Father prayer
- The Beatitudes
- The Golden Rule
- The Good Samaritan
- The Prodigal Son

No one can doubt this Matthean prophecy: "Heaven and earth shall pass away, but my words shall not pass away" (Matt 24:35 KJV).

CONTEXT

I have aligned most of the chapters of this book to debunk the elites' presumptions that the matters discussed in the Gospels are mere concoctions of zealots bent on recruiting new members to their nascent faith. Since the gist of Jesus's teachings are well corroborated and more or less accepted as presented, no rejoinder needs to be offered here to establish the historicity of the basic kernels of Jesus's teachings. This is not to imply that all of the sayings attributed to Jesus in the Gospels are accepted by scholars as actually having origins back to Jesus. Determining which sayings in the Gospels actually go back to Jesus personally as opposed to those attributed to him posthumously is the source of ongoing scholarly debate. But the thrusts of Jesus's teachings are accepted nearly universally as coming from him: love, reconciliation, mercy, forgiveness, and fellowship.

One should not think the words attributed to Jesus are verbatim quotations. The Gospel writers recorded Jesus's sayings in Greek, with a minor exception here or there. However, he spoke Aramaic, an unrelated language. It is nearly impossible to recover the exact words he spoke, again with a possible exception or two.

Here is a historical analog to demonstrate the point: Shakespeare's *Romeo and Juliet* was well known and loved from the time it was first performed. The play was born in a written form, immediately circulated in written form, preserved by a literate society, and recognized at once as masterful. Yet, we cannot now discern which of the following three versions of arguably the most famous pair of lines in the play was the original.

> What's in a name? That which we call a Rose,
> By any other name would smell as sweet.
>
> What's in a name that which we call a rose,
> By any other word would smell as sweete.
>
> What? In a name that which we call a Rose,
> By any other word would smell as sweete.[46]

In comparing Shakespeare's words in *Romeo and Juliet* to Jesus's sayings in the Gospels, validating the authenticity of the former, one would think, would be much easier than the latter. For the Gospels, we do not have any contemporary sources; the speaker was largely an unknown man at the time when the words were uttered; the span of people he spoke to was limited; the duration between when the words were spoken and when were they written down is measured in years; and the world in which he preached was an aural, not a literary, one. If we cannot discern which words in *Romeo and Juliet* are Shakespeare's, how futile the task must be to make discernments regarding Jesus's purported words? Instead of supposing we can extract specific wording, we seek to capture the gist of Jesus's teachings as our figure of merit.

UNIQUENESS OF JESUS'S TEACHINGS

We recall that his teaching's content and methodology were substantively Jewish, likely paralleling those of his contemporary Pharisees. His teachings emanated from many precedents in Jewish tradition, but understanding Jesus's teaching corpus solely being within then-contemporary Jewish thought is a category error. Though much of his teaching remained well within the range of Jewish thought at the time, his mix and manner made his corpus unique. The uniqueness of Jesus's teachings stems from the following:

His obsequious commitment to God by identifying Him as "Father." The term "Father" is used occasionally in Hebrew Scripture for God. In those cases, God is projected as Father, the protector of and provider for Israel. In Scripture, Fatherhood was projected in a national sense over Israel as His family. Jesus's use of "Father" was more personal. The personal connectivity that Jesus makes to God as his Father and the subsequent transfer of that connectivity to Jesus's followers are decidedly of Jesus's origin. When Jesus referred to God as Father, he meant it personally; he did not mean it in the universal sense that God is Father to all, although this meaning is also subsumed within Jesus's personalized use. The use of "Father" by the other Abrahamic religions (in the Sufi tradition of Islam and later Judaism) in the personal sense is a probably a learned behavior from Jesus, via Christians.

Use of parables. Jesus was a master at telling parables. In Hebrew Scripture, parables are rare. The only parable the average person could likely cite from the Hebrew Bible is the parable in which Nathan tells King David the story about the lamb being taken from the poor shepherd by the rich man. Nathan delivers the story as a metaphor. The reader knows the parable represents David's taking of Bathsheba as his wife and the de facto sentencing of her true husband to death (2 Sam 12). David comes to this awareness in Nathan's telling of the story to him. By contrast to the scarcity of parables in the Hebrew Bible,[47] Jesus uses dozens of parables and extended allegories recorded in the Gospels and even extracanonical documents, such as the *Gospel of Thomas*.

Speaking about the "kingdom of God." Jesus infuses the kingdom teachings with urgency.

Speaking on personal authority. Jesus's peer Jewish teachers predicated their teaching on their very extensive learning of the Torah and other religious writings, traditions, and scholarship. The pattern of Jewish religious authority derives from intense Torah study, especially under esteemed teachers. Yet Jesus claims no dedicated study at all under anyone, and, as far as the record reveals, he had no particular religious education or formation. We moderns would say he was his own man.

The centrality of certain virtues. Jesus preached love, mercy, and forgiveness. These values are not alien to earlier or even later Judaism, but their centrality to Jesus's messaging argues for its uniqueness to him.

Social justice. Jesus spoke widely about the virtues of social justice and the need to engage the public writ large to embrace social justice. This pattern is reminiscent of the prophets of old, such as Amos and Jeremiah. Jesus advocated for social justice takes up with verve.

Conversion. Jesus spoke of the need for internal personal conversion (repentance or *metanoia*) to conform to God's ways, not to man's.

Forgiveness of sins and restoration of the people's relationship with God. Then as now, compared to Christian responses, reckoning righteous justice is more a ready response to injustice by Jews than is forgiveness. The understanding of mercy and forgiveness is far broader within Christianity than in Judaism.

The identification of the faith community as a family in fellowship. This is contrasted to the Judaism of the day, where the practice of faith hinged on a patrimonial and familial structure.

CONFIDENCE IN ATTRIBUTION OF TEACHINGS TO JESUS

As noted previously, even the Jesus Seminar—no apologist for orthodox Christianity—accepts a corpus of sayings to Jesus as being authentic. By "authentic," we do not necessarily mean the words attributed to him are direct quotations. Few are. What we mean is that the recorded words capture the substantive meanings and intent Jesus set forth. We moderns would call this form of recording information *paraphrasing*. The ancients did not ascribe origins so legalistically. The words attributed to Jesus in the Gospels are meant to convey his intent, not his specific statements.[48] Capturing words as quotations that were really paraphrases was the modus operandi for biographies written in the ancient world.[49] The scholar Brant Pitre states that, "Joseph Ratzinger (Pope Benedict XVI) emphasizes that the four Gospels 'make no claim to literary accuracy' in the manner of a 'recorded transcript.' However, they do claim to correctly render 'the substance of the discourses' of Jesus."[50] We have confidence in the corpus of the words attributed to Jesus because:

Jesus speaks in parables and stories. These kinds of gems are easy to recall. Stories have a special way of connecting the speaker to listeners. The magic of great storytellers, like Jesus, is that their stories, even after being retold for the hundredth time, still convey freshness.

The words are often pithy or clever, making them memorable.

The teachings frequently shock the hearer, making them resonate in memory. Banal things we forget; exceptional things we remember.

Jesus probably repeated stories. The Our Father in the Sermon on the Mount in Matthew's Gospel (6:9–15) may or may not be the same prayer that Jesus offered in the Sermon on the Plain in Luke's Gospel (11:2–4), but, as every executive knows, the leader needs to be prepared to speak on topics when they arise. The speaker relies upon a cadre of prepared material he can recycle. That Jesus might have repeated teachings in different venues for different audiences should not surprise anyone. If the disciples heard the same teaching in many fora, they would have been more likely to remember it.

Many of the sayings have a commonality to them, allowing them to be tied together in memory. In fact, some scholars argue that the evangelists collected like sayings and arranged them thematically, rather than chronologically, to enhance shared meaning. If so, readers should be reluctant in assuming a strict chronology in the ordering of sayings.

In a few cases, *the authors preserve the original Aramaic words* with Greek translations provided in the text. That the authors sensed the need to preserve a few specific phrases in Aramaic to their Greek-reading audiences is a strong argument for their origin. As a sister point, some renderings now preserved only in Greek are awkward idiomatically, suggesting the reconstituted Aramaic words deduced by translating back into Aramaic may be verbatim. The frequent citation as the "Son of Man" is the best example of this because it seems native to Aramaic but awkward in Greek.

The disciples likely had exceptionally good memories tuned to just this sort of thing. "It is well known that the Orientals (Near East as well as Far East) possessed especially keen memories."[51]

Lastly, in antiquity, *one of the principal tasks of a disciple* (the term's core meaning is *student*) *was to remember the master's teachings.* These apostles may have taken it as their charge to remember and retell Jesus's teachings. The charge may have taken focus when the disciples went out in pairs to preach in Jesus's stead during his public ministry. Therefore, the long-standing pious Christian tradition that the transmission of words attributed to Jesus resulted from apostolic succession may not be a pious myth at all. Indeed, the transmission path may well be the result of a specific plan that Jesus set in place with his apostles for them to remember his teachings after his departure.

THE FOCUS OF JESUS'S TEACHINGS

The center of gravity of Jesus's teachings is the primal virtue of love. Jesus's commitment to love as a central tenet is attested widely and independently. Jesus bound love into the commandment enjoined upon his disciples ("Love one another as I have loved you" [John 13:34]), reconciled Peter by commending him to love the sheep/lambs (John 21), and left it as the great ideal to love one's enemies (Matt 5:44), as three examples. John's Gospel and its presumed paired epistles include the word "love" more than a hundred times. Love is not an alien concept in Judaism, of course, then or now. But within the Judaism of the day, it is a latent, tacit ethic. In Christianity, love could hardly be more explicit.

From modern theories of leadership, we know that a leadership team has fully embraced the leader's values when those values are acculturated and exported to others down the chain of command. I have personal experience with the flow of information down a chain of this sort. I had been my sons' basketball coach for several seasons. As the seasons flowed from one year to the next, I sensed that my counseling words to them had become background noise that they filtered out. To my surprise, I discovered that the boys had actually absorbed my counsel when they became basketball coaches themselves years later and used precisely the same words and drills that I taught them as players.

Such is the conveyance with Jesus's central teachings. The centrality of love in his disciples' words stands as evidence that the virtue was central to Jesus. The transmission down the chain is independent evidence for Jesus's central teaching. In the following passages, we find words from Jesus's disciples that love is the central ethic of Christianity and is the very essence of God. None of these words are attributed to Jesus directly; instead, they reflect the students' understanding of their master's core teaching:

> If I speak in the tongues of men or of angels, but do not have love, I am only a resounding gong or a clanging cymbal. If I have the gift of prophecy and can fathom all mysteries and all knowledge, and if I have a faith that can move mountains, but do not have love, I am nothing. If I give all I possess to the poor and give over my body to hardship that I may boast, but do not have love, I gain nothing. Love is patient, love is kind. It does not envy, it does not boast, it is not proud. It does not dishonor others, it is not self-seeking, it is not easily angered, it keeps no record of wrongs. Love does not delight in evil but rejoices with the truth. It always protects, always trusts, always hopes, always perseveres. Love never fails. . . . And now [in the end] these

> three [things] remain: faith, hope, and love. But the greatest of these is love. (1 Cor 13:1–8, 13 NAB)

God is love. (1 John 4 NIV)

Then there is the most famous of all lines in the Bible, John 3:16, which states that love is foundational to the Gospel. This verse has been translated into more languages than any other:

> For God so loved the world that he gave his one and only Son, that whoever believes in him shall not perish but have eternal life. (John 3:16 NIV)

CONCLUSION

Historians generally accept the basic tenets of the teaching ministry Jesus left us, even if particulars remain debatable. His teachings are sublime. Thomas Jefferson pled to invoke Jesus's morals as a basis for teaching the Native American peoples because of the loftiness and grandeur of his teachings. In the broader sense, Jesus's teachings have had a monumental impact on the formation of the ethics of Western civilization. His name is on the short list of the world's greatest wisdom teachers. Even secularists concede the focus of Jesus's messages. Indeed, some of them adopt many of Jesus's tenets as their own.

Since the core of Jesus's teaching is not particularly controverted, I have not presented much evidence for the historicity of it against the criteria in chapter 2. Rest assured, though, we have significant evidence for the historicity of many of Jesus's central teachings by the criteria of multiple attestation and continuity. We have the added evidence of his central teachings by virtue of how they were conveyed through his disciples, whose writings have come down to us to the present time, via a chain we can track from generation to generation.

9

The Miracles of Jesus

In our post-Enlightenment world, claims of miracles that Jesus performed may evoke more visceral reactions from skeptics than anything else reported in the Gospels—aside from the Resurrection, a purported miracle performed *on* Jesus, rather than *by* him. In our scientific world, we reject miracles as a throwback to a primitive, prescientific era. In this chapter, we start with how skeptics view the reports of miracles and then proceed to assess the reported miracle claims against the rational criteria in chapter 2.

Thomas Jefferson famously used his scissors to cut the miracle stories out from the Gospels. He intended to preserve the otherworldly, sublime teachings and morals of Jesus from the contaminations of the ridiculous miracle accretions that the pious, unenlightened evangelists added. Jefferson's goal was to capture Jesus as the charismatic teacher he was, but Jefferson failed. The miracle stories are so deeply intertwined with the teachings that Jefferson could not expunge the miracles without also stripping away its teaching material.

I examine in this chapter what role the miracle stories play in understanding the public ministry of the historical Jesus. Many probably suppose that the claims of Christianity hang on the miracle stories attributable to Jesus. Under scrutiny, though, this supposition is not correct. As evidence:

- The major tenets of Christianity are captured in Paul's epistles. However, Paul doesn't base Jesus's Lordship on his miracles. The proclamation of Jesus's Lordship exists independent of any claim of miracle working.

- If the Gospel renderings are correct, Jesus is clear that his primary role is as a preacher (or teacher), not as a miracle worker: "'For this purpose [of preaching] have I come'" (Mark 2:38 NAB).

- Jesus personally discounts the significance of his miracles. He does not predicate his ministry upon miracles. He even admonishes some Pharisees and onlookers to not rely upon "signs" (one of the three Greek words we lump in together and call "miracles," the other two Greek words being "power" (or mighty deed) and "wonder")[52] to make judgments: "'Why does this generation seek a sign? Amen, I say to you, no sign will be given this generation'" (Mark 8:12). The Marcan statement is in keeping with the irony that typifies Mark's Gospel account. The pre-Passion narrative of the oldest Gospel has about 40 percent of its verses pertaining to signs or sign-related information provided to "this generation." Adding to the irony is the fact that Mark's Gospel actually contains very little of Jesus's preaching, as compared to the other three Gospels, even after Mark has just described Jesus's primary purpose as preaching.

- When Jesus performs many of his miracles, he does so to amplify his teaching authority, making the miracles supportive of his teaching and keeping with the prioritization assigned to it. Pope Leo the Great makes explicit the subordination of miracle-working to teaching in that miracles were made to edify the teaching, not the other way around:

  > Those who were to be instructed in the divine teaching had first to be aroused by the bodily benefits and visible miracles so that, once they had experienced [Jesus's] gracious power, they would no longer doubt the wholesome effect of his doctrine.[53]

- In Mark—again, the earliest of the Gospels—the apostles answered their invitations to join Jesus without any prior miracle-working. Therefore, their calling could not have been conditional upon any miracle-working.

I cannot leave the reader with impression that the miracle stories are entirely superfluous to the story of Jesus. They surely are part of it. To Jesus's companions, the miracles were an unmistakable part of how they experienced Jesus. From the miracles, the disciples came to understand Jesus's bona fides, the crowds grew in response to hear his teachings, and his renown stretched from Galilee to Jerusalem. The miracles help set up the Passion and Resurrection stories. They are intensely relevant to the Gospels.

HOW SKEPTICS ADDRESS THE MIRACLE STORIES IN THE GOSPELS

No educated, intelligent person can possibly believe Jesus performed miracles. Miracles cannot happen because they violate the laws of nature. The belief in miracles requires a suspension of disbelief. The record of Jesus's miracles in the Gospels reflects an overriding superstition. Their explanation for the miracle stories looks like this: The miracle stories present Jesus in idealized terms. Jesus assumes a supernatural position in keeping with the evangelists' theologies. The miracles retroject Hebrew Bible prophecies onto Jesus. The evangelists started with a resurrected man, blessed with divine election. They backed into their miracle stories to fulfill their understandings and expectations of their Messiah.

OVERVIEW OF THE MIRACLE STORIES IN THE GOSPELS

Recall our presumption: all the stories in the Gospel accounts were fabricated by zealous authors bent on wooing prospective converts to their faith. Rebutting the assumption that all the Gospel miracle accounts were simply made-up tales is particularly difficult because the miracle stories, by and large, serve theological, catechetical, or exegetical ends the evangelists wanted to relate. Furthermore, many of the miracle stories have significant resemblances to miracles reported in the Hebrew Bible, especially those attributed to Elijah and Elisha. So we have to confront the prospect that the reported miracles may be Midrashes (retellings of religious stories, usually biblical stories). We have to be particularly mindful of the charge that the miracle stories are retrojected into the Gospels by the early Church to fortify her evangelization outreach. Perhaps the definitive work on understanding the historical Jesus's miracle stories is the opus from John P. Meier, whose 529 pages of dense prose about miracles is supported by 999 footnotes. In it, the author concludes, as we have here, that retrojection must be dutifully considered in assessing the historicity claims of any miracle account.[54]

Miracles are sorted into four categories: superhuman knowledge (having information not available from natural sources); nature workings; healings, of which raising the dead might be considered a particularly dramatic subset; and exorcisms. (Exorcism, to our modern, secular sensibilities, might be considered treatments of mental illness. In our reckoning, we moderns might re-categorize exorcisms as a subset within healings. Notwithstanding, the ancients did not think in these terms. For our purposes in this chapter, we treat exorcisms as the Gospel writers would have understood them.) Jesus performs multiple miracles of each type in the Gospels. The healings and exorcisms are more easily assessed than the other two types because their incidences are widely reported and can be cross-checked. Since exorcisms usually also end up functioning as healing stories, the two sets run together. In contrast to the multi-attested healings and exorcisms, the nature miracles tend to be one-off propositions. Few nature miracles are multiply attested.

The superhuman knowledge miracles, though not necessarily infrequent (especially in John), are also usually one-off propositions. Accordingly, we do not have independent corroboration for most of them either. To the prospect of superhuman knowledge as prescience, the suspicion of retrojection is most acute. Accordingly, for most instances of prescience we would relegate them as retrojections and consider them no further in keeping to our chapter 2 methodology. However, two instances of prescience appear to survive the severe tests of historicity in chapter 2. One is Jesus's prediction of the destruction of the Temple, which is discussed in the next chapter; the other is Jesus's prediction that Peter would betray his master before the cock crowed. We take up the latter instance here.

Jesus makes the prediction of Peter's betrayal in all four Gospels. Unlike most other instances of prescience, this one has a claim to wide attestation (in all the Synoptics, twice in John, and possibly a second time in Luke, depending how one interprets Luke 5:1–11 in conjunction with the story of an amazing catch of fish in John 21). The prediction of the cock-crowing story also meets many of the other criteria for assessing historicity, including embarrassment, coherence, and discontinuity. A separate reason for asserting the historicity of this event of prescience is that the story of Peter denying Jesus is an entirely extraneous and unnecessary adjunct to the story being narrated at the time: The railroading of Jesus to his trials and his death. As a preemption of a refutation, let us set aside the theory that Peter's betrayal was written into the Gospels to tee up his subsequent rehabilitation. We can set aside this theory because the rehabilitation story is narrated only at the end of John's Gospel. John's Gospel was completed one to three decades after the completion of the Synoptics, which do not record Peter's rehabilitation. So, if the purpose of the betrayal is to set up the rehabilitation in the Synoptics, the punchline remains in absentia for many years—a most unlikely proposition.

THE ARGUMENT FROM MULTIPLE INDEPENDENT ATTESTATIONS

One of the most powerful criteria for assessing historicity of information in the New Testament is applying the test of multiple attestation, that is, the test that an act or statement is recorded independently by multiple authors or in multiple forms or both. The test is useful in refuting our assumption that the Gospel stories were invented. If independent sources are going to make up stories—and our Gospel accounts reflect independent sources—the chances they would coincide is remote. Instead of being independently concocted, multiply attested accounts likely go back to an earlier, more primitive, common source.

As we have in other chapters, we start with the assumption that the Gospel writers simply fabricated their tales. Whereas the Gospels are packed with miracle stories, they are narrated differently in each Gospel such that we apply the test of multiple attestation by groups of like miracles rather than individual miracles. For example, we can make a claim for Jesus's healings of withered limbs from multiple accounts because of the frequency of their occurrence, but we would be reluctant to make a claim about multiple attestation for a specific healing episode relating to a particular healing of a particular withered limb. To make specific claims about remote, isolated events is usually beyond the competence of history.

The healings and exorcisms are the miracles that are most frequently multiply attested. The following table lists thirty-seven miracles attributed to Jesus, ordering them in the presumed chronological sequence in which they occurred. The list does not include miracles pertaining to possessing super-human knowledge. This list includes one post-Resurrection miracle story, where the rest were all attested to Jesus during his public ministry.[55] I have annotated the table to identify the ultimate source for each kernel, as defined in the legend. It happens that all of John's miracle stories that overlap with Synoptic stories always involve Mark (but not always with Matthew or Luke, whose Gospels followed Mark). These facts argue that John may have common or contemporaneous origins with Mark. This is an unexpected result because Mark and John are literarily independent and were completed a generation apart. Their overlap attests to common, ancient sources. The Church has always stated that these common, ancient sources are nobody other than the original witnesses of the events.

Table 9-1. Miracles Attributed to Jesus in the Gospels

#	Miracle	Matthew (Mt)	Mark (Mk)	Luke (L)	John (J)	Type*	By*	Source*
1	Jesus turns water into wine				2:1–11	N	J	J
2	Jesus heals an official's son				4:43–54	H	J	J
3	Jesus drives out an evil spirit		1:21–27	4:31–36		E	Mk, L	Mk
4	Jesus heals Peter's mother-in-law	8:14–15	1:29–31	4:38–39		H	Mt, Mk, L	Mk
5	Jesus heals many sick at evening	8:16–17	1:32–34	4:40–41		H	Mt, Mk, L	Mk
6	Apostles make their first miraculous catch of fish			5:1–11		N	L	L
7	Jesus cleanses a man with leprosy	8:1–4	1:40–45	5:12–14		H	Mt, Mk, L	Mk
8	Jesus heals a centurion's servant	8:5–13		7:1–10		H	Mt, L	Q
9	Jesus heals a paralytic	9:1–8	2:1–12	5:17–26		H	Mt, Mk, L	Mk
10	Jesus heals a man's withered hand	12:9–14	3:1–6	6:6–11		H	Mt, Mk, L	Mk
11	Jesus raises a widow's son in Nain			7:11–17		R	L	L
12	Jesus calms a storm	8:23–27	4:35–41	8:22–25		N	Mt, Mk, L	Mk
13	Jesus casts demons into a herd of pigs	8:28–33	5:1–20	8:26–39		E	Mt, Mk, L	Mk

THE MIRACLES OF JESUS   121

#	Miracle	Matthew (Mt)	Mark (Mk)	Luke (L)	John (J)	Type*	By*	Source*
14	Jesus heals a woman in the crowd	9:20–22	5:25–34	8:42–48		H	Mt, Mk, L	Mk
15	Jesus raises Jairus's daughter to life	9:18, 23–26	5:21–24, 35–43	8:40–42, 49–56		R	Mt, Mk, L	Mk
16	Jesus heals two blind men	9:27–31				H	Mt	Mt
17	Jesus heals a man unable to speak	9:32–34				H	Mt	Mt
18	Jesus heals an invalid at Bethesda				5:1–15	H	J	J
19	Jesus feeds five thousand	14:13–21	6:30–44	9:10–17	6:1–15	N	Mt, Mk, L, J	Mk, J
20	Jesus walks on water	14:22–33	6:45–52		6:16–21	N	Mt, Mk, L	Mk, J
21	Jesus heals many sick in Gennesaret	14:34–36	6:53–56			H	Mt–Mk	Mk
22	Jesus heals a Gentile woman's demon-possessed daughter	15:21–28	7:24–30			H	Mt–Mk	Mk
23	Jesus heals a deaf and dumb man		7:31–37			H	Mk	Mk
24	Jesus feeds four thousand	15:32–39	8:1–13			N	Mt, Mk	Mk
25	Jesus heals a blind man at Bethsaida		8:22–26			H	Mk	Mk
26	Jesus heals a man born blind				9:1–12	H	J	J
27	Jesus heals a boy with a demon	17:14–20	9:14–29	9:37–43		E	Mt, Mk, L	Mk

#	Miracle	Matthew (Mt)	Mark (Mk)	Luke (L)	John (J)	Type*	By*	Source*
28	Miraculous temple tax is found in a fish's mouth	17:24–27				N	Mt	Mt
29	Jesus heals a blind, mute demoniac	12:22–23		11:14–23		E	Mt, L	Q
30	Jesus heals a crippled woman			13:10–17		H	L	L
31	Jesus heals a man with dropsy on the Sabbath			14:1–6		H	L	L
32	Jesus cleanses ten lepers			17:11–19		H	L	L
33	Jesus raises Lazarus from the dead				11:1–45	R	J	J
34	Jesus restores sight to Bartimaeus	20:29–34	10:46–52	18:35–43		H	Mt, Mk, L	Mk
35	Jesus withers the fig tree	21:18:22	11:12–14			N	Mt, Mk	Mk
36	Jesus heals a servant's severed ear			22:50–51		H	L	L
37	The apostles make their second miraculous catch of fish (post-Resurrection)				21:4–11	N	J	J

* N = nature miracle; E = exorcism; H = healing; R = raising from the dead

Note: "By" means the list of Gospels that contain the story. "Source" means the original source the author used; Matthew and Luke had access to Mark such that Matthew and Luke are not considered literarily independent. The original source for common stories is Mark, so I record Mark as the ultimate source. Q is the source common to Matthew and Luke but not to Mark. John is literarily independent of all three Synoptics.

The list is impressive. There are twenty-one healings, nine natural miracles, four exorcisms, and three raisings of the dead. If one were to add to this list of thirty-seven miracles the miracles that were done *to* Jesus in addition to those performed *by* him (the Virgin Birth, the Transfiguration, and the Resurrection), one gets to forty miracles. Voila, forty is the magical number reflecting completion. The number is used in forty days of rain on Noah, forty years in the desert by Israel, forty days in the desert for Jesus at the beginning of his ministry, and forty days between Easter and the Ascension. To get to the perfect number of forty would be almost miraculous in itself. The number could not have been contrived by the Gospel writers because the only way to get to this number is to compile the four Gospels together and assess them as a bundle. These things did not happen during the lifetimes of the Gospel writers.

Setting aside the coincidence, we should know there are many other miracles alluded to but not specifically narrated in the Gospels. Thus, not all of the miracles attested to Jesus are counted in the table. If a miracle is not narrated, it is not counted. There are many allusions in all four Gospels to miracles not specifically reported in them. John ends his Gospel with this leading claim that makes the point in a hyperbolic way: "There are many other things that Jesus did, but, if these were to be described individually, I do not think the whole world would contain the books that would be written" (John 21:25 NAB). So we have undercounts. Perhaps the most prominent example of an undercount of a miracle we know about is the release of the seven demons from Mary of Magdala. The result of Jesus's exorcism of the demons is reported by Luke, but the exorcism itself is not. Then, there is Luke's report of healing of ten lepers (#32 above). Is that one miracle or ten?

Offsetting undercounts, we likely have overcounts, too, due to double counting. The entries might double count an event in one Gospel account that is reported differently in another Gospel. For example, scholars ask whether the two miraculous catches of fishes are different tellings by Luke and John of the same story (#6 and #37 in Table 9–1, respectively [all numbers relate to rows in Table 9–1]) placed in different places in their narratives to support their own stories of faith. (This is one of the few nature miracles multiply attested, if one believes that the underlying event is the same in the two stories.) Many similarities appear in the healing stories, too, such that distinguishing between them is not always straightforward. For example, scholars question whether the healing of the man born blind in John is the same as Jesus giving sight to Bartimaeus in the Synoptics (#26 and #34, respectively). Are either of these sight restoration miracles the same as #16 and #25 (reported only by Matthew and Mark, respectively)? As a last example of a potential double count, the feeding of the five thousand men is the only miracle in each of the four Gospels and the only nature miracle positively multiply attested. Is this feeding the same event Mark and Matthew retell as the feeding of four thousand (#19 and #24)? Many scholars believe so, though the plain language in Mark 8 argues that the two events are distinct.

After taking out the double counts and consolidating like events, a different scholar concludes there are six exorcisms, fourteen healings, three raisings from the dead, and eight nature miracles in the Gospels.[56] Notwithstanding the specific numbers, the list is lengthy and robust. But the count of miracles in the Gospel accounts by itself misses a separate but equally impressive point; the number of different sources of miracle stories. Assuming the stories narrated in Mark were available to Matthew and Luke, we have a majority in the table going back to Mark as a primary source (see the rightmost column in Table 9-1). In addition to Mark, though, we also have unique accounts in Matthew, unique accounts in Luke, unique accounts in John, and unique accounts from Q. That is five different sources in the Gospels alone. But that is not the total of sources attesting to Jesus's miracle-working. That Jesus was a "doer of startling deeds" is specifically reported by the Pharisee Josephus late in the first century. There are also many apocryphal Gospel accounts of Jesus's works. Even the Qur'an reflects Jesus as a doer of miracles: "I [Jesus] have come to you with a sign from your Lord. I make from the clay [something] like the form of a bird, and I breathe into it, and it will be a [living] bird with the permission of God. *And I heal the blind from birth, and the leper, and I raise the dead* with the permission of God" (Sura 3:48–50). The italicized words refer specifically to miracles in Table 9-1. The sentence before the italicized words corresponds to an apocryphal Gospel account, not included in the table. These words demonstrate that the canonical Gospels and the source document Q do not have a monopoly on miracles attributed to Jesus, even among ancient sources.

As we can infer from many passages within the Gospel, Jesus's contemporaries understood him within his lifetime to be a miracle worker. The list of contemporaries may have included Jesus's opponents, as the following two verses suggest. (These two verses from the KJV may fail to meet the evidentiary standard in that they could be considered retrojections. Accordingly, we consider the argument to be suggestive, not authoritative):

> And the scribes which came down from Jerusalem said, He hath Beelzebub, and by the prince of the devils casteth he out devils. And he called them unto him, and said unto them in parables, How can Satan cast out Satan? (Mark 3:22–23)

> And when Herod saw Jesus, he was exceeding glad: for he [Herod] was desirous to see him [Jesus] of a long season,

because he had heard many things of him; and he hoped to have seen some miracle done by him. (Luke 23:8)

Nobody in the Gospels challenges the premise that Jesus is a miracle worker. However, one probably would not expect anything different either. So we acknowledge the absence of information as interesting but not authoritative. Relative to extant sources from antiquity that could take independent positions about Jesus as a miracle worker, we have two ancient sources to consider, namely the Babylonian Talmud (late first to early second century) and the philosopher Celsus (late second century). Neither of these deny Jesus's miraculous abilities. Both, however, attribute Jesus's power to sorcery. The quotation from Mark above (and its parallels in the other two Synoptics) may have been a preemptory rebuttal for the later renderings in the Talmud and Celsus.

So, despite our Enlightenment predisposition to believe miracles cannot happen, the historicity of Jesus as a miracle worker is beyond dispute, by which we mean the people of the day in their memories and records understood Jesus to be a miracle worker. Whether Jesus actually performed miracles per se, we cannot know. All we can assess is whether his contemporaries understood that Jesus was a miracle worker from their experience and traditions. We can assert emphatically that they understood Jesus just so.

Two quotations from Meier's magisterial work are excellent summaries applying the criterion of multiple attestation to Jesus as a miracle worker:

> Multiple sources intertwine with multiple forms to give abundant testimony that the historical Jesus performed deeds by himself deemed by himself and others to be miracles. If the multiple attestation of sources and forms does not produce reliable results here, it should be dropped as a criterion of historicity. For hardly any other type of Gospel material enjoys greater multiple attestation than do Jesus's miracles.[57]

> The statement that Jesus acted as and was viewed as an exorcist and healer during his public ministry has as much historical corroboration as almost any other statement we can make about the Jesus of history. Indeed, as a global affirmation about Jesus and his ministry, it has much better attestation than many other assertions about Jesus, assertions that people often take for granted.... Any historian who seeks to portray the historical Jesus without giving due weight to his fame as a miracle-worker is not delineating this strange and complex Jew, but rather a domesticated Jesus reminiscent of the bland moralist created by Thomas Jefferson.[58]

THE ARGUMENT FROM NOVELTY

Given the proliferation of miracle stories in the Gospels, you might suppose that miracle workers were plentiful in Jesus's time or that miracle stories drew upon a heritage of many multiple precedents and prophecies to draw upon. But, you would suppose wrong. In Jesus's time—and for that matter, later times as well—true miracle workers did not exist. There were a few Jewish holy men who were nearly contemporaneous with Jesus to whom miracles are attributed. The most prominent examples are Honi and Hanina ben Dosa. Honi, the so-called circle drawer, allegedly stayed inside a circle until God brought forth rain to an area affected by drought. Similarly, Ben Dosa made it rain to break another drought. He is also reported to have worked some healings. Note, though, these attributions are made long after the events were recorded, are de-coupled from history, and may be apocryphal. Indeed, the attributions are recorded long after the Gospels were in circulation. It is not impossible the precedent to work miracles came as backpressure from Christians via their Gospel accounts. The backpressure may have resulted in the Jews reframing their own narratives about their heroes to capture them as miracle workers of sorts to make them appear as Jesus's quasi-peers.

The reader does not have to suppose that these Jewish sages' stories are inherently apocryphal. The purported miracles are not substantively different from the thousands of instances from religions all over the world in which God (or Buddha or some spirit or pagan icon) purportedly answers prayers. We have many incidents in our time in which this person or that person claims some miraculous intercession that modern science has not been able to refute. In particular, we need not reject the authenticity of the reports from Honi or Ben Dosa or their peers. Notwithstanding, the miracles attributed to these Jewish holy men, their miracles differ markedly in both kind and degree from the miracles attributed to Jesus. As to degree, the number of miracles and their significance do not rise to the level of Jesus's dealings to make them peers.

As to kind, the difference between Jesus and the Jewish are step-wise. The Jewish holy men are not miracle workers at all. They are agents for the divine power activated through them. Jesus, by contrast, affects divine actions by his own works and authorities. There was no precedent for this kind of story in Jewish literature before Jesus's time. The Hebrew reckoning would have none of it. Only God can work miracles, and men are not God. To attribute divine power to a human would be blasphemous or something close to it. The Qur'an confronts the same issue. In the Qur'an, that Jesus performs miracles is axiomatic. The Qur'an goes to lengths to assure the reader it is Allah working through Jesus (or Isa, his Arabic name) who does the miracle working, not Jesus. (See quotation above from Sura 3.)

A present-day reader is left to determine the source for the idea of Jesus unilaterally performing miracles. Person or persons unknown had to make up the stories, or the authors (or someone in the chain before them) had to observe the events themselves. As with other sections in this book, Jesus's self-authorized divine working would have been unimagined, unprecedented, and perhaps blasphemous to have been invented. It is far more plausible that the Gospel writers are reporting events told to or observed by them, rather than events they just invented that violate their own mores.

One needs to be especially mindful of the possibility of retrojection of the miracle stories. One reported miracle, though, warrants particular attention as we address novelty with respect to nature miracles. As a possible exception, where retrojection does not seem to be a concern, consider the story of Jesus walking on the water (#20 in Table 9–1 above). In this story, some disciples are at sea at night and Jesus walks on the water to where they are. In this story, Jesus addresses the disciples in this way: "Take courage, it is I, do not be afraid" (Mark 6:50 NAB) or even more simply in John's version: "It is I. Do not be afraid" (John 6:20 NAB). This is one of seven Jesus's "I am" statements in the Gospel of John, where seven is a complete number to the Jews of the time. The clear allusion in John and Mark is to the name of God. Several remarkable points follow from the passages. John and Mark are literarily independent. Therefore, if they share stories, the origin of the story's kernel must predate when the sources for the stories split from one another. Determining when the split occurred is rather like the way evolutionary biologists examine species to assess when they diverged from a common ancestor. Mark completes his Gospel in the 60s; the actual source of this walking-on-water kernel is certainly earlier. The date for the kernel could be anywhere from the 30s to the 60s. More fascinating, though, is that John's version is the earlier account. This fact is most surprising because the theology in John's Gospel unmistakably reflects a high Christology, meaning Jesus's Messiahship is made abundantly clear. By contrast, the Christology in Mark is mooted. In John's account of walking on the water, the disciples do not even respond to Jesus's actions. Unlike just about everything else about John's Gospel, where subtlety is at a premium, there is no hyperbole, no exclamation, and no triumphalism in this particular passage. The subtleties suggest that the author of John's Gospel preserved a very raw, unembellished version of the story from at least the time of the Mark-John source split until John's Gospel was written, thirty to sixty years later. The duration suggests a high degree of authenticity in preserving the original kernels of the event.

Whether one accepts the walking-on-water story as actually having happened or not, there is no question a high Christology existed from the earliest writings of the Gospels. Most people assume that Jesus's linkage to the Divine came after some significant passage of time. Not so. Such linkage is built into Christianity. In Mark's account, the event is inserted as a theophany (i.e., an emanation of God) without any prior context. (Mark employs the Messianic Secret motif, in which Jesus conceals his true identity, as noted in chapter 3. Matthew and Luke retain this motif. With the unapologetic theophany kernel inserted in Mark's Gospel, is Mark telling his alert readers that his Secret is a literary device, not a literal statement, to narrate his story? One is never sure in Mark's Gospel whether the Secret is his literary invention or whether it is historical to Jesus. The ambiguity evokes and presages Hamlet's soliloquy in his famous "To Be or Not to Be" speech in that the reader is never sure whether Hamlet is insane or is a genius. Needless to say, in the Fourth Gospel, there is not an inkling of a Messianic Secret.)

Once we recognize the theophany, we are left to answer the obvious question about determining the source for the idea of conflating Jesus with God. We know linking Jesus to God happened within the lifetimes of some of the disciples who knew Jesus in the flesh. The working of the divine by Jesus is one thing, but conflating Jesus with God is quite another. *You just can't make this stuff up* without violating the credibility criterion in chapter 2. Writers who are trying to persuade their readers about the truthfulness of their claims are constrained by the readers' mores. In this case, the writers do not respect the more imposed on Jews against conflating a human (Jesus) with God. Therefore, it seems far more plausible that the conflation was observed, rather than concocted.

As to precedents for miracle working more analogous to Jesus in Jewish history, one has to go back to Elijah/Elisha (about nine hundred years before Jesus) or Moses (about thirteen hundred years before Jesus). The stories about the three prophets were formed by oral tradition and not captured in a written form for hundreds of years after the purported events occurred. This is quite unlike the records of Jesus's miracles, which sprang up virtually overnight. Miracles in the Hebrew Bible are rarely if ever recorded contemporaneous to their posited occurrences. Another striking difference between Jesus's miracles and those of ancient Hebrew prophets is that Jesus's miracles are beneficial to all of their human recipients. (Jesus's two non-beneficial actions are directed to swine and a fig tree, which most scholars deem to be metaphorical narratives rather than actual ones.) Consider the fate of the Egyptians. They suffered the plagues and the Passover wrought forth via Moses. Compare also the apogee of Elijah's miracle stories after Elijah calls down fire on an altar when the 450 priests of Baal were unable to bring down fire themselves (1 Kgs 18:40 ESV): "And Elijah said to them, 'Seize the prophets of Baal; let not one of them escape.' And they seized them. And Elijah brought them down to the brook Kishon and slaughtered them there." That is 450 people!

Lastly with respect to precedent, Q tells us that Jesus sent a message to John the Baptist, who was then in prison, awaiting his execution (see Matt 11:4–5 NAB). The words ascribed to Jesus in his message to John are allusions to prophecies from Isaiah, except the italicized words below, for which there is no prophetic antecedent: "Go and tell John what you hear and see: the blind regain their sight, the lame walk, lepers are cleansed, the deaf hear, *the dead are raised* and the poor have the good news proclaimed to them." Jesus's statement to be conveyed to John the Baptist may be a retrojection, but, if so, being that the extract is from Q, the source is even earlier. Furthermore, the italicized words are a separate attestation to raising the dead (see #11, #15, and #33 in Table 9–1), bringing the total to four sources making the same claim.

THE ARGUMENT FROM PURPOSE

Our hypothesis is that the Gospels were fabricated for specific purposes by clever writers. To test the hypothesis, we would look for the inclusion of contra-information, the omission of expected information, embarrassing events, and forgone opportunities to evidence deviations from the design. We find examples of all of these categories, but, before examining details, let's be mindful of the bigger picture.

The bigger picture is how the miracle stories fit into the stories the Gospel writers are narrating. What is imminently clear is that Jesus is not a magician,[59] he is not some sort of comic-book superhero, and he is not performing acts in the mode of a carnival barker to garner attention to himself. The miracles, with few exceptions, play out to complement his preaching ministry, to assist people in distress, or to boost or instill faith in the recipients and onlookers. If Jesus were speaking our modern language, you can just imagine him saying this after performing one of his miracles, "Hey, this is not about me, it's about you." Jesus sets his miracles as spiritual matters, not earthly ones. This convention is just the opposite of what you'd expect from a supposed miracle worker who was trying to make a name for himself.

If you were a first-century evangelist bent on portraying a miracle worker with special divine powers, you would not bother complicating your story to integrate these superpowers into a teaching ministry. The miracles would stand on their own. Jesus would appear more like Zeus, who has the ability to use his powers at his discretion to whatever ends he desires. It was precisely because the teaching and miracle working are so tightly fused together in the texts that Jefferson could not successfully selectively expunge the miracle stories. He could not take out one without removing the other. Jesus's miracles are frequently performed opportunistically; they are not staged for Jesus's glorification but are performed for the benefit of others as opportunities arise. Indeed, if John's Gospel is correct, Jesus's first miracle fits the mold well. The miracle is performed only reluctantly at his mother's behest at the wedding at Cana. If one were making up the miracle stories, the miracle worker ought to be in the mode of the powerful and supreme, not of a servant. Yet in the Gospel account, we find the depiction opposite to expectations.

As a second point relating to the big picture, here is a trend line you would expect to see if the evangelists were simply writing fiction: The miracle stories would become more embellished and effusive as time goes on. With John, the latest of the Gospels to be written, this trend holds, though the walking-on-water story discussed above argues the other way as a specific exception to the general trend. We have a direct way to assess accretion with the passage of time. In Table 9–1, the numbers of miracles recorded in Matthew, Mark, and Luke are 22, 20, and 21, respectively. These numbers show no trend of escalation. Of the accretions in Matthew from Mark (#8, #16, #17, and #28), they are not particularly more dramatic than Mark's original set of miracles. Luke's Gospel presents the miracles in a slightly more elevated manner than Mark does, but, even in Luke, the accretions are not dramatically more impressive than the original set borrowed from Mark. Some of what might be deemed to be the most dramatic of the miracles in the Synoptics are already narrated in Mark (#12, #13, #15, #19, #20, #25, and #34). Thus, we conclude that the later evangelists evidently remained close to their original sources and did not invent more superlative miracle accounts. Contrary to expectation, the miracle worker in the later Synoptics does not really appear to have been particularly inflated from the original miracle worker in the original source. This fact runs counter to the trend one would expect if the miracle stories were just made up.

The last big-picture point is that the Gospels generally avoid the superstitious. Jesus and the disciples remain rational. Miracles are not subtle things, yet the Gospels generally narrate the miracles subtly. The disciples are not starry-eyed men who fall under the spell of a charismatic magician. They remain earthy, practical, rational men, even in the wake of the miraculous. The Gospel writers stay away from the sensational, as reflected in this periscope from Q, recorded with similar wording in Matthew and

Luke: When Jesus is asked to reply to the Baptist in prison what he should make of Jesus, we have Jesus's reply, "Go and tell John what you hear and see: the blind regain their sight, the lame walk, lepers are cleansed, the deaf hear, the dead are raised, and the poor have the good news proclaimed to them."

The ensuing words in the two accounts, notionally intended as a response to John but really a lesson for the Gospel readers, provide a systematic explanation of the role of Jesus's miracles and clarify John's relationship to himself. There is little triumphalism here in Jesus's measured reply. Furthermore, neither evangelist records whether John received Jesus's message, let alone whether John responded to it. Narrating a positive reply from the Baptist would have been an obvious thing to do, could have steeled the evangelists' message and brought John's story to an orderly close. However, neither writer says anything about a response. One should expect a modicum of a response, even one as simple as, "And John received the message and understood." Again, it appears that both writers independently kept to what was revealed to them via Q, even when deviations or accretions would have made for a better fit to the message they sought to deliver.

In terms of embarrassment relating to miracles, we can find several specific examples in the Gospels. Here are four:

- Jesus is unable to perform miracles under certain conditions. He is rejected by his hometown folks and limited by their lack of faith (Mark 6:5). Even still, he cured a few sick people by laying on of hands. Since the story is an embarrassment, it is likely to be authentic.
- Jesus is perceived to be unable to control his own powers, as is evidenced by the healing of the woman in the crowd (#14 in Table 9–1). This kernel exposes Jesus's vulnerability, which again is an embarrassment and thus likely to be authentic.
- Jesus is asked when the apocalypse will begin. Jesus states that he does not know and that the timing is reserved by the Father. Accordingly, we know from the account that Jesus's prescience has limits.
- This example is one that the later Synoptic writers considered so embarrassing to repeat that Matthew and Luke dropped it from their stories: the story of healing the blind man at Bethsaida (#25 above). In this episode, Jesus puts spittle on the blind man's eyes. After applying the spittle, Jesus asks, "Do you see anything?" The man responds, "I see people looking like trees and walking." Then Jesus repeats the process and undistorted vision results. The sequence implies Jesus was unsure of his success, and he needed two efforts to get it right. An untethered evangelist would not invent the story of their revered Christ being

unable to get the correction correct the first time through. Nor would he invent the cherished Christ engaging with filthy spittle. The embarrassments attest to the kernel's authenticity.

The two-stage sequencing for restoration seems entirely consistent with what an actual sight restoration might entail. This is an interesting point because Mark could not have invented this story. If Jesus were successful in adjusting the eyes to provide optical signals to a brain unaccustomed to receiving them, the information from the eyes would flood into the brain chaotically. The brain would not know how to process the signals. We moderns know but the ancients could not have known that vision is in the brain as much as the eyes. It is imminently plausible that the man's eyes would be healed first and then the images from the eyes are then made coherent by a second action on the brain. Needless to say, if the sequence of eyes-brain healing is correct, the ancients could never have made up this story because they had no understanding of how the eyes and brain work together to create vision for humans. There is no question that the second miracle (or two miracles if one counts the curing of the eyes and brains to be back-to-back miracles, vice one miracle in two parts) is historic.[60] So, literally in this case, Mark just couldn't make this stuff up.

In keeping with the theme of not being able to make this stuff up in conjunction with the Bethsaida event, I have already noted that the connection of spittle to the healing would have been an embarrassment and thus it is likely the detail is native to the story. Who would make up such an odd notion to memorialize their Lord? Probably nobody. But let's just suppose we ask the thought-experiment question, What is the probability that a person who is concocting a story about bringing sight to a blind man would choose to select spittle as the modulating medium? Spittle has no obvious connection to providing vision, and there is no prophesy or expectation of spittle playing any modulating role. So, let us assign that the probability at 1%, just to pick an arbitrary but small number. Now consider the fact that we have the story in John in which Jesus provides sight to the man born blind (#26 in the table above). In this story, Jesus again uses spittle as a modulating medium to effect the miracle. So, then the probability of *both* events of providing vision by the action of spittle, recorded by independent sources a generation apart, is just 1 part in ten thousand, an impossibly low probability to occur by chance alone. The obvious explanation of the low joint probability is that the supposed concocted events are not concocted by the writers at all. Instead, they reflect the common connection that links Jesus, spittle, and the provision of sight that the witnesses of the event(s) record. ("Event(s)" is used here since it possible that the two narrations are different tellings of the same story or are two different events.) Once again, you can't make this stuff up.

CONCLUSION

That his contemporaries understood Jesus to be a miracle worker is beyond dispute. The number of instances and the number of sources satisfy the criterion of multiple attestation in an overwhelming manner. However, this is not the only reason we have confidence Jesus was a miracle worker. There is no essential reason to have concocted the miracle stories. Hebrew Bible prophecies do not require a Christ who was also a miracle worker. Christianity can satisfy its Messianic claims for Jesus without relying upon any miracle stories. Since shortly after Jesus's time, Jews have been suspicious of miraculous claims.[61] So, there were no prior forcing functions operating during Jesus's life to demand the creation of a miracle-working Jesus to qualify as the Christ. Lastly, the way the stories are narrated provide key evidence of their authenticity.

One counterintuitive conclusion of this chapter is that Jesus's Messiahship does not depend upon acceptance of Jesus's purported miracle working. The conclusion of non-dependence predates the Enlightenment—and its predisposition to reject the miraculous as superstitious—by centuries. With the benefit of hindsight, it is almost as if the Gospels anticipated the Enlightenment's predisposition against superstition and preempted it before the Enlightenment began. You can't make this stuff up.

In addressing another Enlightenment predisposition, moderns reject the notion of miracles on ideological lines: Miracles cannot happen; they violate the laws of nature. This modern sentiment is expressed as a universal negative. The logical problem with a university negative is that a single counterexample discounts it. In this chapter, we see that there are a large number of miracles (37?) that are attributed to Jesus. Many of them are highly credible attributions for the reasons identified herein. For the Church to make her case that Jesus is indeed the miracle worker she claim he is (or was) to set aside the universal negative, she need make the case for the validity of only one incident. She need not demonstrate that each miracle claim in the Gospels meets the evidentiary tests in chapter 2, only that some do. And she makes the necessary demonstrations convincingly.

10

How It All Comes Together

My examination of the historicity of the Gospels has so far been limited to a subset of the events in the life and times of Jesus, the emergence of the initial idea of Christianity, and the promulgation of the model of Jesus as the Christ. These events and activities occurred within a few days or perhaps a few months after the Resurrection. But, scholars tell us, Mark, the first of the Gospels to be written, did not reach a final form for at least three decades, and John did not obtain a final form for perhaps six. So we need to track what happened in the intervening years. In this chapter, I address what happened between the time the original Gospels were drafted by their authors until they were compiled and published in the final form that we have today. The path between those dates passed through three conceptual phases, conceptual in that we do not know the actual path that was passed through but we can identify the phases conceptually:

- Phase 1, the development of the manuscripts under the purview of the original set of authors and editors before the close of the Apostolic Age. The Apostolic Age ended when the last of the direct contacts from the apostles and firsthand witnesses died out.
- Phase 2, the dissemination of the Gospels collectively after the original disciples and their first-generation recruits had passed away but before the manuscripts were collected up and bundled as a unit.
- Phase 3, the publication of the four Gospels as an authoritative set.

We need to show that the versions of the Gospels that passed through Phase 1 were then preserved through Phases 2 and 3. We know as a historical fact that the versions that resulted from the close of Phase 3 are the same versions we have now in our time because we have many available ancient manuscripts to compare modern versions against to confirm their authenticity. Therefore, we can end at the end of Phase 3 to validate the authenticity of the Gospels we have in our hands today.

While the Gospels were being developed and taking on their final forms, many relevant events were occurring contemporaneously. Christianity is a religion that evolved in a context, and the historical events of the time are recorded in the Christian Scriptures. The processes from the initial writing of Mark to the publication of the four canonical Gospels as a set likely spanned more than a century. Once the written words of the New Testament were assembled as a unit ("bundled"), the set enjoyed a symbiotic relationship with the Church from the second century on.

Regarding the evolution of the Gospels themselves, we have a reasonable handle on the process of when they were written in their final forms, how and when they were compiled, and how and when they were published as separate documents. Understanding the evolution of the New Testament causes surprise for a certain set of Christians that takes the inerrancy of the New Testament for granted. They suppose the Gospels and, for that matter, the rest of the New Testament, just appeared. The revelation of Scripture to Jews and orthodox Christians was done through the channels of history. This is not a universal attribute shared by all.[62] Some might suppose that the Gospels came in their final form without human agency. This supposition is surely wrong. The Gospels are works of human actions. Whether they might also be works of a higher agent is a theological matter, beyond the scope of this work.

The events occurring while the Gospels were coming together include the beginning of the Church's mission, the persecution of the Church, the first Church council, the martyrdoms of Peter and Paul, the Jewish War that led to the collapse of the Temple, and the split of Christianity from Judaism. Table 10–1 offers a chronology of the development of the Gospels, following the outline of Jesuit Joseph T. Lienhard and Professor Brant Pitre,[63] with other dates included as points of reference.

Table 10-1. Chronology of Events Paralleling the Formation of the Gospels

Event	Approximate Date (CE)
The birth of the Church	30
The conversion of Paul	32–34 (i.e., two to four years later)
First of Pauline letters	Mid- to late 40s
Council of Jerusalem	49 or 50
Completion of Mark's Gospel	60s
Martyrdom of Peter and Paul	64–67
Jewish Roman War	66–70
Collapse of Temple	70 (exact date)[64]
Completion of Matthew and Luke	70s
Split of Christianity-Judaism	80–90s
Completion of John's Gospel	90s
Final editing of the Gospels	100
Identifying the Gospels as a set	120–150
Second Jewish uprising	130–135
Final compilation of Gospels as a group	160–185
Completion of final New Testament	Fourth century[65]

PHASE 1: FAITHFUL CAPTURE OF ORIGINAL WITNESS

Scholars accept that the final versions of the Gospels were put to written form long after the events they reported. The concern that historical critics raise is the lapse of time allowed for accretion of Midrash (retelling of biblical stories), theology, hyperbole, redaction of information, and retrojection. These opportunities detract from us being able to rely upon the information recorded as verifiably historical. Because of the long lapse of time, many historians reject the Gospels outright. Yet to reject the historical content of the Gospels is to assume too much. Much is recorded in the Gospels that is original, authentic, and independently able to be validated, that is, much historical information can be extracted.[66]

As noted before, we have no real understanding of when the Gospels were started, only when they were completed. We have several reasons to know that the authors of the original documents captured their stories faithfully, including the following:

- *Living memories of the writers.* All of the Gospels were completed in the living memory of the apostles or their first-generation recruits. If you were a Christian at the end of the first century, then you probably knew somebody who knew somebody who knew somebody who knew the apostles or original witnesses. So we know the events recorded could be tracked to the lifetimes of the original eyewitnesses or the first-generation successors. Accordingly, if the writers of the Gospels (or perhaps those who dictated to scribes) were not personally witnesses to the events recorded, they knew and spoke to some who probably were. The underlying oral tradition has very few branches from original storyteller to person with pen.[67] The length of the chain from original source to writer is short, perhaps zero, one, or two links long. The Church in the late part of the first century was small but highly networked.[68]
- *Shared messaging.* We know the earliest Christian communities shared their messaging. Their basic story lines were authenticated by retelling and cross-connections of sources. If there were rogue reports conflicting with the known experience of the Christian community writ large, they were set aside. Any patently rogue stories among the early Christians would have confronted testimony from informed sources and likely would have been quashed.

  We know remote communities passed information between themselves because Paul asks the audiences of his letters to share them with other churches (see Colossians 4) and because we have late-first-century, nonbiblical documents corroborating the Gospels and the epistles then in circulation. For example, the first catechism of sorts, the *Didache*, tracks closely to content in Matthew's Gospel, and we have a *Letter from Clement* of Rome, circa 90, referencing a letter of Paul to the Corinthians. So we have nonbiblical information circulated in written form collaborating New Testament accounts. These examples prove documents circulated within Christian circles, evidencing a de facto communications network.
  - The Christian communities were linked by interconnected networks of evangelists. The person-to-person, cross-vetting of stories by these personally knowledgeable individuals provided a degree of norming.
  - The Christian community ethos included fellowship and honoring the apostles and eyewitnesses. These tendencies would have worked to help normalize the stories. Paul even made it a point in 1 Corinthians to criticize Church members for having false

gospels and false prophets, meaning he was attempting to train the faithful on what he understood to be true. One can suppose other evangelists did the same.

- The Christian community came together to assure common messaging from the top down at the Jerusalem Council in 49 or 50. Among the understandings shared by the leadership was building a consensus on the common experiences of the life of Jesus. These shared experiences lay at the root of the stories collected in the Gospel accounts.

• *Independent validation.* That the Synoptics overlap considerably provides some independent confirmation of their veracity. As noted in chapter 3, Matthew and Luke are not literarily independent from Mark. Actually, 90 percent of the verses in Mark appear in some form in Matthew and 60 percent appear in Luke. These facts are an overwhelming validation of the basic Marcan text by the writer's contemporaries. Then, separately, we have Matthew and Luke, who independently picked up the content in Q, which provides us more authentication from contemporary sources. Lastly, we have other early Christian documents collaborating details in the Gospels, such as the aforementioned *Didache* and *Letter of Clement* and other documents of the early leaders of the Church, such as the *Gospel of the Hebrews*, which provides a non-canonical version of the risen Jesus presenting himself to James the Just, the so-called brother of Jesus.[69]

• *Martyrdom.* By the time the Gospel stories are being formulated, the Church is under great persecution. The fundamental claims in the Gospel are well articulated by now, irrespective whether the claims were memorialized in writing or not. In the case of Peter, to take the most prominent case, we can assert with great confidence that he would not have chosen martyrdom for claims he knew *personally* were false. It is one thing to memorialize the martyrdom of Thomas More, for example, and quite another to memorialize Peter's martyrdom. Thomas More had no personal experience of Jesus in the flesh; his martyrdom stemmed from a faith rooted in others' witness. Thomas More's Jesus might be an idealized, literary figure in whom More wants to believe. Not so for Peter. Peter had the most privileged position to witness the life, death, and Resurrection of Jesus. His heroic witness rested on his own personal experience. If he were being martyred, it was for what he saw, heard, and witnessed firsthand, not from what he read in a book or what he heard from somebody else.

After Jesus's name, Peter's name appears more frequently than any other in the Gospels. If he was martyred for Jesus, it must have been for the Jesus whom Peter knew, not from some second- or third- or nth generation account. People don't die for ideas they know are lies. So we can say with confidence that Peter died for what he understood to be true. And we know Mark and Matthew were diligent in making their narratives comport with Peter's.

Of course, Peter was not alone among firsthand witnesses to the Resurrected Jesus to suffer martyrdom. James (one of the three inner-circle apostles), James the Just (the so-called brother of Jesus), and Paul are other firsthand witnesses who wore the crown of martyrdom. (Pious Christian legend has it that all of the apostles were martyred, except John, who lived to a ripe old age. But the fates of the apostles beyond Peter are less well attested.) The testimonial of the martyrs' firsthand witness is powerful evidence for the truth of the Gospels they preached.

- *Character of the first witnesses.* If the whole of Christianity is a fiction, its principal deceiver would be Paul. Paul is the person who identifies Jesus as the Cosmic Christ. Paul shares the ethics of Jesus and the other leaders of the Church. Consider these words from Paul's hand and ask yourself whether they sound like the words of one whose basic character was based on deceiving people (Col 3:5–14 NIV). If he were a deceiver, he deceived nobody more so than himself:

> Put to death, therefore, whatever belongs to your earthly nature: sexual immorality, impurity, lust, evil desires and greed, which is idolatry. Because of these, the wrath of God is coming. You used to walk in these ways, in the life you once lived. But now you must also rid yourselves of all such things as these: anger, rage, malice, slander, and filthy language from your lips. Do not lie to each other, since you have taken off your old self with its practices and have put on the new self, which is being renewed in knowledge in the image of its Creator. Here there is no Gentile or Jew, circumcised or uncircumcised, barbarian, Scythian, slave or free, but Christ is all, and is in all. Therefore, as God's chosen people, holy and dearly loved, clothe yourselves with compassion, kindness, humility, gentleness and patience. Bear with each other and forgive one another if any of you has a grievance against someone. Forgive as the Lord forgave you. And over all these virtues put on love, which binds them all together in perfect unity.

- *Dating of the Gospels.* As stated, we know more about when the Gospels were completed than when they were initiated. The distinction between the two dates can be significant because an original base manuscript may have been edited and compiled later, perhaps much later, than the stories underlying it. After the document was published in its final form, we ended up with only the edited versions, and earlier versions are subsequently lost forever. Mark and John appear to have been edited to add to or revise information that was not in the original form, whatever the "original" may have been.

Similar editing may have occurred for Matthew and Luke as well, as they seem to have their own seams in them. For Mark and John, both have accretions as additional endings to the original narratives, meaning there were older strata in circulation before the final documents came together. Interestingly, for John's Gospel, the last chapter was inserted after the penultimate chapter, but every extant version we have of the Gospel has both chapters. Accordingly, if one finds an element that has a relatively late date in a text, it says nothing about the age of the other text in the document. The following points suggest the dates scholars typically assign to the Gospels may be too late. The Gospels, or at least portions of them, are older than generally supposed.

Mark

Mark's Gospel seems to follow Peter's eyewitness account. Now, a clever writer can create the illusion of proximate characters, so the fact that Mark's words are so personalized to Peter is suggestive of authenticity, but not proof. Yet the document makes no comment about Peter's death. One might suppose Peter's death would have been acknowledged in the document, given Peter's centrality to the Gospel. The absence of any such statement leads many to believe the document must predate Peter's death. This would make Mark's Gospel earlier than usually reported (not later than about 67). Again, though, this argument is suggestive, rather than conclusive.

With respect to the secular events we attempt to correlate to date Mark, nothing in Mark's Gospel fixes the document in time with any great precision, with two possible exceptions. The first exception to dating of the text is that the separation of Christians from Jews has not yet happened. The invective tone directed against "the Jews" in John's Gospel (his code word for the Jewish leaders in Judea) does not appear in Mark. So we know Mark's Gospel was prepared before the 80s or 90s. The second possible exception is the treatment in Mark 13, the so-called Apocalypse of Mark. In this chapter, Jesus speaks about the destruction of the Temple, the end times, and the persecution of the Church. Working backward, the persecution of the Church began almost immediately after Pentecost, so this does not help us to date the document. The prophecies of the end times could have been native to Jesus or could have been retrojected by the writer, so these words do not help us date the text much either. It is the prophecy of the destruction of the Temple that stands out. The building of the Second Temple by Herod the Great began in the lifetime of Jesus's immediate ancestors. The Romans destroyed it in 70 CE. Jesus is recorded in Mark 13:2 as saying the following: "Then Jesus asked [a disciple], 'Do you see these great buildings [of the Temple Mount]? Not one stone will be left here upon one another; all will be thrown down.'" Jesus's purported words predate the destruction of the Temple by about forty years. Many secularist scholars presume these words were added after the destruction of the Temple in order to fortify Jesus's bona fides as a prophet; therefore, they claim the words in the Gospel account came after 70 CE, but this reasoning is specious. There are at least four problems with the argument, besides the obvious one from scholars who discount any possibility Jesus might be the prophet his followers took him to be:

1. If the words are retrojected to Jesus, why would the writer have chosen to write them metaphorically? If the writer went to all of the trouble to make up the prophecy and insert it after the fact, wouldn't he have written the words to be literally true? After all, even today, there are stones stacked atop one another from Herod's Temple, where Jews pray at the Western Wall. Presumably, a reader of the text post-70 CE knew the Temple had been destroyed, but he would also have known that many stones remained that were left atop one another, too. Jesus's words may be metaphorically true, but they are not literally true.
2. Nothing in Jesus's prophecy really differs from the same kind of prophecy Jeremiah made about the destruction of the first Temple. Jesus may well have been making the same point Jeremiah made about the Temple of Jeremiah's day, too, when he prophesied it would be destroyed because of Israel's impertinence.[70] And Jesus would have had reason to make such a pronouncement about the Temple of his day as well; in many pious Jews' eyes, the Second Temple was built by a Roman hack, the petty but ruthless King Herod, a Jew in name only. Herod's Temple reminded many contemporary Jews that Israel was a vassal state of the Romans, yet these same people understood their land to be the eternal gift to the Hebrew people from God. The Romans and their

Jewish compatriots, including the puppets in Jerusalem, trampled on their belief. In this sense, Jesus would be echoing Jeremiah and doing so quite deliberately. If we are willing to accept Jeremiah's gloom-and-doom prophecy as authentic in his own day, why not also accept Jesus's, which bears great similarity?

3. Given its centrality to the religious cult of the day, if the Temple had already been destroyed when the Gospel writer wrote these words, where is, "I told you so"? The satisfaction of the prophecy in the life of the hearers would have been epic and would have paid huge dividends for the evangelists' goal in seeking converts. Yet, there is not a specific word about the Temple's actual destruction in Mark's Gospel. Consider this paradox: The writer goes out of his way to plant the retrojected prophecy with Jesus, but takes no credit for its fulfillment. Is this reasonable?

4. Setting aside the three prior arguments, even if the prophecy is a retrojection, it says nothing about the dating of the rest of the document regardless. The hypothetical person who implanted the supposed retrojection could have done it years after the basic Marcan account was drafted and circulated, so a late dating of chapter 13 does not imply a late dating for the rest of the document.

Matthew

Matthew has a similar Temple destruction story in it, and the arguments above apply similarly. An additional point about the Temple is also relevant. In the Matthean tale of Jesus's temptation in the desert (Matthew 4), the devil takes Jesus to "the highest point of the temple." It is hard to understand the reference to the highest point of the temple ("pinnacle" in Luke) if the temple were already destroyed, suggesting that these Matthean words also predate the destruction of the Temple.

Another item adding insight into an earlier date for Matthew is the well-known story of Peter's confession of Jesus's Christhood. In Matthew's Gospel, we have these two verses at 16:18 and 16:19. Jesus says, "You are Peter and upon this rock I will build my church and the gates of the netherworld will not prevail against it. *I will give you the keys to the kingdom of heaven; and whatever you loose on earth shall be loosed in heaven*" (NAB). The first sentence would serve an important purpose in that the sentence makes it clear that the church that Peter leads, if still living, or led, if dead, is the right path for Jesus's believers to follow. This statement has currency after Peter's death. Now, consider the second verse (shown in italics for emphasis). What would be the point of these words, a personal blessing to Peter, if Peter were already dead? There is no transferability clause to pass the blessing down from Peter to anyone else in the Gospel. So this verse has no currency, at least by itself, if Peter is dead. Therefore, this sentence, even if it were purely the author's invention, could not have been penned any later than Peter's death, which we note is earlier than the date generally accepted for the completion of Matthew's Gospel. It is also earlier than the destruction of the Temple.

Luke

Luke also has the Temple destruction story and the temptation-of-Jesus tale. Another point arguing for an earlier date for Luke is the fact that the Acts of the Apostles, which follows the exploits of Paul and was written as a sequel to Luke's Gospel, ends with Paul still alive. Acts was apparently completed before Paul was martyred, which suggests an earlier date for Luke than has been supposed. Again, this date is before the destruction of the Temple as well.

John

John's Gospel is completed after the rift between the Jews and the Christians, so a late date for completion of John seems correct. However, the late date does not mean the whole document is of late origin. John, like Mark, exhibits clear evidence of editing after the substrate of the manuscript had been completed. The Prologue, the Epilogue, the appearance of the disciple whom Jesus loved, and the story of the woman caught in adultery are examples of matters that may have been pulled into John's text. The additions suggest an earlier, more primitive narrative within the document. How much earlier? We cannot say, but we can assert that some of the John text is older than the newer verses because much of John retains a primitive character about it. So, again, the recorded witness is earlier than has been generally assumed.

The arguments above provide some evidence that the manuscripts we call the Gospels were faithful to the sources of information the writers had available to them, and, furthermore, the sources of the stories were close to the events recorded. This is not to provide assurance that every event and word attributed to Jesus were recorded perfectly correctly. Instead, we have some assurances that the basic story lines and the kernels of many of the stories have been preserved.

PHASE 2: FAITHFUL RETENTION OF THE GOSPEL ACCOUNTS

At the end of the first century CE, the Church had a set of four distinct documents whose core messages dated to an earlier era. The core messages were recorded by folks from their living memories. Sometime near the end of the first century CE, the Church took it upon herself to begin to use the Gospels in a more formal manner. As discussed with Phase 1, each of the four documents circulated separately. It does not appear that the Church disseminated them purposefully as an organized set. At some point, editorial control of the documents, whether officially or unofficially, passed to the Church because the original writers and editors had passed away. We ask ourselves, then, whether the Church remained faithful to preserving the integrity of the documents presented to her, once the documents reached their final forms. We have to accept the inherent ambiguity coming from ancient history about what it means to have a document in its "final" form because we have no way to make categorical judgments. The four documents probably arrived at their final forms at different times and places as well. These facts complicate our ability to isolate a date for the nucleation of the final Gospel accounts. We will simply go with the consensus of scholarly opinion and assert that this time probably came at some point between the completion of John's Gospel and the rise of Marcion (to be discussed shortly). This puts the timing in the range of circa 90 and 144; an informed, narrower range would be 100 to 120.

In that narrower span of the years 100 to 120 CE, we are two or three generations removed from the life of Jesus and just past the living memories of the first disciples and their direct recruits, excepting that there may have been a precious few who could have been evangelized by the Apostle John or his first-generation recruits who were still alive. Pious tradition has it that John may have lived to late in the first century. This claim is not impossible, as a death as late as the 90s probably would have made John an octogenarian. Therefore, at the time we are discussing, there are either no or at most only a few folks alive who can provide personal input as to the integrity of the events recorded in the documents. What this means, at least in principle, is that the persons who gained editorial control of the documents, whether these people were specifically identifiable or not, had some degrees of freedom to recast the narratives in whatever way might have supported their evangelical aims at the time. No longer were there any agents who could enforce an orthodoxy that derived from personal witness or firsthand teaching since all of these people who might have performed these functions were in their graves.

We understand that the folks with editorial control had wide discretion, but even they had constraints about what they could insert into or redact from the Gospel accounts they now owned. The people with editorial control could not have invented a Jesus out of whole cloth, for example. They certainly could have edited stories provided to them to include useful tidbits or purge undesired information. The supposed editing would make the editors' Jesus conform to their personal beliefs and theologies. To state the obvious, these editors, whose existence we hypothesize, would have been highly incentivized to refine the stories in their documents to support their evangelical efforts. Put another way, the editors were subject to the same sorts of pressures as the original writers. Both sets of people wanted to publish their works specifically to support the evangelical mission of the Church. A cynic would argue, "Precisely. That is why the Gospel accounts are so unreliable. They went through a series of editorial changes that erased their primitive character. What is left and available to us cannot be relied upon to make any claims of historicity."[71] However, the facts of history tell another story, as I argue below.

I have already observed in previous sections that the Gospel accounts include content that would have been suboptimal for the evangelists' purposes of spreading the good news. I showed that, instead of being optimized to provide fodder for the evangelists, the writers of the Gospels kept close to their sources, even when doing so was contrary to their goals. Employing a more modern concept, I can say that the writers showed a remarkable degree of journalistic integrity in keeping to their sources. The editors may have exhibited even more journalistic integrity than the original writers; unlike the evangelists, subsequent editors would not have been constrained by having to conform to the living witnesses of the events of Jesus's life.

Here are some facts arguing for the faithful preservation of the Gospels during what I identify as Phase 2:

Preservation of Embarrassing Material

Now we are into the second century. Many of the models of Jesus have been solidified, apostolic succession has been institutionalized, and the Church has already built her hierarchical character. By this time, if not earlier, the Church had vested interests in capturing Jesus's legacy in the most favorable light. The editors had ample time to purge items of embarrassment or explain them away, yet we know this did not happen as the following examples attest:

- Jesus links even his closest friends to Satan for their disbelief. Why would the Church want her leaders to be compared to Satan? Wouldn't she have suppressed or softened the words, given the opportunity?

- The disciples remain clueless about what Jesus meant. If Jesus were the great teacher he was made out to be, why would the disciples not have heard the message? Wouldn't the editors want to portray the disciples in an enlightened manner? The disciples and their first- or second-generation followers are the purported sources for the Gospel tales, of course, so why would the editors portray their human links so negatively?

- Some teachings in the Gospels are ambiguous. If they were ambiguous, why retain them? Why not clarify them? Or discard them? Here is one, as a classic example: "Truly I say to you, all sins shall be forgiven the sons of men, and whatever blasphemies they utter; but whoever blasphemes against the Holy Spirit never has forgiveness, but is guilty of an eternal sin" (Mark 3:28–29). The reader is left asking what are blasphemes against the Holy Spirit.

- There is an episode in which Jesus is declared to be out of his mind (Mark 3:21). Why not suppress this detail? Or explain it to a positive end? The writer makes no attempt to do so.

- After speaking in his hometown, his neighbors planned to throw Jesus off a cliff (see Luke 4:29). Why retain this piece of information? Wouldn't the writer have suppressed this story if he were writing for evangelical impact?

- In one scene, Jesus discounts the connections to his family (Matt 12:46). Denouncing one's family would have been totally contrary to the mores of the day. Why not purge this detail or explain it? The story remains naked with no explanation.

- Jesus is remembered in one occasion as being unable to perform miracles because the people were too faithless (Matt 13:58). Given Jesus's exalted status, why not rewrite this story to capture Jesus's position in a more favorable light, to make a theological point, or to explain the incident? Such rewriting did not occur.

- The disciples are reflected in cowardly terms after the Resurrection. Why retain this negative caricature when the editors had the chance to rewrite the stories and redeem the disciples? They are, after all, remembered in greatly heroic terms by the Church of the second century.

None of these details would have been retained by the editors if they were editing for maximal evangelical impact. Instead, the editors preserved the documents presented to them. These items would have been considered embarrassing to the Church, so we can take it that they must be true. The editors certainly would not have installed fabricated points of embarrassment into their documents.

Noninsertion of Text after the Fact

None of the Gospel writers mentions the destruction of the Jerusalem Temple in 70 CE. Possibly the texts predate 70 such that this event's noninclusion would be understandable. What is not possible, though, is the second-century editors being unaware of the Temple collapse. By the end of the first century, everyone targeted for evangelization would have known this fact. Yet, like the writers before them, the editors take no effort to revise the Gospel texts to take advantage of the Temple's demise for what evangelical benefits could be motivated by the event.

Avoiding mention of the Temple collapse is a specific example where known historical facts are not back-written into the Gospels. Contrary to what one might suppose, the Gospel stories, with few exceptions, are not told in flashback. Instead, they are written in the present tense, as if the reader were living the stories out in real time with the characters in the stories. There are very few instances in which the evangelists inserted information from a later era into a story, even when such insertions would have been most useful. Some of the post-Resurrection material in John is a rare exception proving the rule. The evangelists and later editors kept their stories Jesus-centric and written in the present tense, even if the events were now many decades in the past. This is another example where the editors set upon themselves a set of constraints to contain their texts in ways they need not have done. They have self-imposed constraints that structure their arguments to remain centralized on Jesus—not the follow-on events—and on the texts provided to them. Just to take a hypothetical example, consider the italicized words as a prospective insert to the well-known Doubting Thomas story (John 20:27–28):

> Then Jesus said to Thomas, "Put your finger here and see my hands, and put your hand into my side, and do not be unbelieving but believe." Thomas answered and said to him, "My Lord and my God." *Thomas would use the very hand thrust into Jesus to baptize thousands of souls, who would came to believe in Jesus's name in the east beyond the Indus valley.*

These kinds of words could have been added to huge evangelical advantage in showing the reach and truth of the Gospel. Its inclusion would have conveyed no downside. After all, who could disprove the claim, even if it were concocted? (One tradition holds that Thomas did indeed go to India to evangelize, which is why this example was selected for illustrative purposes. This belief is widely held in some western provinces in India even today. So the scenario here, described as hypothetical, may not be so hypothetical after all.) Alas, we have few such vignettes in the Gospels where future information is grafted onto the preexisting text. The absence of exactly these kinds of things, which we might cast as low-hanging fruit, is a testament to the focus the Gospels kept on the actual, historical Jesus. The Gospel editors did not develop their works as ideal evangelical tools. If they had, we would have been gifted with a different set of information from what has been passed down to us in our modern Bibles.

The italicized words above are a fiction to make a point. Retrojection of information into the Gospels could have been easily done with huge positive effect and no downside. We need not limit ourselves to insertion of fictional information either, by the way. For one historically accurate example not recorded in the Gospel account, consider the story beginning at Mark 3:31 (NIV). This is a perfect example illustrating how tightly the writer of the text and the subsequent editors kept to the original story. Consider the story as recorded and what could have been relayed in the Gospel account but was not, even though the words could have kept to known historic facts (my added words in italics):[72]

> Then Jesus's mother and brothers arrived. Standing outside, they sent someone in to call him. A crowd was sitting around him, and they told him, "Your mother and brothers are outside looking for you."
>
> "Who are my mother and my brothers?" he asked.
>
> Then he looked at those seated in a circle around him and said, "Here are my mother and my brothers! Whoever does God's will is my brother and sister and mother."
>
> *Years later, those who would do God's will would include his family members, such as Jesus's kinsman James, who would shepherd the community of believers in Jerusalem and be martyred for Jesus, in addition to as a whole new family connected through Jesus by his apostles and their followers, who are now situated all over the world.*

The editors could have enhanced this passage for positive effect. They did not, even aware that the italicized words were historically accurate at the time they were edited. The lack of additions indicates the editors did not alter what was available to them.

The lack of this kind of italicized phrase inserted into the text attests to the fidelity the editors kept to the original words. The editors had great opportunity to insert add useful words, but they did not. We can surmise that the editors prized the original words so dearly they did not want to alter them. (From the view of the historian, the lack of accretions, unfortunately, affords no help in dating the texts.)

Whereas the lack of these inserts says much about the fidelity of the redaction process leading to compiling the Gospels, we twenty-first-century readers lament their absences, too. We would love to know, for example, what happened to the people who were recipients of Jesus's healings, to Mary of Magdala, and to the apostles. These points, though, are lost to history.

As a complement to the points above where we find the lack of expected accretions, consider the possibility that scribes altered texts after they were written to support later theological understandings. However, any such instances at all are rare. Consider this anecdote to serve as an example.[73] Tom Bissell, a self-described apostate, makes the claim that Luke's story of Jesus's baptism was recrafted by scribes to combat an Adoptionalism thesis that arose as part of the Christological debates scores of years after Luke's Gospel was compiled. (Adoptionalism undercuts the later Christian orthodox view that the Son of God was always a son. Adoptionalism argues that Jesus only became a son by adoption.) The original Lucan words (Luke 3:21–22) for the pronouncement from heaven at Jesus's baptism, Bissell claims, were, "You are my Son, today I have begotten you." These words were revised by later scribes to "You are my Son with whom I am well pleased." The alteration, he goes on to assert, was done by nefarious scribes to bury any support for Adoptionalism that could be inferred from the former words. Bissell is correct that the former words are in some early Lucan editions, as footnotes to study Bibles duly indicate. The footnote in the NAB (St. Joseph edition) is "*'You are my beloved Son; with you I am well pleased'*: this is the best-attested reading in the Greek manuscripts. The Western reading, 'You are my Son, this day I have begotten you' is derived from Ps 2, 7" (italics in original). What Bissell misses, however, is that the suspected later words in Luke are exactly the same words that appear in Mark's and Matthew's versions of the same event, which, presumably, are the more original words. As a result, instead of being a nefarious action by later scribes, the anecdote evidences the degree of continuity that scribes provided.

There could have been scribal impact on the texts for grammar, word choice, order of events, and other matters, but the collective impact of scribal actions is marginal. Not a single important Christian doctrinal position depends upon the outcome of any disputed scribal action.

Lack of Attribution of Matters to Jesus

As a specific variant to the section above, the editors of the Gospels would have had reason to document already-resolved matters within the Christian community and make the settlements attributable to Jesus. By the time the second century started, some of the pressing doctrinal points of the previous century had been resolved, yet the resolution of these points took time to work out. There would have been every reason to back-read into the Gospels some preemptions to lead to the resolution of the issue with specific words going back to Jesus. Alas, the editors did not insert this kind of information.[74]

Take the person of Paul and his theology. Questions about Paul's apostleship were on the front burner in the middle decades of the first century. Wouldn't it have been ideal for editors to put onto Jesus's lips a prophecy about Paul's arrival? By the second century, of course, Paul was a revered character. After the fact, the ambiguity of Paul's apostleship could have been set aside by the insertion of just a few words into the Gospel accounts. However, as simple as these words would have been to add, they do not appear. In fact, neither Paul nor any specific predictions of Paul's arrival are reflected in the Gospel accounts.

Paul's theology would come to dominate the Christian Church, but when his teachings began to take sway is a little hard to pinpoint exactly. We can surmise that it was no later than the end of the Council of Jerusalem in 49 or 50 CE. An earlier date cannot be ruled out. In Paul's discourses, justification by faith and the call of the Gospel to Gentiles as well as to the Jews were two polarizing positions. Both would eventually be adopted as Christian norms, but these issues were controversial in the middle decades of the first century. By the time Luke writes his Gospel, he could have retrojected into his narrative some words to be ascribed to Jesus to settle the matter with authority. The editors in the second century could have added supporting text since, by then, these questions were settled matters. However, neither Luke nor subsequent editors make changes to the text to reflect the established point of doctrine. They put no such words onto Jesus's lips. Luke, in particular, seemed to have had a great incentive to steel Paul's legacy and tie it to Jesus in the flesh, but he doesn't. Luke's incentive would have been to dispel the opinion some held that Paul was not a true apostle since he never met Jesus in the flesh. Luke would have wanted to anchor Paul's apostleship since Paul was his mentor.

Luke is not making history; he is recording it, which is precisely what Luke says he is doing in the first words of his Gospel. The editors stay with the Lucan account presented to them, even though they would have had every reason to extend the narrative.

Treatment of Gentiles in the Gospels

By the beginning of the second century, that the Christian community was a merger of Jews and Gentiles was an established fact. When the Gospels were being written, though, this point remained equivocal. The editors of the Gospels in the second century could have easily redacted the Gospel to make them track to the Church of their time and not keep to the events in Jesus's time. For example, as an obvious retrojection to have included in the second-century renditions of the Gospels, the editors could have placed a demand from Jesus during his public ministry onto the original Church to engage in outreach to Gentiles. This would have been hugely important, of course, by making the Church accessible and welcoming to Gentiles. Needless to say, if not already true many years before the editors were compiling the Gospels, the Gentiles were the overwhelming target of Christian evangelical efforts during the second century, so the editors had every incentive to tee up the Gospel accounts to facilitate the Gentilization of the Church. But the editors did not take advantage of this obvious opportunity in any substantive way. Instead, the editors retained the primitive character of earlier witness captured in the Gospel accounts, which are almost always stories related to Jews and Jewish practices and mostly exclude mentions of interactions with Gentiles.

How do the Gospels treat the Gentiles? As it happens, they do not treat Gentiles much at all. Jesus grows up a stone's throw away from a large, modern Hellenized city-Sepphoris—full of Gentiles, yet the city's name never appears in the Gospels. A tiny Jewish hamlet like Nain with, at most, a few dozen residents gets a call out, but a veritable metropolitan Gentile town in the same area is never mentioned. This is the general pattern. Jesus's interactions are overwhelming connected to fellow Jews, not to Gentiles, and Gentiles appear in Gospel accounts sparingly. The Gospels were being written after the Council of Jerusalem, which endorsed baptizing Gentiles. Accordingly, one would have expected that the Gospels would have been written to expand the opportunity to evangelize the Gentiles. The writers could have included significant passages of Jesus's ministry with Gentiles as a foreshadowing of the apostles' ministry to them. But, alas, there is no significant set of Gentile-based stories. The incidents in which Jesus migrates to pagan territories and the story of the Magi in Matthew are two of the few cases, the latter one probably relegated as a retrojection. The personal nexus from Jesus to Gentiles remains tenuous. For our editors in the second century, though, it is already a settled point that Jesus is the Christ for Jews and Gentiles alike. Remember, Gentiles outnumber Jews by an order of magnitude in the Roman Empire.

The editors knew their opportunities and futures rested with the Gentilization of the Church, so the editors rewrote the Gospels to make them more appealing to the Gentiles, right? Well, actually, no. Instead of opening the gospel to Gentiles, we get this remarkably harsh passage from Matthew's Gospel (15:21–28 NIV, italics added for emphasis):

> Leaving that place, Jesus withdrew to the region of Tyre and Sidon. A Canaanite woman from that vicinity came to him, crying out, "Lord, Son of David, have mercy on me! My daughter is demon-possessed and suffering terribly."
>
> Jesus did not answer a word. So his disciples came to him and urged him, "Send her away, for she keeps crying out after us." He answered, *"I was sent only to the lost sheep of Israel."* The woman came and knelt before him. "Lord, help me!" she said. He replied, "It is not right to take the children's bread and *toss it to the dogs.*"
>
> "Yes it is, Lord," she said. "Even the dogs eat the crumbs that fall from their master's table." Then Jesus said to her, "Woman, you have great faith! Your request is granted." And her daughter was healed at that moment.

Wherever one wants to place this extract on the scale of being a retrojection—it could be argued either way—identifying Gentiles as "dogs" could never be interpreted as a term of endearment. The editors retained these words, knowing full well the evangelical outreach to Gentiles was already under way. If the editors were simply reporting events for evangelical advantage, why would they allow the inclusion of these words, which reflect so poorly upon the targeted audience?

Noninclusion of Updates

Editors would have had opportunities to include updates to the text to add clarity or refine statements in the original, and there would have been great incentive to do so. There are statements in the Gospel accounts the editors could have rewritten to reflect changes in circumstances. Here is a classic example, where the editors would have had every reason to alter the words, but they did not. The verse is from Matthew 16:28 (KJV) with parallels in the other two Synoptics:

> "Verily I say unto you, There be some standing here, which shall not taste of death, till they see the Son of man coming in his kingdom."

On first reading, this verse seems to disprove itself to those who were reading it in the second century. The verse says Jesus is returning soon such that some of those standing with him will not die. The folks in the second century were fully aware the generation seeing Jesus in the flesh had already died. So, they would have known that the statement can't be true. Any decent editor would have purged the sentence entirely or added some context, perhaps something like this addition in italics:

> "Verily I say unto you, There be some standing here, which shall not taste of death, till they see the Son of man coming in his kingdom." *Jesus meant that they would experience Jesus risen from the dead and claim his kingdom before their deaths.*

But, again, the editors kept the ambiguous words as written and made no effort to adjust the words to reflect current conditions. This is evidence of the deference the editors offered to the words provided to them.

The Net Impact of Editors

The items above demonstrate that our would-be editors do not appear to have edited the Gospel accounts at all. Given the foregone opportunities, we conclude that the supposed "editors" are not editors at all, but merely scribes. It appears that the Church, which took over editorial control of the Gospels after the close of the Apostolic Age, chose as her editorial policy the faithful replication of the material presented to her, even when doing so was not to her advantage. The scribes committed to faithful reproduction of the words because they felt some compunction to preserve the texts as written. They must have believed the texts had characteristics that put them in a category where changing them was highly discouraged. This fact of history sounds remarkably like the Church's continual claim that she has faithfully retained her sacred texts from generation to generation.

PHASE 3: FAITHFUL COMPILATION OF THE GOSPELS

In Phase 1, which took us through the end of the Apostolic Age, we discussed how the original four documents became finalized. In the process of publishing them in final forms, corrective mechanisms existed to assure that the words captured in the documents corresponded to the events they recorded. In Phase 2, which took us through the wider-scale distribution of the documents, we found that the persons who scribed the documents for distribution exercised great care to retain the words provided to them. The editors—or, as we have deduced, the scribes—replicated their copies from one generation to the next, not necessarily perfectly perhaps but with no evident intent to change the kernels of the transmitted stories. We conclude from these facts that the words captured and distributed in the second century were reasonable facsimiles of the same words written two or three generations earlier.

So far, we have limited our discussion to the preservation and integrity of the *words* in the documents on a document-by-document basis. This brings us to an obvious question: What can be said about the documents when they became bundled as a set? Those of us in the twenty-first century know, of course, there are four canonical Gospel accounts and the Church bundled them together as a unit. Presenting them as a unit introduces a new set of queries about the relationships between the documents themselves and the Church. This is Phase 3 in the evolution of the Gospels, the last of the phases we need to consider. After this phase, we should have great confidence that the Gospel accounts recorded in our modern Bibles track directly to the documents coming from this era.

We are now up to approximately 120–150 CE. The four Gospel accounts have been circulating as separate or at least uncoordinated accounts. The Church chose to gather the accounts together in some manner at this time. Looking backward through history, we would say the Church was at the incipient stages of setting the canon for her Scripture. The New Testament still wouldn't be formally set for a couple hundred years, but the process of bringing the Gospel accounts together was now under way. We know this was true because of, among other reasons, the occasion of a man named Marcion in the middle of the second century. Records relating to him and his theological approaches date to circa 144 CE. Readers who don't recognize the name shouldn't be alarmed; Marcion's impact on the evolution of the Church and the Bible was not a result of what he accomplished but rather what he failed to do.

Marcion recognized two facts important to us: there is really only one Gospel, not many; and the God identified by Jesus as his loving, personal

Father looks very unlike the angry, jealous, unpredictable God of the Hebrew Bible. Whereas Marcion's reckoning of these facts may be correct, how he convolved them becomes the point of the story, leaving him merely as a footnote to history.[75] Marcion came up with the bizarre theory that God the Father of Jesus overthrew the Hebrew God, relegating the Hebrew God and His Hebrew Bible to the dustbin of history. Marcion also took it upon himself to develop his own set of Scriptures reflecting the true image of the Father whom Jesus had identified to his disciples. Marcion would merge all of the stories of Jesus into one definitive account, drawing on the Gospel of Luke as his primary source. Marcion would give us a harmonized Jesus. The Church rightly rejected Marcion's theories as heretical. Even so, Marcion's heresy raised two fundamental questions for the Church to resolve:

- *How would the Church reconcile her identity to her Jewish origin?* In the second century, Christianity is clearly distinct from Judaism. The Church is rapidly being Gentilized. The Judaism that Jesus lived is now a history lesson. The Jesus of history was buried; the Jesus of Christ is risen. Jesus exists now under the banner of a developed theology of the Cosmic Christ, the Redeemer, who is the second Adam and who liberates fallen humanity from its sinful destiny. The Church asked herself, *Why retain her historic Jewishness? Why not start afresh? Why be anchored to a seemingly irrelevant past?*
- *How would the Church consolidate her images of Jesus to provide a harmonized message?* How can we have four different accounts? They differ from one another, sometimes in important and seemingly unresolvable ways. The Church must have asked herself whether she would homogenize the stories of Jesus and issue a unified message.

The answers to these two questions would drive the Church's self-understanding and her emergent Scripture. In particular, the answers would say as much about the Church as they do about the canon she was beginning to set.

Retaining the Hebrew Scripture

In Jesus's time, Judaism was anchored to four *T*s: Torah, tribe, tradition, and temple. By the second century, the Church's linkages to the four *T*s had faded:

- Torah had been supplanted by the new law of Jesus.
- The tribe, the nation of Israel, has been replaced by the new Israel, the Church, whom the Church understood to be the body of Christ. The

tribe is no longer a specific tribe of people but is the mystical community of believers, open to all.
- The traditions of the Jews have been replaced by the new rituals of the Church, including and especially the Eucharist (the communal breaking of bread) and baptism.
- The temple has been destroyed. Not even second-century Jews could rely upon the temple and its cults. Christians had their new temple, the body of Christ. Interestingly, the basis for the mystical body predates the collapse of the Temple in 70 CE. We know with certainty that the idea of Jesus's body being a new temple existed before the Temple in Jerusalem was demolished, because Paul wrote about the mystical body in 1 Corinthians, which predated the collapse of the Temple by more than a decade.

Based on these facts, the Church must have asked herself whether it should shed her Jewish roots and move out smartly on her own, untethered to a Jewish past? Once divorced from the confines of Judaism, which we can tentatively date to 80–90 CE, the Church had the option to anchor herself as she desired. In this sense, the Church could have written her own Scriptures to correspond to where she found herself in history and not be beholden to ancient and often difficult-to-apply Scriptures.[76] In this sense, the Church could have made herself a better witness to the message she received from Jesus by striking out on her own. If she were to remake herself, now divorced of Judaism, how much opportunity would there have been to bring in pagan myths or understandings? Divorcing Christian Scripture from Hebrew Scripture had to have entered the Church's mind. As Nietzsche observed, the God of the Hebrew Bible is a God of justice, and the God of the New Testament is a God of mercy. To conflate the two, he observed, would be utter "temerity." The divorce from Hebrew Scripture could have opened the door to a whole new slate of Gentiles and made it easier to attach Christianity to whatever the local folks might have desired.

Needless to say, the Church did not do that. Instead, the Church doubled down and committed herself to her Jewish origins and accepted the Hebrew Bible en toto. These words from 2 Timothy, purportedly by Paul, make the adoption of Hebrew Scripture axiomatic, remembering that when these words were written, the Hebrew Bible contained the only documents that were understood to be Scripture, though the New Testament writings would accrue this designation in time as well (italics added for emphasis):

> And that from a child thou hast known the holy scriptures, which are able to make thee wise unto salvation through faith

in Christ Jesus. All scripture *is* given by inspiration of God, and *is* profitable for doctrine, for reproof, for correction, for instruction in righteousness: That the man of God may be perfect, thoroughly furnished unto all good works. (2 Tim 3:15–17 KJV)

The adoption of the Hebrew Bible by the Church has been called the biggest corporate takeover in history. The Church executed the takeover even while she had the opportunity to untether herself from its Jewish origins. The rationale for the Church retaining the Hebrew Bible, even if doing so without modification may not have served the Church's evangelical outreach especially well, is as follows:

- The Church's history was not hers to create. The origins of Christianity were unshakeable and went back to the first witnesses. The origins went back to the historic Jesus, his apostles, and the first believers. The Church was committed to this origin. She could have made up a new origin myth or recrafted the Jesus story to extract Jesus from his roots, but the Church did not, would not, and could not do so.
- The Hebrew Bible is a thick set of books. What fraction of it really plays an essential role in Christians' understanding of their faith? Not half, for sure. Maybe 20 percent? Ten percent? Yet the Church kept 100 percent of the Hebrew Bible. (Actually, she kept more than 100 percent. The Church retained the Greek and Aramaic materials in the Old Testament. The Jews, by contrast, did not complete the process of down-selecting their canon until a later time, when they chose to canonize only Hebrew-origin text. As a result, the "Old Testament" and the "Hebrew Bible" are not quite synonyms. Interestingly, when the Protestant Reformers got around to setting their Old Testament canon in the aftermath of the Reformation, they followed the Jewish convention for selected texts. They did not follow the conventions of the early Church, which is one reason that not all Christian Bibles are alike.) The Church was the new Israel, which subsumed the old.
- Jesus could never be something other than the Jew he was (or, as Christians would say, still is). His ministry and life were thoroughly Jewish. He came to fulfill the Law, not condemn it, as Matthew put on Jesus's lips.

> "Do not think that I have come to abolish the Law or the Prophets; I have not come to abolish them but to fulfill them. For truly I tell you, until heaven and earth disappear, not the smallest letter, not the least stroke of a pen, will by any means disappear from the Law until everything is accomplished. Therefore

anyone who sets aside one of the least of these commands and teaches others accordingly will be called least in the kingdom of heaven, but whoever practices and teaches these commands will be called great in the kingdom of heaven." (Matt 5:17–19 NIV)

- As mentioned in chapter 7, the adoption of the model of Jesus as Christ became normative to Christianity quite soon after the Resurrection. The model implied a commitment to the traditions and heritages that bore the prophecies of the Messiah. Jesus cannot fulfill Messianic prophecies if there are no prophecies, and there are no prophecies without the Hebrew Bible.

As a matter of history, the irony of ironies is this: when the Church had a decisive opportunity to make herself more inclusive by shedding her Hebrew/Jewish past in making Jesus known "to the ends of the earth," the Church took not the path of inclusion but a path of exclusion. She made herself more particularized and more structured to preserve her own origins, which meant retaining her Hebrew/Jewish character. We know this as a point of history because Christianity at the time had confronted a bastardized set of Jesus stories that had been merged into some existing philosophical traditions. The new set of literature, called *Gnostic*, created a competing understanding of the life and times of Jesus. In the rival interpretation, Jesus conveyed special understandings (or "knowledge," which is the etymological root of the term *Gnostic*) of a mystical sort to his followers. This mystical knowledge, as Gnostics told the story, could be passed down and used to free people from their wretched material bodies. In the Gnostic scheme, knowledge and spirit are in tension within man and the material world. Gnosticism spread widely and developed its own scriptures. The best known is the *Gospel of Thomas*. A library of Gnostic literature was uncovered at Nag Hammadi in Egypt in 1945, one of the great literary and archeological discoveries of the twentieth century.

The Gnostic heresy was put aside by Christians for other reasons too, but especially because the Church realized that fundamental understandings of Gnosticism were false. The falsehoods included: (1) the denial of the universal call of salvation (the Greek term *catholic*, which means "universal," was the term used at the end of the first century by the bishop of Rome for the true Church; the term *catholic* [lowercase c] appears in the Nicene Creed for this reason), as Gnosticism was predicated on secret knowledge available only to particular people; and (2) the belief that the material world is inherently evil, contrary to the Hebrew belief that creation is very good, as revealed by God.

The fallout of all this is that the Church may have had an opportunity to shed her Jewish roots, but she did not. The Hebrew-Jewish connection, the Church understood, is the link to salvation history. The drama beginning with the fall of the first Adam would be completed with the rise of the second Adam, Jesus.

The Nonharmonization of the Gospels

Quick, how many Gospels are there? Four is the common answer, referring to the canon of the New Testament. This number, however, does not count the many noncanonical Gospels, which, if added in, would raise the number significantly. However, there really is only one gospel; it is just expressed in multiple ways. As discussed in chapter 4, the four Gospel accounts were written by different authors for different audiences at different times and in different places. By the middle of the second century, those nuances are lost to history, and the differences giving rise to separate accounts don't matter as much to the people of the second century or, for that matter, to those of us in the twenty-first century either. Many of the stories told in two or more Gospel accounts are complementary. One can extract different meanings and different twists from the different readings, enhancing the understanding of the matter recorded. However, in some instances the stories are utterly irreconcilable. The baptism of Jesus by John is a case in point. Accounts appear in each of the four Gospels. As long as the Gospel accounts circulated separately and were not bundled together, as was true until the mid-second century, the conflicts between accounts may have been missed or ignored. Once the four accounts were bundled together, however, the conflicts became obvious. The reader of the bundled accounts has the problem of the man who has two watches telling him two different times. Which one of the watches is correct?

Bundling the Gospels became something of a self-inflicted wound to the Church. Why would she publish unreconciled accounts? What did she do to harmonize the accounts?

The surprising answer is that she did very little to harmonize them. The Church retained the four Gospels as written and made no substantive effort to harmonize them. (The limited exception is the localized attempt in Syria to roll the three Synoptic accounts into the template of John's Gospel. This solution lasted for two hundred years but was never widespread and never took on anything like an official sanction by the whole Church.[77]) Those of us with modern, Western minds find the ambiguity of nonharmonization to be intolerable. We have to ask, well, which of the accounts is right?

The Church would have suffered the same sort of intellectual dissonance we moderns do, though perhaps less so since the atomized, cause-and-effect, reductionist world we have is not the one in which the ancients lived. But the Church persisted with four nonharmonized accounts. Why would the Church choose not to harmonize them? The answer rests in how the Church understood her sources and how the Church would have put together her canon, that is, the Scriptures it considered to be authentic and normative for Christians. The content of the canon of the New Testament would not be settled for a few centuries. The protracted portions of the debate centered, though, not on the selection of the Gospels but on other books that would make up the New Testament. The criteria the Church used for the selection of Gospels to include in the canon were as follows:

- The work had to derive from apostolic succession.
- The work must resonate with the other books of Scripture.
- The work could not include doctrinal or fundamental errors, like the Gnostic Gospels did.
- The work must conform to the rule of faith, meaning the work comports with what the faithful were already joined to.

The Church coalesced around the four Gospels quickly and never looked back. In 130, there was no set canon of the Gospels; by 180, it was fixed. Canonization of some of the remaining twenty-three books of the New Testament was not as straightforward. Many of the authentic Pauline epistles were readily accepted; other works would be debated over long periods for inclusion. Martin Luther reopened the inclusion of certain works in the New Testament during the Reformation. He sought to remove the Letter of James from the New Testament, although he reluctantly relented by retaining it.

In the end, the Church retained the four Gospels because she believed they contained authentic source material the Church felt necessary to keep—and to keep separate without harmonization. That the Church had the opportunity to make up a harmonized account but consciously choose not to is clear evidence that the Church assumed her role as the preserver of history, not the maker of it. Quite clearly, the Church rejected revisionism, even when employing it to render a single, cogent account of Jesus would have been a valid goal. It is as if the Church were prescient enough to avoid historical re-creations of Jesus for her time and place. Luke Timothy Johnson explains the hazard of attempting to create a new image, based on historical reconstruction:

> Historical reconstructions are by their very nature fragile and in constant need of revision. They cannot sustain the commitment of the human heart and life. Even the most casual survey of all the Jesus reconstructions offered just in the last twenty years, furthermore, discovers a bewildering variety of conflicting portraits of Jesus, and a distressing carelessness in the manner of arriving at those portraits. If historians cannot be pious at least about their own trade, why should their suggestions be taken as the guide to religious piety?[78]

Fortunately for us as benefactors of history, the Church kept to her source materials and did not attempt to harmonize them.

The Preservation of the Gospels

We have seen that the scribes took great care in faithfully copying one version to another of their documents from the Apostolic Age through the canonization of the Gospels. We see also the Church was careful in bundling the four Gospel accounts. The Church made no attempt to revise the four documents so they might fit together better. All of this is to say the Church was methodical in keeping to her sources for her Scripture.

The last piece of the puzzle is making the case that the versions of the documents we have now have a claim to historical continuity. We need to argue that the documents beginning as a separate narratives at the beginning of the second century would be the same documents that were bundled together to become the four first books of the New Testament.

The Gospels of the New Testament gained wide circulation quickly. They were translated from their native Koine (or "common") Greek into Latin, Syriac, and other Oriental languages very soon after they were written.[79] The New Testament stands as the best-attested set of work of antiquity by a tremendous margin. The number of ancient copies (or portions) of the New Testament is unprecedented, compared with any other work from antiquity. The degree of consistency among the versions is impressive. There is a contra narrative, from Bart Ehrman and others, that there are more variations in the ancient versions of New Testament than there are words in the New Testament. The point is just a distraction that misses the bigger reality. In *The Case for Christ,* author Lee Strobel interviews the prominent New Testament scholar Bruce Metzger, who puts this in perspective when he states in his interview that:

> "The number [200,000 variants among ancient versions of the New Testament] sounds big, but it is misleading because of the

way variants are counted.... If a single word is misspelled in two thousand manuscripts, this is counted as two thousand variants."
[Strobel:] "How many doctrines are in jeopardy because of variants?"
[Metzger:] "I don't know of any doctrine that is in jeopardy."[80]

Metzger makes the point that, even if we lost all of the ancient Greek manuscripts, the New Testament could be reassembled from ancient manuscripts written in other languages that have survived from antiquity by translating the surviving manuscripts back to their native Greek. The fidelity of the New Testament as a matter of literary history has no peer. This comment from Matt Slick establishes this fact, leaving no allowance for equivocation:

> The New Testament documents are better-preserved and more numerous than any other ancient writings. Because they are so numerous, they can be cross checked for accuracy . . . and they are very consistent. There are presently 5,686 Greek manuscripts in existence today for the New Testament. If we were to compare the number of New Testament manuscripts to other ancient writings, we find that the New Testament manuscripts far outweigh the others in quantity. There are thousands more New Testament Greek manuscripts than any other ancient writing. [Note: The next more prevalent ancient manuscript is Homer's *Iliad* with 643 copies.] The internal consistency of the New Testament documents is about 99.5 percent textually pure. That is an amazing accuracy. In addition, there are over 19,000 copies in the Syriac, Latin, Coptic, and Aramaic languages. The total supporting New Testament manuscript base is over 24,000. Furthermore, another important aspect of this discussion is the fact that we have a fragment of the gospel of John that dates back to around 29 years from the original writing (John Rylands Papyri A.D. 125). This is extremely close to the original writing date. This is simply unheard of in any other ancient writing.[81]

These facts mean that

- The written Gospels could not be isolated from the evangelical mission of the Church.
- The scribes who copied the documents did so with a remarkable degree of care.
- The scribes understood that copying the words faithfully was a sacred honor.

CONCLUSION

In Phase 1, we discovered that the four documents that became the four canonical Gospels were preserved and cross-checked for accuracy as they were developed and as they took final form. The Church would have had tremendous incentive to inject herself into the written words to insert important information and to expunge other undesired information. She never did so but instead kept to the documents as presented to her.

In Phase 2, we discovered the Gospels bundled together as a unit, knowing full well that they were not harmonized, even when harmonization would have advanced the Church's evangelical claims. But instead of reworking the narratives and creating something new, the Church retained the nonharmonized documents and used them as the base of the canon for her New Testament.

In Phase 3, we discovered that the written New Testament propagated down through history has been faithfully recorded from generation to generation.

In earlier chapters, we argued that the Church could just not have made up the things that were recorded. In this chapter, it is almost the reverse: the Church could have made things up to suit her ends as she came to compiling and publishing her New Testament, but she did not.

Some of us moderns might believe that preserving the integrity of the accounts for so long is preposterous. Recall, though, when the Dead Sea Scrolls were found in 1948, the discoverers found an essentially intact scroll of the book of Isaiah. This version remained in hiding, undisturbed from about 73 CE until 1948 CE. The scroll was protected from the elements in a cave in the desert in a low-humidity environment. The discovered version of Isaiah essentially duplicates the version we have today in modern Hebrew Bibles.

All these points suggest that the four Gospel accounts we have in our modern Bibles are faithful renderings going back to originally sourced material.

11

The Gospel Truth about the Gospel Truth

I started the journey with the assumption that the Gospels were contrivances of zealous evangelists who were bent on converting the first-century Roman-Greco populations to join their ranks. I assumed that the Gospel writers made up their tales. Then I tested this assumption against a set of seven historical claims the Church makes about Jesus's life, death, and the events immediately surrounding his death. Those claims are

- Jesus's followers banded together after his death to found the Church.
- Jesus was a teacher.
- The Gospel accounts reflect the personal witness of first-century CE disciples.
- Jesus was a miracle worker.
- Jesus was resurrected from the dead.
- Jesus was (or is) the Messiah.
- Jesus's death achieved an atonement for the sins of his believers.

I assessed these claims or their proxies for historicity against the logical criteria established in chapter 2. I made arguments for applying evidentiary tests for authenticity while skirting possible retrojection of information. I devised a systems approach for assessing the historicity of the Gospel accounts, and I kept to it religiously (pun intended). The criteria are not

Christian criteria, faith criteria, or self-selecting criteria. They are logical, objective criteria—the tools of the historian.

In assessing the Gospels via the methodology established in chapter 2, I stacked the deck against the Gospel accounts by discounting most of the words and stories in them. Only a small set of kernels of stories survived the screening criteria. An individual with whom I work at NNSA and who has a theological background takes great exception to stacking the deck so desperately against the witness of the Gospels. He realizes that the methodology begins with the premise that the evangelists are duplicitous in the extreme. This imagery contrasts with the heroic witness these men shared with the world. Notwithstanding all of these severe impediments and perverse starting points for discounting witness in the Gospels, I still end up validating the kernels for these seven primal Church claims. The methodology is as if I attached balls and chains to a runner's ankles, but the runner still managed to win the race. I demolish the hypothesis the writers were clever enough just to go off and make up their narratives. The writers stayed true to their primitive sources and faithfully relayed the events observed by or reported to them. They were recorders of history, not its makers. As I have recounted throughout this book, they didn't just make this stuff up.

The conclusion speaks volumes to the credibility of the Church in preserving historical accuracy. If the Church faithfully preserved the events in the Gospels amenable to scrutiny by historical methods, then, it stands to reason, the Church probably applied a similar level of rigor in preserving the narrative matters not amenable to historic scrutiny as well.

Jesus puts the lie to the adage that there are no great men of history, only great deeds. Jesus is a great man and a man of great deeds as well. With regard to the prospect of just making up the basic story of Christianity, this quip answers the objection elegantly:

> I am reminded of Talleyrand's famous answer to an earnest [French] revolutionary, who asked him for advice on how to start a new enlightened religion to replace Christianity. [Talleyrand responded,] "I recommend that you be crucified and rise again on the third day."[82]

The Gospels, as delivered to us, were not something the Church would have or could have made up. Christianity is approaching its two thousandth birthday. It is the world's largest religion and its first truly global religion. The Church took four centuries to articulate her creeds. Yet if you wind the clock back to the first days of the Church—long before creeds, the organic Church, theology, doctrine, Scripture, or philosophical musings—the Church made an outlandish linkage. A small group of outcasts articulated an initial idea of Christianity virtually overnight. Perhaps what is most amazing is not Christianity's stunning growth from obscurity to its rise as an unparalleled influence on the world stage but rather how rapidly the nucleus of the faith gelled together. The foundational initial idea of Christianity was formulated and promulgated in a substantive way in, at most, a few months, though likely it was even shorter than this. The development of the central idea of Christianity represents stunning alacrity for a new concept coming from nowhere that was an unnecessary, unprecedented, and contrarian one in the first place. As Tertullian said about the story of Christianity: it is impossible; therefore, it must be true.

There remain matters of the Christian faith that lie beyond the reach of rational inquiry, such as:

- Jesus is with us until the end of time.
- Jesus is the Son of God.
- Jesus is divine, true God from true God.
- Jesus's suffering provides a modality for the forgiveness of sins.
- The Church is the mystical body of Jesus.
- The Holy Spirit dwells in believers.

These are matters of faith, revelation, and theology. They may comport with reason, but they cannot be deduced from reason alone. When it comes to these matters, we have to revert to the same question about Jesus we asked in chapter 1, which is precisely the same question Jesus asked his friends two thousand years ago, "Who do you say that I am?"

The pious Christian can make the same dramatic proclamation Peter spouts in Matthew's Gospel: "You are the Christ, the Son of the living God." She understands that Jesus's question is not a question on a history exam; it is a question of conviction.

The thoughtful skeptic must pause to offer an answer to Jesus's question. If a certain man can rise from the dead, can work mighty deeds, and can teach with authority and vision like none before, then the skeptic might want to be a little deferential in accepting any claims such a man makes. Each of the four Gospels has Jesus claiming himself to be divine. In Mark, the claim is subtle; in John, it pulsates. A person who claims divinity for himself is insane, right? But how many insane people perform miracles at their direction? How many of them rise from the dead? How many of them can preach a wisdom proclamation that stands at the foundation of a culture? Based on these attributes, the skeptic might reconsider the Church's proposition that the Jesus of history is the Jesus of faith. Perhaps this seemingly preposterous proposition may be not so preposterous after all.

Epilogue

The Fruition of the Gospel Truth

The subtitle of this book is *You Can't Make This Stuff Up*. The subtitle arose owing to the number of attributes we know about the historic Jesus that were not matters an evangelist would have just concocted. Here is the syllogism underlying the title: (a) The claim of an event having occurred is either made up or not; (b) We know that the claimant would not have made up some particular claims for some particular events; (c) Therefore, the particular event must have occurred or was transmitted to the claimant as presented. The following events or attributes fall into the category of things a claimant would not have made up, as some examples: death of a hero by crucifixion, the apostles' continual bungling and faithlessness, Jesus's totally unexpected corporeality at his Resurrection, the linkage of Jesus's death-Resurrection to the forgiveness of sins, and the identification of Jesus as Christ when his messiahship looks nothing like the messiah his contemporaries had envisioned. Given the lack of incentive to make these points up, there is a high probability that they convey historicity.

We have completed assessing the seven primal, historical claims of the Church against the criteria of historicity. Having done so, one cannot help but wonder how the you-can't-make-this-stuff-up premise might apply to the evolution of Christianity in the bigger sense, not just the historical portions recorded in the Gospels. Open the aperture more widely and view, not the historical Jesus claims of Christianity, but its theological ones through this same lens of "You can't make this stuff up."

At the base of Christian theology for the vast majority of Christians, we have Jesus as the second person of the Godhead in the Trinity, taking on human form as true God–true man and redeeming his fellow humans as their Messiah by his death, Resurrection, and atoning for believers' sins. Recognizing that Christianity derives directly from Judaism, how much of this theological conceptualization would have been foreseen by Jews before Jesus? Zero. To most Jews, then as now, this kind of theology is scandalous, yet Christians can and do argue how the Hebrew Bible envisions Jesus as its fulfillment.

As C. S. Lewis stated, Christianity has an authenticity to it precisely because it is not something one would ever dream up. In the parlance of this volume, you just can't make Christianity up.

The Church understands Jesus as the singularity in human history, the end point of what would be known as *salvation history*. Looking backward, we see the beginnings of salvation history more than a millennium before Jesus's time. The story begins in human time with Abram and in mythical time to Adam. The witnesses to the Resurrection could not have known then how the events they were seeing would fit together into the multigenerational drama of salvation history. The culmination of this history was far too afield from those ordinary men in those first days of the Church to comprehend its significance. The believers simply went with the flow, probably oblivious to the broader theological contexts. The fit of their portions of salvation history would reveal itself only in the elegance of the unfolding of time. They just could not have made the story hold together as exquisitely as it does. It is too rich, too coupled with the Hebrew Bible, too nuanced, too insightful, too original, too profound, and too philosophical for a group of illiterate, untrained, uneducated men to have devised it. They could not have pulled the pieces together virtually overnight around a campfire. How could they have had the insights to formulate the intricacies of salvation history in their confused state? Yet, it seems as if that is precisely what they did, even if unconsciously. We recall Benedict XVI's words:

> The anonymous community [of the early Church] is credited with an astonishing level of theological genius—who were the great figures responsible for inventing all of this? No, the greatness, the dramatic newness, comes directly from Jesus; within the faith and the life of the community it is further developed, but not created. In fact, the "community" would not even have emerged and survived at all unless some extraordinary reality had preceded it.

The Church did not make up salvation history. The Church honors her founders for their heroic virtue, but let's not kid ourselves into believing they were brilliant enough to dream up the profundity of salvation history.

Salvation history was revealed to the incipient Church and interpreted by successive generations in the fullness of time. The fullness spanned centuries in some cases. Notwithstanding, the initial idea of Christianity, which came together impressively quickly, has been faithfully retained since the earliest days of the Church.

The emergence of Christianity was a story that actually played out on a real stage, in real time with a real audience, with actors performing to the director's script. The players recited their lines and played their roles on cue. Only the director had the script in advance, only he had the last scene of the last act, and only he knew what attended the curtain call.

In this vein, only the director can make this stuff up, not the actors.

All of the Gospel accounts are clear that the apostles and the earliest disciples were dazed and confused and maybe even oblivious to what the Resurrection was all about when it was thrust upon them. That is to say, the apostles and the earliest disciples did not have the prescience or intuition to understand then how linking the Resurrection to the forgiveness of sins would be the revolutionary idea that founded the world's greatest religion. With the Resurrection linked to the forgiveness of sins, the redemption of man from his depravity became realizable. What that means for all time is that we have the gospel, that is, the good news. The rest, to be literal and trite, is history.

Here are some ramifications of how the initial idea of Christianity kicked off the new religion. The initial idea addressed a whole suite of questions the Church probably was not even cognizant she was being asked. She couldn't have made up the initial idea to provide these insights at the time because she hadn't had the presence of vision to do so. The Church couldn't have made this stuff up. But the axioms that flow from the initial ideas make for a sound intellectual foundation, notwithstanding the Church's obliviousness to founding a new religion, let alone a theological basis for one. Christianity was not founded to answer these foundational questions; it just happened that way. One might suppose that the answers were developed in advance by a Designer. The Church did not make up these answers; she received them from the script's author, God Himself. These answers include:

JOY

Once the Church fully appreciated she had a means for obtaining the forgiveness of sins by Jesus's death, she realized, for the first time since the proverbial fall of Adam, there was a means to restore humanity's fundamental relationship to God. All the prayers, penance, and almsgiving the apostles and first disciples had applied before Jesus's Resurrection would have, at best, only temporarily restored them to a rightful state before God. The mediating role of Jesus offered a unique, structural means to bridge the gap between heaven and earth in perpetuity. Jubilation! Though the realization of the mediation of Jesus's death and Resurrection for all people took time to roll out, once the acceptance of the mediating role of Jesus was understood, it was all but inevitable that the logic of redemption of the Israelites could be extended to the Gentiles as well. Thus, we are heading down the path for the makings of the first worldwide, universally applicable religion.

DIVINE ELECTION

There are three fundamental questions of Judaism remained open for a thousand years that found answers with Christianity. The Church offered new, unforeseen, and compelling responses to long-standing unresolved riddles. The riddles were: (a) If the Jews are the chosen people, what are they chosen *for*? The Jews understood they were elected, but for *what*? They know they are light for the Gentiles, but how does the light get *cast*? (b) How does Israel parlay its election to everyone? We know that Abram (later called Abraham) was both blessed and a blessing to the world. Traditional Judaism is unclear about how Abraham's blessing would be exported to everyone. It is simply taken as a matter of faith that it would be done. The Church offered an unexpected answer. (c) What is the game plan for God's reconciliation with man? Judaism sports no answer about how it was going to happen, but the Church does.

On this point, one might wonder how modern Jews think about Christianity. This short anecdote is telling: A Jewish friend of mine was asked by her school-age daughter, "What is Christianity?" The mother replied, "It is Judaism for Gentiles." Hers was a fascinating reply, even if it would be off-putting both to Orthodox Jews and orthodox Christians. Yet some real wisdom is captured in her five-word sentence. Her response describes a universalization of the original covenant with Israel to all humans while not disrupting it. In other words, the formerly parochial divine election of the Jews gets transmitted as a gift to all humanity.

COORDINATION OF JUSTICE AND MERCY

Jews—and Christians and Muslims too—understand God to be both just and merciful. But being both simultaneously is almost a contradiction in terms. If God is all merciful to those who seek him, how can he also exact justice simultaneously? Clearly, one cannot have it both ways. Or can he? God's ways are not our ways. He can be and is merciful, and, if you follow the story of the Prodigal Son, you might even say he is merciful to a fault. Yet, God demands justice, too. He and we require justice in response to sin. If he and we did not demand justice, what kind of place would this earth be? It would be a dystopia, awash in lawlessness. Sin would prevail, and might would make right. In such a place, people would have to make no account for their misdeeds; indeed, there might not be anything labeled a misdeed. Such a condition would not be amenable for human society to progress, let alone flourish. With Jesus's death, justice is available, once and for all, for all people and for all time. Thus, mercy can be made available to all because the price of justice has already been paid. Mercy and justice can now logically coexist, both temporally and locally, whereas they really could not before.

SUFFERING

Suffering inheres as part of the human condition. That it does so has never quite been adequately explained to anyone's complete satisfaction. No philosophy or religion has really been able to address this riddle successfully in all its dimensions. Judaism and Christianity are no exceptions. The Christian community saw in Jesus's Passion that suffering can serve a higher purpose. In their Hebrew Scripture, Jews find suffering featured prominently, perhaps no more prominently than in Isaiah's Song of the Suffering Servant (see Isa 42:1–4; 49:1–6; 50:4–7; 52:13–53:12). The earliest Christians connected this particular set of prophecies to the Passion of Jesus. The fit of the Song of the Suffering Servant to the Passion of Jesus is unmistakable.

Christians understand their Jesus to be Isaiah's long-predicted Suffering Servant. In a tale that displays the connection between the ancient prophecy and the New Testament events, consider this short tale:

A Jewish-Christian was proselytizing in Israel a few years ago. A non-Christian Jew, who was targeted for evangelization, was convinced that the Jewish-Christian's version of Isaiah was fabrication. He believed it was fabricated because the evangelist's version of Isaiah supported the evangelist's claim. He reasoned, the version must be fake because the Hebrew Bible does not support Christian beliefs. The target of the evangelist went back to his "safe" non-Christian Hebrew Bible, only to find the Jewish-Christian's version and his versions matched exactly.

Early Christians garner an understanding that suffering is part of the human condition. Christians understand that Jesus shares in human suffering, and, thus, he offers solidarity with his followers. This is where we get the word "compassion," whose etymology literally means "sharing in pain." Does this solidarity alleviate man's suffering? Not necessarily, but it provides a context for understanding and accepting suffering as inherent on this side of heaven.

GRACE

In the accounting of sin prior to Jesus, one is restored only as much as his prior actions made an atonement to make him restored. Then there is the next day. Sin is revisited. The sinner separates himself from God again. One chases his tail in a sense. Christianity offered a different understanding, one predicated on superabundant grace, where "grace" is an unmerited gift. The restoration of the relationship between God and man is solely of God's doing. Man's role is but to accept salvation. Man's efforts to save himself are feckless.

COMBATING EVIL

In the Jewish economy of the forgiveness of sins, if it works as supposed, the individual is restored by being atoned of his sins. In the atoning process, what is accomplished in abating the origins of evil? Nothing. By contrast, the atonement of Jesus offers the pretense of actually having conquered the source of sin and evil. In the Church's view, the victory over evil has already been won. The continuation of evil still in this world persists only in its last gasps as the end of the age nears. The Christian understanding of atonement has a more heightened sense of Manichaeism (or dualism) than does its Hebrew understanding. In Christianity, the source of evil is quashed; in the Hebrew rendering, the source of evil is unabated.

Given how elegantly the pieces of the puzzle fit together, one might be inclined to consider that the claims of Christianity were back-written into history and then the whole thing was written with the forgiveness of sins and the restoration of mankind as the endgame of the project. However, this is exactly opposite to how things really unfolded. The unfolding followed the sequence of Jesus's unexpected death, his unexpected Resurrection, and then the search for an understanding of the two prior events.

We know from psychologists that seeking and obtaining forgiveness for wrongdoing can be hugely cathartic and healthy for one's psyche. I recall hearing a Jewish psychiatrist speaking on the radio telling the audience there is nothing more mentally healthy for a person who is truly contrite to receive forgiveness in a concrete way. The psychiatrist singled out the Catholic rite of confession/reconciliation in this regard. The opposite of a healthy mental state is incessant wallowing in being unable to achieve forgiveness. The classic demonstration of mental unhealth, which results in sin eating away at the perpetrator's soul, is remembered in *Hamlet* (act 3, scene 3). Given its timelessness, *Hamlet* remains one the most critically acclaimed plays in the English language, even now at the ripe young age of 400. In this scene, the usurper uncle, Claudius, who has murdered his brother to take his brother's throne and his wife, can find no solace in his existence because he is incapable of repenting his sins. He, therefore, lives an inherently and insurmountably dark existence:

> O, my offence is rank it smells to heaven;
> It hath the primal eldest curse upon't,
> A brother's murder. Pray can I not,
> Though inclination be as sharp as will . . .
> My fault is past. But, O, what form of prayer
> Can serve my turn? "Forgive me my foul murder"?
> That cannot be; since I am still possess'd
> Of those effects for which I did the murder,
> My crown, mine own ambition and my queen . . .
> Try what repentance can: what can it not?
> Yet what can it when one cannot repent?

The Church could not have understood the mental health therapy she proffered as she rolled out her understanding of salvation history. But roll it out she did; the positive mental effects came along for the ride. Salvation history is God's script, not man's. Alas, *you can't make this stuff up!*

Endnotes

Chapter 1

1 Moore, "Evangelicals Won't Cave," 30.
2 Cupitt, *Meaning of the West*, as quoted in "Douglas Murray's 'Strange Death of Europe' Aska the Most Difficult Question," *Financial Review*, July 21, 2017ps://www.afr.com/work-and-careers/management/douglas-murrays-strange-death-of-europe-asks-the-most-difficult-question-20170710-gx87ay
3 Meier, *Marginal Jew*, 1:837.
4 Wright, *How God Became King*, 26.
5 Garraty and Gay, *Columbia History of the World*, 218–19.
6 Wright, *How God Became King*, 106.

Chapter 2

7 Lewis, *Mere Christianity*, 41–42.

Chapter 3

8 Ehrman, *Jesus before the Gospels*, 194.
9 See Stark, *Rise of Christianity*, for an excellent review of how Christianity emerged, as described by a sociologist.
10 See the appendices to Levine and Bretter, *Jewish Annotated New Testament*.

Chapter 4

11 Pitre states that the Gospels look a lot like other biographies written by secular sources in the same time period in terms of focus, length, thematic (versus chronological) ordering, and the manner in which events are recorded (*Case for Jesus*, 70–77).
12 Karl Keating relays the efforts of the scholar Jean Carmignac to translate the Greek version into Hebrew. He concluded, contrary to all expectations, the translation was surprisingly easy. Given that Hebrew and Greek have very little in common, this was quite a remarkable result. What Keating surmised is the ease of translation into Hebrew derives from the fact that Mark was originally penned in Hebrew so that the extant versions we have in Mark reflect their Semitic origin. This explains the unexpected simplicity in the back-translation. The reason the extant Greek in Mark is awkward is because it was not originally written in Greek. A majority of scholars believe, though, that Mark originally wrote in Greek and Matthew and Luke followed Mark, using Greek as well (Keating, *Nothing but the Truth*, 102).

A contra theory with a minority following, based on widely spread ancient traditions, holds that Matthew's Gospel was written in Aramaic in Palestine for his fellow

Palestinian Jews and that this document became the original source for Mark. I stick with the majority of scholarly opinion. In the end, we have well-honed theories but few well-substantiated facts.

[13] Keating, *Nothing but the Truth*, chapter 8, "Upstart Theories."

[14] The Son of Man title, scholars have concluded, is an authentic title Jesus used for himself. Jesus spoke Aramaic, but the Gospels are all written in Greek. Scholars know the "Son of Man" name is included in the Hebrew Bible, namely in Daniel's apocalyptic and mysterious passages, but it is also included elsewhere, such as in Ezekiel. Though the apocalyptic meanings from Daniel might be conveyed in Jesus's use of the term, Jesus's breadth of the term's use is both much wider and more nuanced than Daniel's. It remains a mystery exactly what Jesus intended by the term or, for that matter, if he meant just one thing. Scholars attribute three meanings to it (see, e.g., Benedict XVI, *Jesus of Nazareth*). One might wonder whether the ambiguity itself was intended by Jesus, trying to convey to his disciples the otherness and inscrutability of Jesus's mission. The wonder is matched by the many actions and remarks from the disciples demonstrating they never really understood Jesus or his mission entirely. Surely, they were mesmerized by Jesus, even if not convinced they knew how all of his pieces fit together. As an example of the disciples' cluelessness, nowhere in the Gospels is there a phrase from a disciple during Jesus's earthly life that links his death to the forgiveness of sins. We ought to find the omission odd since it is the central tenet of Christianity. The only person referenced in the Gospels who links Jesus to the forgiveness of sins in the sense of the atonement is in a dream that Matthew imputes to Jesus's mother's fiancé Joseph (Matt 1:21). Note, though, that the linkage is not related to Jesus's death, and, moreover, it is believed Joseph would have been dead many years before Jesus began his public ministry, so we have no way to authenticate the link to Joseph historically.

[15] Burton Mack has an excellent telling of how Q was reconstituted by careful reading of the Synoptics in his book *Q, The Lost Gospel*. The content in the cited section closely follows the introduction of Meyer, *Secret Teachings of Jesus*.

[16] See the bibliography for sources on the *Gospel of Thomas* as well as other inferior-quality documents. Meyer's book *Secret Teachings of Jesus* provides an English translation of four Gnostic Gospels, the best known being the *Gospel of Thomas*. This Sayings Gospel has many parallels to the sayings in the Synoptics, providing a hint of the antiquity and authority of the canon's authenticity from outside of the Bible.

[17] See Funk, *Honest to Jesus*. At the end of the book is an appendix the Jesus Seminar concludes are the authentic sayings of Jesus. John's Gospel gets a total of three lines, which is less than the Gospel of St. Thomas. On the whole, the Jesus Seminar assigns only 18 percent of the words attributed to Jesus in the Gospels as actually having come from him.

[18] Lewis, *Christian Reflections*, 155, as quoted in Keller, *Reason for God*, 110.

CHAPTER 5

[19] Crosson, *Who is Jesus*, 153.

[20] Schwienhorst-Schönberger, "Marcion on the Elbe," 23.

[21] Johnson, *Real Jesus*, 135.

[22] The discussion here comes from the Jesuit magazine *America*, "The Empty Tomb Hypothesis," April 1, 2013, in an article featuring the scholarship of William Lane Craig.

[23] Some of the arguments in this chapter parallel an excellent discussion that Timothy Keller provides in *Reason for God*, chapter 11. However, his approach does not directly employ criteria for assessing the historicity of biblical claims. He does not consider the possibility of retrojected information.

[24] Josephus, *Antiquities*, 4:219: "From women let no evidence be accepted, because of the levity and temerity of their sex."

[25] Bretter, "New Testament between the Hebrew Bible (Tanakh) and Rabbinic

Literature," in *Jewish Annotated New Testament*, 5055.

²⁶ Levine, *Entering the Passion of Jesus*, 47.

²⁷ The lack of sensationalism in the Resurrection accounts is notable. Sensationalisms mostly reside in the Matthean account. Where they do appear, they pertain more to Jesus's death than to his Resurrection. Interestingly, there are no words of sensationalism that are attributed to the resurrected Jesus.

²⁸ Pitre makes an intriguing argument in his book *The Case for Jesus* that the Jonah story is truly a prophetic story that presages the Resurrection of Jesus. Setting aside whether he might be right or not, it is pretty clear the people whom Jesus spoke to during his life would have never understood the Jonah story as a prelude to the Resurrection. So, even if we can see how to connect the dots after the fact, the people living at the time likely did not.

²⁹ The 2001 Pontifical Biblical Commission, *The Jewish People and Their Sacred Scriptures in the Christian Bible*, as quoted in Schwienhorst-Schönberger, "Marcion on the Elbe," 24.

³⁰ United States Catholic Conference, *Catechism of the Catholic Church*, article 992.

³¹ In Mark Movesian, "Religious Rights," review of Samuel Moyn's *Christian Human Rights*, as the review appeared in *First Things*, January 2016.

CHAPTER 6

³² Gelernter, "Why Should a Jew Care?"

³³ Ehrman, *Did Jesus Exist?*, 264ff.

³⁴ Reardon states in "As It Is Written . . . " (p. 64), "Unlike so many theologians of later times, Paul did not inherit a Christian worldview. His vocation, rather, was to create such a thing from his own experience. . . . Paul's mind was essentially formed by the doctrine he inherited from Christian tradition" from his nearly a decade under Christian tutelage before embarking on his first missionary journey.

³⁵ I have couched the story of the martyrdom of Stephen as a candidate for retrojection, consistent with the methodology of this book. Notwithstanding, many historians accept the historicity of the story. The historian Alain Decaux, for one, dates the event specifically to 34 CE (see Decaux, *Paul*, 1).

³⁶ Sherwin-White wrote in *Roman Society and Roman Law in the New Testament*, 189–190, "Herodotus enables (us) to test the tempo of myth-making, and the tests suggest that even two generations are too short a span to allow the mythical tendency to prevail over the hard core of the oral tradition."

³⁷ Benedict XVI, *Jesus of Nazareth*, 324.

³⁸ Soloveichik, "'May God Avenge Their Blood,'" 14.

CHAPTER 7

³⁹ A footnote to the New American Bible states that the words in parentheses do not appear in all ancient manuscripts.

⁴⁰ Rich, *Judaism 101*.

⁴¹ The quip that follows from Douthat, "To Change the Church," applies here if one takes the liberty to substitute "New" for "Old" Testaments, as I have, to illustrate the point.

⁴² David Novak ("Letters," 6–7) responded to comments to an intriguing article he wrote in an earlier issue of *First Things* on how Jews and Christians might harmonize their different understandings of being covenanted with the same God. The next line in his response in *First Things* is worth reading, too: "Nevertheless . . . I am grateful to God that because of the ministry of the Jew, Jesus of Nazareth, many Gentiles . . . have been covenanted with the Lord God of Israel."

⁴³ Augustine, *City of God*, book 17, chapter 16, p. 386.

44 Of the epistles attributed to Paul in the New Testament, scholars accept some of them as being authentically from Paul, some as being authentically from someone other than Paul, and some whose authenticity cannot be settled. We consider the corpus of the three sets to be "Pauline epistles" and stave away from pedantic debates about actual authorship.

45 It is not unprecedented for Christian doctrine to be codified by looking back to confirm the basis for the answer already reckoned. The person to whom this book is dedicated had a Jesuit friend who identified his job as follows: "When the Church declares that, 'This is what the Church has always taught,' it is my job to determine when 'always' began."

CHAPTER 8

46 See the editor's introduction to *The Tempest*. The editor discusses how determining the original words in Shakespeare's work is impossible.

47 The only other candidate as a parable in the Hebrew Bible is an obscure and debated one located at Judges 9:7–15, as stated by Shea, "Parables in the Boat and in the House." David Stern notes there are more than a thousand parables in rabbinic writings recorded from a time beginning just after the life of Jesus. Whether the use of parables was a widespread oral practice among Jesus's contemporaries that were later recorded or whether Jesus was at the forefront of the practice cannot be discerned. Notwithstanding, it remains undisputed that the earliest widespread reports of employing parables goes to Jesus's use as recorded in the Gospels, especially in Matthew and Luke. See Stern, "Midrash and Parables in the New Testament," 566.

48 Pitre, *Case for Jesus*, 81.
49 Ibid.
50 Ibid, 82.
51 Stravinskas, *Catholic Church and the Bible*, 39.

CHAPTER 9

52 Mary Fairchild, *37 Miracles of Jesus*.

53 Leo the Great, as recorded by Snow, "Heal Our Wounds," 23. There is an interesting parallel to Islam here. Muslims consider the Qur'an to be their miracle. If Jesus's teaching is superior to his miracle working, then Jesus's teaching could be considered miraculous, too. However, one should not overextend the parallel between Islam and Christianity here. In Christianity, Jesus's person is an inherent part of the message; in Islam, Muhammad's role is solely as the messenger of the Qur'an, where the person of Muhammad is only obliquely included.

54 Meier, *Marginal Jew*. Many of the arguments and much of the information in this chapter derive from inputs from Meier's work.

55 Mary Fairchild, *37 Miracles of Jesus*. As noted in a previous chapter, the chronology is particularly difficult to unpack because the evangelists arranged their stories for literary effect, not to preserve chronological order. I make no claim whether the order is correct or not, but I applaud the table's developers to attempt to de-convolve the miracle stories and place them in a reasoned order. The table is available online in open source at http://blog.adw.org/wp-content/uploads/2018/03/37-Miracles-of-Jesus-in-Chronological-Order.pdf (accessed March 28, 2020).

56 Meier, *Marginal Jew*, 618.
57 Meier, *Marginal Jew*, 622.
58 Meier, *Marginal Jew*, 970.
59 See Meier, *Marginal Jew*, chapter 18, esp. 537–53. With respect to discussing Jewish magicians and alleged miracle workers of the one hundred to two hundred years before his time (including the time in which Jesus lived), Josephus, writing at the end

of the first century, derides most of them. Jesus is exceptional in this regard. Josephus is not dismissive of Jesus's wondrous deeds, nor does the author attribute anything magical to Jesus. As a side note, Josephus speaks about a group of Jews of the late first century being somewhat expert at exorcisms. Interestingly, the one specific case of exorcism that Josephus does narrate, Elezear's, sounds very much like an experiment in magic with the whole scheme of special rituals and incantations. Jesus's exorcisms look nothing like the one Josephus describes for Elezear. Jesus's exorcisms do not depend on concoctions, incantations, amulets, or anything other than Jesus's authority.

[60] Mano, "Bethsaida Miracle," 26.

[61] Vermes, "Jewish Miracle Workers in the Late Second Temple Period," 537: "For the rabbis [post 135 CE] the study of Torah was more important than visionary."

CHAPTER 10

[62] The revelation of Scripture to Jews and orthodox Christians was done through the channels of history. This is not a universal attribute shared by all religions. Consider the Qur'an for Islam, the Book of Moroni for Mormons, and the Scriptures for the Hindus.

There are different schools of Islam. One of the most prominent Sunni schools, especially prominent in the Arab world, is the Ash'arite school. The school rose to prominence within Islam in the ninth century. This school holds the Qur'an is uncreated, i.e., it is co-eternal with Allah, having no human contingency or agency whatever. For the followers of this school, the Qur'an is an ahistorical document.

Mormonism provides another interesting example. Its Scripture was purportedly revealed to Joseph P. Smith via tablets he translated into English. In this regard, Mormonism shares the attribute of Islam in that its Scriptures are ahistorical, meaning they did not evolve on the floor of human experience. Instead, they just appeared.

A last example is the Hindu Scriptures. They are an assembly of myths whose recorded events did not occur on the stage of human history, and they are set in mythical, not real, time.

[63] Lienhard, *The Bible*, and Pitre, *Case for Jesus*.

[64] The first breach of the Jerusalem city walls happened on August 10, 70 CE, which was Av 9 on the Jewish calendar that year. The collapse of the city and the Temple ensued shortly after.

[65] We have historical reasons to believe that the date the four books came together in a substantively final form as a collective group before 185. See Ehrman, *Jesus before the Gospels*, 119–24. Irenaeus of Lyon declared there were four and only four Gospels named Matthew, Mark, Luke, and John in 160.

[66] This book focuses on the life and times pertaining to Jesus. Therefore, I have made no reference to the geographic, ritual, and historical information embedded within the texts. The New Testament is the most comprehensive set of information available about life in the Holy Land in the Late Second Temple period. Its descriptions of towns, places, and architecture have proven to be highly reliable. These facts are incidental to establishing the historicity of the stories pertaining to Jesus and the rise of the Church, but the veracity of information informs the reader of the care the evangelists took in writing up the incidental background information.

[67] In doing research for this book, I discussed the reliability of oral tradition in forming the Gospels with a professor of Old Testament at Catholic University. The university hosted a seminar for the fiftieth anniversary of *Dei Verbum*, the Catholic Church's definitive statement about Scripture, in November 2015. He laughed. He pointed out that the so-called oral traditions of Gospel writers span just a few decades—within the memory of the writers and not oral tradition at all! He laughed because, as he pointed out, the oral traditions within the Hebrew Bible are three hundred years or more in the making, not

just a few decades. The oral traditions in the Hebrew Bible span many lifetimes.

[68] For an intriguing understanding of the growth of the Church, consult Stark, *Rise of Christianity*. Stark is a sociologist who shows that the Church remained quite small at least until mid-second century.

[69] From St. Jerome's translation of the ancient *Gospel of the Hebrews*, as reported in Barnstone, *The OTHER Bible*: "James had sworn that he would not eat the bread from that hour in which he had drunk the cup of the Lord until he should see [Jesus] risen from among them that sleep. And shortly thereafter the Lord said: Bring a table and bread. . . . He took the bread, blessed it and brake it and gave it to James the Just and said to him: My brother, eat your bread, for the Son of man is risen from among them that sleep" (335). The commentary for this extract comes from Ron Cameron, *The Other Gospels*, (Philadelphia: Westminster Press, 1982) p. 83–86. He claims its origin somewhere in the 50–150 CE range, with a bias toward the earlier end of the period.

[70] This argument follows the discussion from Pitre, *Case for Jesus*.

[71] This is precisely the argument that Ehrman makes in his book, whose subtitle says it all: *Jesus Before the Gospels: How the Earliest Christians Remembered, Changed and Invented Their Stories of the Savior*.

[72] The martyrdom of James the Just is recorded by Josephus. It is a case where we have collaborating documentation of New Testament events from contemporary, non-Christian sources. The ministry of John the Baptist is another story recounted by Josephus comporting with New Testament accounts.

[73] Bissell, *Apostle*, 327.

[74] Timothy Keller follows this same line of reasoning in his *Reason for God*. As I have argued here, Pastor Keller argues, too, that there would have been lots of opportunity to set unto Jesus the resolution of important doctrinal questions that were then present when the Gospels were written and edited. He points out, relative to the debate whether Gentiles needed to be circumcised, the Gospel writers (and Luke in particular, for whom the issue was more central) do not engage Jesus in this debate. Obviously, the Gospel writers exercise a restraint in a kind of self-suppression so as, apparently, to keep true to the source material available to them. These source materials evidently did not include any discussions of circumcision, and thus the writers remained silent on the point as well.

[75] Linehard, *The Bible*, 16–17.

[76] For those looking five hundred years out from the events here, you will observe the rise of Islam. Islam asserts its absorption of the Hebrew Bible and the New Testament (Torah and Injil, as the Qur'an would invoke them, respectively). Indeed, many Bible stories find their way into the Qur'an. However, Muslims basically reject the earlier testaments as frauds, claiming the writers of the Hebrew Bible and the New Testament corrupted the revelations provided to the Hebrew prophets and to Jesus; so the Bible is rejected by Muslims as false Scripture. Muhammad (or perhaps the immediately following rightly guided caliphs) and their co-religionists chose to untether Islam from earlier Scriptures. This decision is precisely the opposite of what Christians in the second century chose to do.

[77] Ibid., 34–35.

[78] Johnson, *The Real Jesus*, 141.

[79] There is some scholarly opinion that Matthew's Gospel may have been written first in Hebrew or Aramaic but later translated into Greek. This is a minority opinion. I keep to the prevailing scholarly opinion that the originals were produced in Greek.

[80] Strobel, *The Case for Christ*, 64–65.

[81] Slick, "Manuscript Evidence for Superior New Testament Reliability."

CHAPTER 11

[82] As quoted in Movsesian, "Religious Rights."

Appendix A

A Case Study of a Systems Approach: A Review of Josephus's Words about Jesus

INTRODUCTION

The earliest, extant, non-Christian words we have on Jesus are from the Jewish historian Flavius Josephus, remembered simply as Josephus. He wrote a twenty-volume history of the Jews, *Antiquities of the Jews*, in Greek in either 93 or 94 CE. Josephus wrote at about the same time when the last books of the New Testament were being written and in particular probably just soon after the Gospel of John reached its final form. The words about Jesus in *Antiquities* amount to about a paragraph. This appendix focuses on how those few words contribute to understanding the historicity of the Gospels.

Josephus had been a Pharisee, a general, a politician, a negotiator, a traitor, a witness to the destruction of the Temple in 70 CE, and, ultimately, a historian who served the emperor in Rome. Scholars believe that *Antiquities* was translated directly into Latin and Syriac and possibly other languages, too. The only known existing versions of *Antiquities* seem to have come down to us through Christians, a bit of an irony since Josephus's work was addressed to pagans to explain Judaism to them. The earliest copies of *Antiquities* we have available to us date back to the eleventh century, and they derive from Western sources. Notably, the eleventh century was long after Christian ascendancy in the West and a millennium after Josephus lived.

TESTIMONIUM FLAVIANUM

So much discussion relates to the few words that the relevant passage in *Antiquities* gets its own name, *Testimonium Flavianum*. Humanities professor Schlomo Pines at the Hebrew University sets the tone for our discussion with the introductory words to his academic paper that analyzes it:

> Few historical texts, or none, have been more often quoted, more passionately rejected and denounced as literary forgeries, more devoutly defended, more carefully edited and more variously emended than the so-called *Testimonium Flavianum*, a short passage in Josephus' "Antiquities of the Jews" (xviii, 63–64) dealing with Jesus.[1]

The issue with the *Testimonium*, like the issue with the words in the New Testament, is that we would love to have authentic, verifiable words that go back to the primary source, but, instead, we have what we have. What we have is two distinct extant versions. The more widely available version and the one more frequently cited is listed first below, known as the *textus receptus*. It is the version that has been passed down and preserved in Greek. Scholars believe the text goes back at least as far as ca. 311 in its current form. The famous Church historian Eusebius preserved this version in his work[2], and it is this text that has enjoyed primacy for hundreds of years. The other extant version came down from an Arabic source, and its currency goes to Professor Pines in 1971, who rescued it from relative obscurity. The Arabic version, dubbed the *Agapius* version after the name of its source (an eastern bishop named Agapius, who lived in the tenth century), is listed second. Its route involved these translations: Greek to Syriac and to Arabic, where the original sourcing for the Syriac version (no longer available) goes back to an unknown date but likely before 311. The *textus receptus* version is considered superior to the second because it is not based on any translations between languages, it is centuries older than the second (fourth versus tenth centuries), and it is better attested by other sources.

As for context, the words about Jesus in the *Testimonium* fall between events that are dated by the University of Chicago to be between the years 28 to 33.[3] The range is precisely where the description of Jesus ought to be. Furthermore, the literary style in the *Testimonium* matches Josephus's broader style, so most scholars believe the passage itself in the *Testimonium* does indeed go back to Josephus, setting aside for the moment whether the entire passage is authentic or not. We also have independent evidence authenticating the passage as described in the next paragraphs.

Many scholars take it as a given that later Christians interpolated the original words in Version 1 to make them more closely harmonize with the Christian understandings of their day by adding favorable words to the text, as the New York Times reported in 1971:

> [M]odern Christian scholars are almost unanimous in considering the passage on Jesus in the Greek texts of "The Antiquities of the Jews" by Josephus to be "too Christian"—that is, a forgery by church leaders of the third and fourth century designed to bolster the historical legitimacy of their faith.[4]

Version 3 is the theoretically recreated, un-interpolated words from Josephus, drawing upon Version 1. Scholars conclude that Christians interpolated the words in Version 1 because of the existence of three sets of words (in italics below) that Josephus, a non-Christian Jew, would never have written himself. As noted earlier, some would argue that the Christian interpolations are so severe in Version 1 that the whole of the *Testimonium* is a forgery and should be discounted. This is where Version 2 comes in. Version 2 tells much of the same narrative as Version 1, but Version 2 lacks the supposed Christian accretions. Accordingly, Versions 1 and 2 evolved after their diverging from a common ancestor. Perhaps because the words in Version 2 were preserved in Syriac-to-Arabic, the Greek- and Latin-speaking Western churches exerted no effort to censure them, some would say.[5] The existence of Version 2 provides evidence that the *Testimonium* existed before the supposed Christian interpolations interspersed their words into Version 1. The existence of Version 2 assures us that the passage itself about Jesus truly goes back to Josephus because the divergence of the two streams implies a common ancestor, which was the original passage in *Antiquities*.

First Version

The extant version comes down to us through Greek via a familiar translation into modern English. In this version supposed interpolations are italicized, and words in Version 1 but not in Version 2 are underlined. This version is a commonly accepted English translation and is the point of reference for the other two versions.

> About this time there lived Jesus, a wise man, *if indeed one ought to call him a man*. For he was one who performed surprising deeds and was a teacher of such people as accept the truth gladly. He won over many Jews and many of the Greeks. *He was the Christ.* And when, upon the accusation of the principal men among us,

<u>Pilate had condemned him to a cross, those who had first come to love him did not cease.</u> *He appeared to them spending a third day restored to life, for the prophets of God had foretold these things and a thousand other marvels about him.* And the tribe of the Christians, so called after him, has still to this day not disappeared.[6, 7]

Second Version

This extant version comes down to us through Arabic. This version is translated by Prof. Pines:[8]

> At this time there was a wise man who was called Jesus. And his conduct was good, and he was known to be virtuous. And many people from among the Jews and the other nations became his disciples. Pilate condemned him to be crucified and to die. And those who had become his disciples did not abandon his discipleship. They reported that he had appeared to them after his crucifixion and that he was alive; accordingly, he was perhaps the Messiah concerning whom the prophets have recounted wonders.

Third Version

The presumed original words, starting with Version 1, are theoretically recreated by removing words thought to have been added by Christian interpolators. This translation is Meier's:

> About this time there lived Jesus, a wise man. For he was one who performed surprising deeds and was a teacher of such people as accept the truth gladly. He won over many Jews and many of the Greeks. And when, upon the accusation of the principal men among us, Pilate had condemned him to a cross, those who had first come to love him did not cease. And the tribe of the Christians, so called after him, has still to this day not disappeared.[9]

JOSEPHUS'S WORDS COMPARED AGAINST THE CLAIMS OF THE CHURCH

We can relate the seven primitive claims of the Church to the three versions of the *Testimonium* to get an indication what a first-century, non-Christian source said in relation to them.

Table A-1. Comparison of *Testimonium* Versions against the Church's Claims

#	Claim	Version 1	Version 2	Version 3
1	Jesus's followers banded together after his death to found the Church.	Confirmed.	Confirmed.	Confirmed.
2	Jesus was a wisdom teacher.	Confirmed.	Confirmed.	Confirmed.
3	The Gospels' accounts reflect personal witness of first-century CE disciples.	Partly confirmed. There is no indication of Gospel accounts particularly, but there is confirmation of disciples' personal witness underlying the stories.	Partly confirmed. See entry for Version 1. Version 2 explicitly identifies sourcing for the account, unlike Version 1.	Partly confirmed. See entry for Version 1.
4	Jesus was a miracle worker.	Confirmed.	Confirmed, but only as witnessed by the disciples.	Confirmed.
5	Jesus was resurrected from the dead.	Confirmed.	Confirmed but only as reported by the disciples.	Not confirmed
6	Jesus is the Messiah.	Confirmed.	"Perhaps"	Confirmed but weakly and indirectly. Jesus is not called the Messiah, but his followers are "Christians," which makes for the indirect confirmation.
7	Jesus's death achieved an atonement for the sins of his believers.	Not confirmed.	Not confirmed.	Not confirmed.

CONCLUSIONS ABOUT JOSEPHUS'S WORDS

The interesting points are that all of the versions support or partially support several of the Church's seven claims (depending how one counts: 5

or 6; 4, 5, or 6; and 4 or 5 for Versions 1, 2, and 3, respectively). Further, none of the versions states anything contrary to Christianity. The table provides overwhelming evidence of the historicity of some of the claims of the Church from a first-century non-Christian. We can, therefore, take credit for Josephus's work in advancing the historicity of the Gospel accounts. However, the significance of Josephus's endorsement is mooted by the fact that he does not identify what was the content of Jesus's teachings, what were the "surprising deeds" Jesus did, or what came with identifying Jesus as the "Christ," whether directly or indirectly. With regard to the "surprising deeds" report, we note that Josephus comments elsewhere in *Antiquities* about other alleged Jewish miracle workers. He dismisses them as frauds or hucksters. In contrast, he is not dismissive of Jesus's deeds. Is the absence of any dismissal commentary meaningful? Perhaps, but we cannot say for sure.

Irrespective of whether one accepts or rejects the interpolation theory, one walks away with the only known near-contemporary, non-Christian source about Jesus supporting many points of the Gospel accounts' historicity. Further, none of the accounts provides anything information that contravenes anything in the Gospel accounts of Jesus. Moreover, we can find plausible reason to believe that the core words in *Antiquities* go back to Josephus personally.

Appendix B

Design Parameters for the Four Gospels

APPENDIX B

Table B-1. Design Parameters for the Gospels

Parameter	Matthew	Mark	Luke	John
Purported author. See Note A.	The Apostle Matthew, the tax collector, also thought to be known by the Jewish name Levi	John Mark, the first name being a Jewish name and second being a Roman-Greco name	Luke, physician and companion of Paul of Paul's missionary journeys	The Apostle John (or perhaps one or more scribes who worked with and for him)
When documented was completed. See Note B.	70–80 CE	60–70 CE	70–80 CE	~90 CE
Where document was thought to have been composed	The Holy Land	Rome	Syria	In Greece or a Greek Island, perhaps Patmos
Model of Jesus developed by the author	The Messiah as the fulfillment of Hebrew prophecies with Jesus cloaked in divine royalty, authority, and power.	The Father's Suffering Servant.	The compassion of the Father.	The preexistent and eternal God-man.
Target audience of the Gospel	Palestinian Jews	Roman peoples, especially the oppressed; focuses on Gentiles but reaches diaspora Jews as well.	Hellenized people—Diaspora Jews and Gentiles	All mankind with a special focus on human's spirituality

As Table B-1 shows on the following page, each evangelist wrote his Gospel to serve a particular niche as to time, place, audience, and characterization of his Jesus.

NOTE A

Technically speaking, all of the Gospels were written anonymously. We cannot be sure about the authorship of any of them. However, as Brant Pitre[10] points out, from the copious texts we have going back to as early as the second century, there are exactly *zero* copies that do have an attestation other than the same authorship we have today. Pitre argues that there may never have been a time when the Gospels did not have specific authorship attributed to them. In his view, there never was an anonymous Gospel. Indeed, the named author has from an early date been thought to be central to affirming its pedigree and thus its authority.

With respect to the Gospel attributed to Matthew, he was a tax collector for the Romans before being called by Jesus. Unlike most of the apostles, he was literate. Many of the apostles are thought to have performed their missionary work in and around the Holy Land (a later Roman name: Palestine). Matthew may have been one of them. Being literate, he would have been a perfect choice to have rendered an account to his fellow Palestinian Jews. Most modern scholars believe that the Gospel was composed in Greek, drawing upon an available version of Mark's Gospel, also available in Greek. As an alternate theory, in *Church History* we have from Eusebius, a fourth-century bishop, Matthew is identified as having composed the original in Hebrew (or Aramaic, the then-Semitic dialect of the Jews). It was translated into Greek at some point, claims Eusebius. None of the original Hebrew/Aramaic versions, if they ever existed at all, has survived. An initial Hebrew composition is consistent with the back-translation ability of the extant Greek back to Hebrew, as theorized by Jean Carmignac, a biblical scholar who one of the first translators of the Dead Sea Scrolls. We really have no authoritative evidence that Matthew (probably also known as Levi) actually wrote the Gospel with his name attached to it. How his name became associated with the document is unknown, but it may relate to the fact he was perhaps the only literate apostle (not including Paul, who became an apostle after Jesus's death). Though Matthew was an apostle, he lives in near-obscurity in the Gospel accounts—as is true for most of the apostles.

For Mark, there are many reasons to believe that the Gospel has a direct relationship to witness of Simon Peter, who was martyred circa 64–68 CE. As reported by Eusebius, John Mark (known to us as Mark) was believed to be a secretary of sorts for Peter when Peter was in Rome (see 1 Pet 5:13), and John Mark recorded the stories in the waning days of Peter's life or perhaps shortly after Peter's martyrdom. John Mark also traveled with Paul for a spell, though their work together seems to have ended badly (Acts 15:38–39). A pious tradition holds that the Last Supper was served in John Mark's mother's house. In any event, this John Mark was an early member of the Church, had Palestinian roots, and had strong ties to Jerusalem and then later to Rome. Whether he wrote the Gospel attributed to him, we cannot say with certainty, but it is certainly plausible.

Of the historical basis for the attributions of the Gospels, the basis for Luke's may be the strongest. Luke traveled extensively with Paul. Late in Acts of the Apostles, the sequel to Luke's Gospel, we see a first-person account of Paul and Luke traveling together, which is attested to separately in Paul's letters. Luke was a God-fearer, that is, a pagan convert to Judaism. The Greek is exquisite. The attention to detail and the ordering of information are done so elegantly its author must have been learned and articulate. These details comport with what is known about Luke as a physician. The historical style of this Gospel puts it on par with the excellent secular biographies (called *bios*) that were written contemporaneously.

With respect to John's Gospel, the author of this manuscript may be the same person or persons who wrote the Letters attributed to John and perhaps the Revelation (aka the Apocalypse) of John. There is shared mysticism in the documents. John the Apostle is piously identified as the author of the Gospel. He had a central seat in the life and times of Jesus. John was thought to have been the youngest of the apostles, and the only one who survived to old age, being remembered as the only apostle not to suffer martyrdom (not including Judas). Owing to his personal proximity to Jesus, John was perhaps indeed the "disciple whom Jesus loved," but, on this point, one cannot be sure. Most scholars refer to the document as being the product of a Johannine community, rather than an individual. The actual leader of the community or the inspiration for it may be the origin of the name to whom this Gospel is attributed. In the ancient world, documents often were attributed to the people who inspired the works, rather than the actual writers themselves. Since there is so much puzzlement about the origins and authorship of this Gospel, many scholars simply call it the "Fourth Gospel" and fret no more about its origins being, as they are, no longer accessible to us.

NOTE B

Timing is an important matter in establishing historicity because, all things being equal, earlier reports are preferred to later ones. Scholars debate the timing of when the documents were completed. Table B-1 reflects scholars' consensus. However, one needs to understand that the question answered in the table is really not the right question. The right question is, When were the source materials gathered up? Unfortunately, the answer to this more meaningful question is not readily accessible to us. The answer needs to be teased out from the text and its context. Here is a modern analogy about dating information that is illustrative: Anna is cleaning out her grandmother's house and finds the centennial anniversary cookbook from her grandmother's country church. The cookbook was printed in 1961. Within the cookbook, Anna comes upon a recipe titled "Grandma's Favorite Cookies." *When was the recipe originally crafted?* she wonders. The fact that it was compiled in 1961, the date on the cover, does not really help her much in dating the original recipe. The recipe likely goes back two generations before 1961, perhaps longer. We have an analogous problem in dating the Gospels. We have more confidence when the documents reached final publication (like 1961, in this example) than when the stories within them were collected. Scholars thus tend to report the former date, even though everyone knows the other date is the far more important one.

We use the estimated completion dates, for that is the best date we have. Even so, the proxy dates may render misleading conclusions. Many years may have lapsed between the time when the information was sourced and when the Gospels were completed. The time lapse could be especially large if one allows time for editing and promulgation of the documents after they were first drafted. As such, the dates in Table B-1 ought to be interpreted not as the dates when the textual material in a Gospel were crafted but rather the latest reasonable dates for when the final edited versions of documents were published. The distinction is important in the sense that the source materials embedded in the texts are of greater antiquity than the date for the completion of the Gospels. What this means practically is that the "real" dates for writing the Gospels are earlier than reported dates, perhaps by years, and thus the reported information is probably more primitive than one might suppose. The distinction becomes even more pressing when one considers that the Gospels were possibly written in stages, preserving the older kernels along the way. If this theory is correct, some of the kernels may be much older than final version of the Gospel we have.

The distinction about publication date and source date is a crucial one, which no one can unravel completely. The information we would need to ascertain dating was lost nineteen hundred years ago. That notwithstanding, the distinction about the setting and the timing for the Gospels becomes hugely important regarding how one chooses to interpret the so-called Marcan Apocalypse (Mark 13), a story that also appears in Matthew and Luke (as discussed in chapter 10). The important point is that dating the origins of the Gospel stories is a controversial point that cannot be settled precisely.

Bottom line: The four Gospels portray distinctly different Jesuses, and we often blend them together. The interested reader ought to consider them separately to understand the richness of each evangelist's nuances and literary conventions.

Appendices Endnotes

1. Pines, *Arabic Version*, 5.
2. Eusebius, *History of the Christian Church*.
3. University of Chicago, online version of *Antiquities*.
4. Grose, "New Evidence," 1.
5. Grose, "New Evidence," 1. "As Professor Pines notes, version of Josephus preserved only in an Arabic text is more likely to have escaped church censorship than the official text passed down through the ages."
6. Meier. *Marginal Jew*. Fr. Meier provides an expansive discussion of the *Testimonium*. His analyses underlie much of the line of argumentation in this appendix.
7. An online English translation of *Antiquities* is available from the University of Chicago. See note 3. Its translation of Version 1 is as follows to compare to Meier's in the main text; readers can see for themselves the impact that translators can have. There are some differences in wording choices, but the meanings of the two translations closely comport.

   > Now there was about this time Jesus, a wise man; if it be lawful to call him a man. For he was a doer of wonderful works; a teacher of such men as receive the truth with pleasure. He drew over to him both many of the Jews, and many of the Gentiles. He was [the] Christ. And when Pilate, at the suggestion of the principal men among us, had condemned him to the cross, those that loved him at the first did not forsake him. For he appeared to them alive again, the third day: as the divine prophets had foretold these and ten thousand other wonderful things concerning him. And the tribe of Christians, so named from him, are not extinct at this day.

8. Pines, *Arabic Version*, various.
9. Meier, *Marginal* Jew, 60.
10. See Pitre.

Bibliography

Akin, Jimmie. "Horus Manure: Debunking the Jesus/Horus Connection." *Catholic Answers Magazine*, November–December 2012.

Aland, Kurt, ed. *Synopsis of the Four Gospels, English Edition*. USA: United Bible Society, 1985.

Armstrong, Karen. *A History of God*. New York: Ballantine, 1993.

Aslan, Reza. *Zealot: The Life and Times of Jesus of Nazareth*. New York: Random House, 2013.

Augustine. *City of God*. New York: Image, 1958.

Barnstone, Willis, ed. *The OTHER Bible*. San Francisco: HarperCollins, 1984.

Belloc, Hilaire. *The Great Heresies*. Rockford, IL: Tan, 1991.

Benedict XVI, Pope. *Jesus of Nazareth*. New York: Doubleday, 2007.

Bissell, Tom. *Apostle: Travels among the Tombs of the Twelve*. New York: Vintage, 2017.

Buckley, William F., Jr. *Nearer, My God*. San Diego: Harcourt Brace, 1992.

Cahill, Thomas. *The Gift of the Jews: How a Tribe of Desert Nomads Changed the Way Everyone Thinks and Feels*, New York: Talese, 1998.

Cooper, James Fenimore. *The Last of the Mohicans*. New York: Signet, 1962.

Crossan, John Dominic. *Who Is Jesus?* New York: HarperCollins, 1996.

Cupitt, Don. *The Meaning of the West: An Apologia for Secular Christianity*. London: SCM Press, 2008.

Decaux, Alain. *Paul, Least of the Apostles*. Boston: Pauline, 2003.

Douthat, Ross. *To Change the Church: Pope Francis and the Future of Catholicism*, New York: Simon & Schuster, 2018.

Erhman, Bart D. *Did Jesus Exist? The Historical Case for Jesus of Nazareth*. New York: HarperOne, 2013.

———. *Jesus before the Gospels: How the Earliest Christians Remembered, Changed, and Invented Their Stories of the Savior*. New York: HarperOne, 2016.

Eusebius. *History of the Christian Church*. https://librivox.org/search?title=Eusebius+History+of+the+Christian+Church&author=CAESAREA&reader=&keywords=&genre_id=0&status=all&project_type=either&recorded_language=&sort_order=catalog_date&search_page=1&search_form=advanced.

Fairchild, Mary. "37 Miracles of Jesus." https://www.learnreligions.com/miracles-of-jesus-700158.

Francis, James Allan. "One Solitary Life." *The Real Jesus and Other Sermons*, 121. Philadelphia: Judson, 1926. https://www.celebratingholidays.com/?page_id=4456.

Funk, Robert W. *Honest to Jesus: Jesus for a New Millennium*. San Francisco: HarperCollins, 1996.
Garraty, John A., and Peter Gay, eds. *The Columbia History of the World*. New York: Harper and Row, 1988.
Gelernter, David. "Why Should a Jew Care Whether Christianity Lives or Dies?" *First Things*, March 2015.
Goldberg, G. J. "Critique of the Argument of Meier in *A Marginal Jew* in Light of the New Evidence." http://josephus.org/meierCrt.htm.
Grose, Peter. "New Evidence on Jesus' Life Reported." *New York Times*, February 13, 1972.
Hershkowitz, Nathan. "Jewish Genius." *Commentary*, May 2017. https://www.commentarymagazine.com/articles/reader-letters/jewish-genius-2/.
Jefferson, Thomas. *The Life and Morals of Jesus of Nazareth*. London: Dover, 1902.
Jenkins, Philip. "Going South: A Review of *From Every Tribe and Nation*." *First Things*, August–September 2015.
———. *Hidden Gospels: How the Search for Jesus Lost Its Way*. New York: Oxford University Press, 2002.
John Paul II, Pope. *Crossing the Threshold of Hope*. New York: Knopf, 1994.
Johnson, Luke Timothy. *The Real Jesus: The Misguided Quest for the Historical Jesus and the Truth of the Traditional Gospels*. New York: HarperOne, 1996.
Johnson, Phillip E. *Reason in the Balance: The Case Against Naturalism in Science, Law, and Education*. Downers Grove, IL: InterVarsity, 1995.
Josephus, *Antiquities*. penelope.uchicago.edu/josephus.
Keating, Karl. *Nothing but the Truth: Essays in Apologetics*. San Diego: Catholic Answers Press, 1999.
Keller, Timothy. *The Reason for God: Belief in an Age of Skepticism*. New York: Penguin Books, 2009.
Lane, Craig William. "The Empty Tomb Hypothesis." *America*, April 1, 2013. https://www.americamagazine.org/faith/2013/03/19/accounting-empty-tomb-quest-risen-historical-jesus.
Levine, Amy-Jill. *Entering the Passion of Jesus: A Beginner's Guide to Holy Week*. Nashville: Abingdon, 2018.
Levine, Amy-Jill, and Marc Zvi Bretter, eds. *The Jewish Annotated New Testament*. Oxford: Oxford University Press, 2011.
Lewis, C. S. *Mere Christianity*. New York: HarperCollins, 1980.
Lewis, Scott M. *The Gospel According to John*. Collegeville, MN: Liturgical, 2005.
Lienhard, Joseph. *The Bible, the Church and Authority*. Collegeville, MN: Liturgical, 1995.
Longnecker, Dwight. "A Catholic Dating Service: Strong Evidence of the Historicity of the Gospels." *Catholic Answers Magazine*, September–October 2015.
Mack, Burton L. *The Lost Gospel: The Book of Q & Christian Origins*. San Francisco: HarperSanFrancisco, 1993.
Malone, Matt. "Of Many Things." *America*, April 13, 2015. https://www.americamagazine.org/issue/many-things-87.
Mano, D. Keith. "The Bethsaida Miracle." *National Review*, April 21, 1997.
Martens, John W. "The Challenge of the Word." *America*, September 21, 2015.
Meier, John P. *A Marginal Jew: Rethinking the Historical Jesus*. Vol. 2. New York: Anchor Yale Reference Library, 1994.

Meyer, Marvin W., trans. *The Secret Teachings of Jesus: Four Gnostic Gospels*. New York: Vintage Books, 1984.
Moore, Russell D. "Evangelicals Won't Cave." *First Things*, October 2015. https://www.firstthings.com/article/2015/10/evangelicals-wont-cave.
Movsesian, Mark. "Religious Rights: A Review of Samuel Moyn's *Christian Human Rights*." *First Things*, January 2016. https://www.firstthings.com/article/2016/01/religious-rights.
Novak, David. "Letters." *First Things*, April 2019. https://www.firstthings.com/article/2019/04/letters.
O'Reilly, Bill, and Martin Dugard. *Killing Jesus*. New York: Holt, 2013.
Patella, Michael. *The Gospel of Luke*. Little Rock: Liturgical, 2006.
Paul VI, Pope. *Dei Verbum*. http://www.vatican.va/archive/hist_councils/ii_vatican_council/documents/vat-ii_const_19651118_dei-verbum_en.html.
Pines, Shlomo. *An Arabic Version of the Testimonium Flavianum and Its Implications*. Jerusalem: Jerusalem Academic Press, 1971. http://khazarzar.skeptik.net/books/pines01.pdf.
Pitre, Brant. *The Case for Jesus: The Biblical and Historical Evidence for Christ*. New York: Image, 2016.
Podhoretz, John. "From 1945 to 2015." *Commentary* 140.4 (November 2015). https://www.commentarymagazine.com/articles/john-podhoretz-2/from-1945-to-2015/.
Reardon, Patrick Henry. "As It Is Written . . ." *Touchstone: A Journal of Mere Christianity* 31.1 (January–February 2018).
Reilly, Robert R. *The Closing of the Muslim Mind: How Intellectual Suicide Created the Modern Islamist Crisis*. Wilmington, DE: ISI, 2010.
Rich, Tracey R. *Judaism 101*. http://www.jewfaq.org/.
Sabar, Ariel. "Unearthing the World of Jesus." *Smithsonian Magazine*, January–February 2016. https://www.smithsonianmag.com/history/unearthing-world-jesus-180957515/.
Sabin, Marie Noonan. *The Gospel According to Mark*. Collegeville, MN: Liturgical, 2005.
Samir, Samir Khalil. *111 Questions on Islam*. Genoa: Casa Editrice Marietti S.p.A., 2002.
Schall, James V. "What, Indeed, Is the Quran?" *Crisis Magazine*, January 9, 2018. https://www.crisismagazine.com/2018/what-indeed-is-the-quran.
Schweitzer, Albert. *The Quest of the Historical Jesus*. Cambridge: Black, 1906.
Schwienhorst-Schönberger, Ludger. "Marcion on the Elbe." *First Things*, December 2018.
Shakespeare, William. *Hamlet*. https://www.folgerdigitaltexts.org/download/pdf/Ham.pdf.
———. *The Tempest*. Edited by Peter Holland. New York: Penguin, 1999.
Shea, Mark. "Parables in the Boat and in the Home." *Catholic Answers*, November–December 2015.
Sherwin-White, A. N. *Roman Society and Roman Law in the New Testament*. Oxford: Oxford University Press, 1963.
Slick, Matt. "Manuscript Evidence for Superior New Testament Reliability," December 10, 2008. https://carm.org/manuscript-evidence.
———. "Regarding the Quotes from the Historian Josephus about Jesus." Christian Apologetics and Research Ministry, May 2019. https://carm.org/regarding-quotes-historian-josephus-about-jesus.
Snow, Patricia. "Heal Our Wounds." *First Things*, May 2018.

Soloveichik, Meir Y. "'May God Avenge Their Blood': How to Remember the Murdered in Pittsburgh." *Commentary*, December 2018.
Spong, John Shelby. *Resurrection, Myth or Reality: A Bishop's Search for the Origins of Christianity*. San Francisco: HarperSanFrancisco, 1995.
Stark, Rodney. *The Rise of Christianity: A Sociologist Reconsiders History*. Princeton: Princeton University Press, 1996.
Stern, David. "Midrash and Parables in the New Testament." In *The Jewish Annotated New Testament*, edited by Amy-Jill Levine and Marc Zvi Bretter, 565–69. Oxford: Oxford University Press, 2011.
Stoner, Peter W., and Robert C. Newman. *Science Speaks: Scientific Proof of the Accuracy of Prophecy and the Bible*. Chicago: Moody, 2005.
Stravinskas, Peter M. J. *The Catholic Church and the Bible*. San Francisco: Ignatius, 1996.
Strobel, Lee. *The Case for Christ: A Journalist's Personal Investigation of the Evidence for Jesus*. Grand Rapids: HarperCollins Zondervan, 1996.
U.S. Conference of Catholic Bishops. *Catechism of the Catholic Church*. New York: Doubleday, 1995.
Vermes, Geza. "Jewish Miracle Workers in the Late Second Temple Period." In *The Jewish Annotated New Testament*, edited by Amy-Jill Levine and Marc Zvi Bretter, ##-##. Oxford: Oxford University Press, 2011.
Whealey, Alice. "The Testimonium Flavian in Syrian and Arabic." *New Testament Study* 54 (2008) 573–90.
Wright, N. T. *How God Became King*. New York: HarperOne, 2012.

Author Index

Aquinas, Thomas, 2
Aslan, Reza, 6, 195

Benedict XVI 4, 78, 84, 111, 169, 176, 177
Bultmann, Rudolf, 3

Crosson, John Dominic 19
Craig, William Lane, 50, 176, 196
Cupitt, Don, 2, 175

Ehrman, Bart, 24, 73, 161, 175, 177, 179
Eusebius, 182, 189, 193, 195

Fairchild, Mary, 178, 195
Francis, James Allan, 1, 2, 195
Funk, Robert, 111, 176, 196

Gelernter, David, 71, 177, 196

Habermas, Gary, 50

Jenkins, Philip, 5, 196
John Paul II (Pope), 30, 104, 196
Johnson, Timothy Luke, 49, 160, 176, 180, 196
Josephus (Flavius), 29, 31, 103, 104, 124, 176, 178–183, 186, 193, 196, 197

Keller, Timothy, 176, 180

Lane, Craig William, 50, 176, 196
Levine, Amy-Jill, 59, 175, 177, 190, 198
Lewis, C.S., 22, 23, 44, 168, 175, 176, 190, 196
Lienhard, Joseph, 135, 179, 196

Meier, John P., 5, 18–21, 117, 125, 175, 178, 193, 196
Moore, David, 175, 197

Newman, Robert C., 17, 198
Novak, David, 101, 102, 177, 197

Reimarus, Samuel, 3, 4
Rich, Tracey, 99, 197

Pines, Shlomo, 182, 184, 193, 197
Pitre, Brant, 43, 111, 135, 175, 177–180, 189, 193, 197

Shakespeare, 90, 109, 178
Schweitzer, Albert, 4, 73, 197
Slick, Matt, 162, 180, 197
Soloveichik, Meir Y., 177, 198
Spong, John Shelby, 6, 48, 198
Stoner, Peter W., 17, 198
Strobel, Lee, 11, 161–62, 180, 198

Wright, N.T., 5, 6, 8, 175, 198

Subject Index

Apocalypse (apocalyptic), 37, 64, 73, 74, 95, 96, 131, 141, 176, 190, 192
Apostolic Age, 153, 154, 161

Caiaphas, 28, 29, 61
Council of Jerusalem, 136, 138, 150, 151
Covenant, 72, 87–88, 94–96, 99, 170
Criteria for historicity, 18

Damascus (or Road to), 32, 76, 77, 88,
Dei Verbum, 179
Didache, 80, 137, 138

Election, 26, 75, 84, 86, 96, 117, 170,
Elijah (Elias), 33, 56, 86, 94–96, 105, 117, 128, 129
Exorcism, 117, 122, 123, 125, 179,

Fourth Gospel, 36, 40, 68, 128, 190

Gnostic, 39, 158, 160, 176,
Gospel of Thomas, 39, 110, 158, 176
Grace, 172

Hanina ben Dosi, 126
Hebrew Bible, 17–18, 26, 33, 37, 40, 58, 61–63, 72, 82, 84, 94–101, 106, 110, 117, 128, 147, 155–58, 168, 171, 176, 178–180
High Priest, 29, 34, 61, 84
Historicity (definition), 11
Honi, 126

Initial Idea of Christianity (definition), 68
Isaiah, 33, 95, 96, 100, 102, 129, 163, 171,

James (Apostle), 28, 139
James the Just or brother of Jesus, 54, 55, 138, 139, 148, 160, 180
Jefferson, Thomas, 3, 4, 114, 115, 125, 130, 196
Jeremiah, 33, 95, 96, 105, 111, 141, 142
Jesus Seminar, 4, 6, 80, 111, 176
John (the Baptist), 26, 95, 96, 105, 129, 131, 180
Judas (Iscariot), 28, 76, 190

Kingdom (of God or Heaven), 26, 73, 74, 110, 142, 153, 158

Love, 16, 19, 22, 41, 47, 72, 80, 90, 109–140, 184
Luther, Martin, 160

Maccabees, 33, 64, 65, 71, 94–96
Marcion 144, 154, 155, 177, 197
Messiah, 3–5, 7, 13, 17, 18, 33, 43, 61, 64, 67, 69, 79, 97–107, 158, 164, 167, 168, 184, 185, 188
Messianic (or Marcan) Secret, 37, 128, 176, 197
Midrash, 136, 178, 198
Miracle, 2, 4, 7, 13, 14, 16, 21, 27, 37, 39, 71, 74, 82, 95–97, 102, 114–133, 146, 166, 178, 179, 185, 186, 195, 196, 198

Model, 12, 26, 40, 85, 93, 97–99, 101, 104–108, 158, 188,
Mormon(ism), 56, 70, 179, 180,
Moses (Mosaic), 33, 40, 56, 60, 86, 87, 88, 94–96, 128,
Muhammed, 24, 56, 178,

National Nuclear Security Administration (NNSA), 11, 163
Nicene Creed, 15, 158

Parable, 20, 82, 110, 178
Paul (Saint and apostle), 23, 29–32, 42, 51, 52, 54, 55, 63, 66, 72, 75, 78, 87, 88, 103–105, 115, 135–37, 139, 143, 150, 151, 156, 177, 178, 188–190, 195,
Peter (aka as Simon or Cephas), 28, 40, 53, 54, 60, 62, 72, 75, 97, 100, 104, 105, 113, 118, 135, 136, 138–140, 142, 143, 166, 189, 190
Pharisee(ism), 7, 18, 26, 31, 63, 65, 81, 82, 90, 110, 116, 124
Pilate, Pontius, 15, 29, 37, 61, 184, 193
Primitive (claim), definition of 12–14
Prophet, 14, 40, 82, 86, 96, 102, 141,
Prospective (as opposed to retrospective), 50, 62

Q (Quelle), 36, 39, 120–22, 124, 129–131, 138, 176, 196,

Quest (for the historical Jesus), 3–5, 196, 197
Qur'an, 56, 124, 126, 178–180,

Resurrection (why a capital letter), 45
Resurrection Experience, 30, 45, 47–50, 67, 74, 76
Retroject (definition), 17
Retrospective (versus prospective), 62

Samaritan, 20, 27, 40, 108
Sanhedrin, 76–78, 88, 97
Scalia, Paul and Antonin, 2, 3
Singularity, 24, 68, 69, 74, 83, 86, 96, 107, 168,
Son of Man, 5, 46, 81, 82, 97, 104, 105, 112, 153, 176, 180
Stephen (Saint and martyr), 75, 177
Synoptic, 36, 37, 40, 41, 81, 87, 91, 94, 118, 119, 122, 123, 125, 130, 131, 138, 153, 159, 176,
Systems engineer(ing), 10, 11, 16, 17, 22, 44, 164,

Talleryand, 67
Tanakh, 58, 99, 103, 176
Tertullian, 23, 67, 166,
Theology, 4, 16, 32, 38, 41, 75, 78, 79, 91, 100, 106, 127, 136, 150, 155, 165–68
Thomas (Apostle or the Gospels attributed to him), 39, 110, 147, 148, 158, 176,